DEMOLISHING DOUBT

DEMOLISHING DOUBT

DISCOVER HOW YOUR DEEPEST QUESTIONS CAN LEAD TO LIFE-GIVING FAITH

CLIFFE AND
STUART KNECHTLE

ZONDERVAN BOOKS

Demolishing Doubt

Published by Zondervan, 3950 Sparks Drive SE, Suite 101, Grand Rapids, MI 49546, USA. Zondervan is a registered trademark of The Zondervan Corporation, L.L.C., a wholly owned subsidiary of HarperCollins Christian Publishing, Inc.

Requests for information should be addressed to customercare@harpercollins.com.

Zondervan titles may be purchased in bulk for educational, business, fundraising, or sales promotional use. For information, please email SpecialMarkets@Zondervan.com.

ISBN 978-0-310-37083-3 (audio)

Library of Congress Cataloging-in-Publication Data

Names: Knechtle, Cliffe, 1954- author | Knechtle, Stuart, 1988- author
Title: Demolishing doubt : discover how your deepest questions can lead to life-giving faith / Cliffe Knechtle and Stuart Knechtle.
Description: Grand Rapids, MI : Zondervan Books, [2026]
Identifiers: LCCN 2025054699 (print) | LCCN 2025054700 (ebook) | ISBN 9780310370802 hardcover | ISBN 9780310370826 ebook
Subjects: LCSH: Jesus Christ—Biblical teaching | God—Biblical teaching | Belief and doubt
Classification: LCC BS544 .K54 2026 (print) | LCC BS544 (ebook)
LC record available at https://lccn.loc.gov/2025054699
LC ebook record available at https://lccn.loc.gov/2025054700

HarperCollins Publishers, Macken House, 39/40 Mayor Street Upper, Dublin 1, D01 C9W8, Ireland (https://www.harpercollins.com)

Cover design: Studio Gearbox
Cover photos: Shutterstock
Interior design: Sara Guild

Printed in the United States of America

26 27 28 29 30 LBC 5 4 3 2 1

CONTENTS

FOREWORD

SEAN MCDOWELL

My faith was rocked. Doubts had crept in like never before. What happened? Please allow me to explain. I think you will be challenged and encouraged, and you'll also see why this book is so vital for your own faith journey.

I was a curious college sophomore stumbling around on the internet. I don't recall what I searched for, but I came across an atheist website. While I had previously engaged many non-Christians in conversation, this was the first time I encountered some really smart atheists—doctors, lawyers, scientists, engineers, philosophers. They argued with depth and sophistication that the Bible was fiction, that evolution disproved the existence of God, and that the resurrection was a myth. To put it mildly, *it rocked my faith*.

Not only was I intellectually rocked, but I was emotionally rocked as well. I felt it in my gut. Over the next few days, questions flooded my mind: Was I only a Christian because I was raised this way? Am I really committed to truth, or am I merely following what is convenient? Are there good responses to these arguments?

While there is far more to the story than I can share here, I do want to highlight one game-changing conversation I had shortly thereafter with my father. At this time, in the mid-1990s, my father was one of the most influential apologists alive. Like Cliffe and Stuart's (although before the existence of social media), his evangelistic ministry has reached millions of people worldwide.

Even though I was hesitant, I knew I needed to share my doubts with my dad. We were sitting in a small café in Breckenridge, Colorado, and as best as I can remember, I said something like this: "Dad, I want to know what's true, but I am not sure I think Christianity is true." To say I was nervous would be an understatement.

And yet without hesitancy, my dad responded, "Son, I think that's great. You can't live on my convictions. You need to search for truth yourself and follow it. If you seek truth, I am confident you will follow Jesus, because Jesus is the truth. Your mom and I will love you no matter what." I hesitate to overdramatize this experience, but it was a significant moment for me. I look back at it as one defining moment in which I began to yearn to find and follow truth, no matter the cost.

How does this relate to your journey and *Demolishing Doubt*? First, it is *good* to have questions about God. As Cliffe and Stuart say repeatedly in this book, it is natural and normal to have questions about the Bible, the afterlife, and more. Despite what you may have heard, it is *not* a sin to doubt. Honest doubt can often be good. It was for me, and it can be for you too.

Second, God is not threatened by your doubts. God is big enough for your questions. In fact, he invites them! God told the prophet Isaiah, "Come now, let us reason together" (Isaiah 1:18 ESV). Jesus invites us to love God with our hearts, souls, and *minds* (Mark 12:28–34). My dad's response to me is similar to God's response to you: Bring your questions!

Third, there are answers if you are willing to seek them. In *Demolishing Doubt*, Cliffe and Stuart offer positive evidence that

God exists and they respond to the toughest questions critics raise about the Bible. They don't pretend to have it all figured out. In fact, they are honest enough to talk about their own doubts. But even amid their own questions, they convincingly show that Christianity is a reasonable faith that truly changes lives today.

Let me end by saying this: *I love this book*. I love that it's full of stories. I love that both Knechtles write from their personal experience as pastors and evangelists. I love that they write as a father-son team who clearly love each other—as well as their readers. I couldn't put *Demolishing Doubt* down. And I suspect your experience will be the same.

Whether you are a believer or a skeptic, I hope you will read this book with an open heart and an open mind. Study it. Discuss it with a friend. Share your thoughts online and engage others in conversation. Go for it. The life-giving faith of Jesus is waiting for you.

Sean McDowell

INTRODUCTION

"Thanks for coming today, although I don't think you oughta be here." The red-bearded fellow in the straw sun hat drawled his words as he spoke. "We have an institution of learning here, and your stories—they're beautiful and all, but they don't contribute to the rational discourse promoted at this university. They're exclusionary."

Standing next to the iconic UT Tower in Austin, Texas, I took a quick glimpse at the several dozen students sitting on the West Mall steps shaded by overhanging mesquite trees. Some of them were snickering at his tongue-in-cheek "welcome." A couple others nodded in agreement as they held signs that read "Good Without God," "Secular Student Alliance," and "Free Hugs from Atheists." Still others just gazed intently at the two of us, waiting for my response.

"Is there a religion department here at the University of Texas?" I asked him calmly.

"No," he replied with a grin. The other students began to chuckle aloud, knowing full well there was. "I mean, there *is* a religious *studies* program here."

"All right, so you have a religious *studies* program," I said, mimicking his unclear point of emphasis. "So are you hinting that a pursuit of the rational does not include discussion about God or religion? What are you talking about?"

"The things you're saying are uncritical of the ideology you're promoting." Still speaking slowly, he waved his hand toward the students on the steps. "It's not doing any service to the folks here who wanna know if it's real or not. You just claim what you're saying is real, and we have to take your word for it. You talk about Jesus dying on the cross and all this proof for God . . . but that's just a bunch of nice stories. They're not evidence for anything real."

Just a bunch of nice stories? Is that all religion is? Could God be nothing more than a figment of our imagination? Is the Bible just an outdated collection of legends no different than some fantasy novel? Did Jesus even exist, much less do all the miracles recorded in the New Testament? And what's the point of even having such debates? Why can't everyone just believe whatever they want to believe?

If you're reading this now, you've probably heard at least a few of those questions before. Maybe you've always been skeptical about religion and such issues. Perhaps you recently started struggling with these ideas for the first time. Maybe you're heading off to college next year and wondering how to prepare yourself for the ideological melting pot you're about to encounter. Or perhaps you're the loving parent of a teen or young adult who is facing a lot of disbelief and confusion right now.

No matter the reason, we're really happy you chose to pick up this book and join us on this journey from the valleys of disbelief to the peaks of faith, including all the obstacles we'll see along the way. We don't know precisely where you've been in your life or what you've experienced. And we can't say for sure that we've been there either. But one thing we do know is what *doubt* feels like, the deep-seated uncertainty that eats away at you inch by inch, leaving behind only fear and distrust in its wake. There are few things worse than feeling completely incapable of making heads or tails about what's true and what isn't.

Sometimes it's like trying to drive a car blindfolded.

That feels especially relevant in this day and age. You can barely go an hour without running into a chorus of voices on social media offering their various opinions about God, religion, and morality. This virtual echo chamber can make it nearly impossible to stay the course through the depths of one's doubt, much less think straight in general. No wonder some folks just throw in the towel to cynicism and proclaim that none of this is worth the trouble. How are you supposed to untangle what your beliefs are in a world where's there are *so many ideas* out there?

If you're frustrated, disoriented, or just plain unsure where to start when it comes to navigating your beliefs, you're not alone. Lots of folks are in the same boat. And guess what? We've been there too. So let me tell you right off the bat that cynicism isn't the answer. Succumbing to nihilism (the idea that life is meaningless) isn't a viable solution. As tiresome as it may sound right now, wrestling with your doubts is *absolutely* worth it. In fact, there's nothing *more important* in life than figuring out what you believe about God. It's a life-changing quest that can radically transform who you are and how you live the rest of your life. But it's not a quest you have to venture alone, nor an obstacle you need to demolish on your own.

We're traveling this road with you.

Who We Are

For those of you who aren't familiar with us, we're Cliffe and Stuart Knechtle. We're a father-and-son team out of Fairfield County, Connecticut, who, for the past decade, have been visiting university campuses and hosting open-air discussions with students from all walks of life about their religious beliefs.

When I (Cliffe) first started this dialogue-based mission more than forty years ago—today known as *Give Me an Answer*, a name derived from the title of my 1986 book—I had no idea what to expect. Having recently graduated from Gordon-Conwell Theological Seminary, I knew I wanted to go into ministry and talk with people about God—it's a passion I've had since I was teenager. But at twenty-six I still wasn't sure what that was supposed to look like. At the time, I was doing evangelism for InterVarsity Christian Fellowship in inner-city Boston. But deep down, I felt drawn to college students. I loved their energy, candor, and willingness to discuss deeply personal topics like God, ethics, and human suffering. I've always been someone who's been full of such questions too. So I appreciated the authentic way undergraduates tested the world around them and sought to take personal responsibility for their beliefs. Somehow I knew that was where I was called to be.

The spiritual guidance I needed came in the form of my closest mentor, Leighton Ford. A renowned evangelist, preacher, and author who worked for decades as a ministry partner of Billy Graham, Leighton took me under his wing when I was freshman at Davidson College. When I expressed interest in ministry, Leighton helped me decipher my calling. As an undergrad, I would stay on weekends at the Ford household with Leighton, Jeannie, and their family. He was like a second father to me.

It was Leighton who, in my moment of doubt, perceptively heard God's voice and advised me to go to college campuses; set up shop outside the student union, library, or quad; and start talking with undergraduates about their beliefs. At first, I didn't know how to respond to his idea. I kept seeing in my mind one of those ranting, Bible-thumping, apocalyptic preachers—you know, the kind you try to avoid eye contact with when you walk by.

But that's not what Leighton was suggesting. What if, he wondered, instead of preaching sulfur and brimstone at students, I engaged them in open conversations full of truth, respect, and love?

What if instead of screaming out a fiery sermon, I actually listened to what people had to say and honestly addressed their questions? What if instead of shoving Christianity down people's throats, I empowered them to think more intentionally about their beliefs concerning God?

It was from that advice that *Give Me an Answer* was born.

Ever since then, I've had the joy of sharing thoughtful conversations with tens of thousands of university students from nearly every corner of the United States. Naturally, every single discussion hasn't been sunshine and roses or ended with a friendly handshake. I've had a few water bottles tossed in my general direction. I've received my fair share of ridicule and untimely gestures too. And there have been plenty of debates that got way too heated too fast. (I've learned a *lot* about patience and humility in the past few decades!) But those moments are far overshadowed by the many profound, positive interactions I've had with young men and women who, in the face of doubt, reconnected with their faith. Students who, after losing their sense of direction, came to rediscover new meaning to life. Skeptics and agnostics who walked away challenged to rethink their beliefs and examine for themselves whether there's more out there in this universe than mere matter and energy. And I've learned a lot from all of them along the way too.

In 2015, my son Stuart started joining me on my college campus trips. I can't tell you enough how much of a blast it's been to share this calling with Stuart (and, on occasion, his brother Robert, who still joins us on campus visits). The joy, laughter, and deep relationship-building moments we've had over the last decade have made these years incredibly special for me. I would never have dreamed when I started doing this that I'd someday be following this passion with my son by my side.

When Stuart jumped on board, some of our ministry partners encouraged him to explore using social media as a ministry tool. I'll openly admit that I wasn't too sure about the idea at first. Eventually, however, Stuart and I warmed up to the idea, and much to his credit, Stuart took the reins and ran with it. After a few years, our online following began growing larger and larger. Soon we noticed our crowds doubling or even tripling in size, with many students approaching us and mentioning our social media content. Before we knew it, we had fan accounts remixing our videos and more interview requests than we could comfortably handle. People even began to recognize us in public. To call the last couple years "surreal" would be an understatement.

At the end of the day, though, we're not doing this to rack up likes or achieve social media stardom. Don't get me wrong, we appreciate the support. But that has never been the end goal. What ultimately matters to us is embracing this unbelievable opportunity to engage skeptics in thought-provoking dialogue and encourage believers who struggle with doubt. We want to empower truth seekers as they search for life's answers and bring the good news of Jesus Christ to this world. That's what we're really all about.

What Is This Book About?

Throughout my life and ministry, I've spoken one phrase more than any other. It might be as close to a catchphrase as I've got. Four simple words that, although not the most comfortable to say, are absolutely central when it comes to growing in truth and faith.

I do not know.

Admitting we don't know something isn't a painless thing to do. It's a real knockout punch to our pride. When someone comes along who challenges what we believe or makes us second-guess something we're so sure about, our usual impulse is to either get incredibly defensive and confrontational or feel utterly defeated. We tend to either plug up our ears and disregard any and all criticism, no matter how valid it might be, or we surrender to skepticism without a fight. The problem is that neither of those reactions represents a good response. Neither of them gets us (or our conversation partners) any closer to the truth.

We need to face our doubts. We can't ignore, suppress, or run away from them. Nor can we just wallow in them. We have to learn to work through our doubts and be comfortable with the phrase "I don't know." And that's exactly what this book is about. *Doubt.*

Doubt has gotten a bad rap in our culture. Expressing uncertainty is considered a huge weakness. There's a misconception that if you're an intelligent and successful person, you've got all the answers figured out. We value the veneer of confident self-assurance. We like strong and decisive leaders with clear, bulletproof ideas. Doubt calls all that into question. It's a point of vulnerability, a concession that you don't know something for certain, that you might just be wrong. And last time I checked, nobody likes to be wrong. I know I don't.

However, there's a lot more to doubt than that. For starters, doubt isn't always a bad thing. Doubt compels us to investigate for ourselves whether something is true beyond our presumptions or assumptions. If I wasn't sure whether the milk in the fridge was still good, I'd be crazy to just unscrew the cap, shrug my shoulders, and take an overconfident gulp. Call it blind arrogance. Call it pure foolishness. Either way, it wouldn't be pretty. Any rational person would check the expiration date on the carton, smell its contents, or ask someone when it was purchased. In other words, they'd investigate the source of the doubt. They'd explore whether there was any basis to their skepticism.

Ignoring our doubts can run a far more substantial risk than just drinking sour milk. So many of the important things in life require us to scavenge for truth through well-placed skepticism. You can't make a groundbreaking scientific discovery without conducting loads of experiments to confirm the results. You wouldn't invest your life savings in a company unless you felt convinced it was a safe investment.

In all these cases, honest skepticism isn't a bad thing. It pushes us to look beyond what we currently know, weigh carefully whether the evidence we have is credible, and seek out the most probable answers to our lingering uncertainties. Doubt isn't a bad feeling to just disregard; *it's an opportunity for growth.*

But why, then, does doubt seem like such a dirty word when it comes to faith? There's an onslaught of reasons why some believers feel unsettled by doubt. Some aren't sure how to even express their uncertainties because they've never witnessed someone publicly struggle with such things. Others panic that they'll be ostracized or judged because of their doubts. Still others fear that admitting their doubts will result in their betraying God or sliding into nonbelief. There's a lot of shame, guilt, and social pressure surrounding doubt. No one likes admitting that they're really not sure what they believe.

That's why it's so important to remember that doubt isn't something to be feared or scorned. Doubt is totally *normal*. I have doubts—*plenty* of them. Stuart has doubts too. Jesus's disciples had them as well, even after they saw him resurrected from the dead (Matthew 28:16–17). Truthfully, I don't understand how any person could express deep, authentic belief in God and somehow make it through this life without encountering skepticism at some point. As I've been telling students for decades, I can't say I'm absolutely certain that God exists or that Jesus rose from the dead, because, frankly, I can't say I'm 100 percent certain about *anything* in this world! The idea that we hold all the answers is a naive illusion. There's so, so much we as human beings will never know. There's always room for humility. There's always room for doubt.

But you know what else? It's often those episodes of skepticism that later emerge as the moments when our faith experiences its deepest and most fulfilling growth. Transformation, life, and renewal can be found in our doubts. But only if we seize those moments by the horns. We can't just take them lying down. We can't simply dwell in our uncertainty or disbelief. *We need to demolish those doubts before they become unhealthy.*

Unhealthy doubt occurs when you find yourself falling into unbelief faster than you can pick yourself up. It's when the rough terrain on the trail leaves you unable to move forward. It's when doubt morphs from an opportune moment for growth to a long-lasting cynical despair that you begin to call home. That's when doubt becomes dangerous and has to be demolished.

In the pages to follow, we're going to embark on a winding journey from disbelief to faith, demolishing doubt along the way. It's an adventure we've taken with thousands of people over the years, and now we'd like you to join us on that same quest. We'll start by examining several arguments suggesting that our universe cannot be reduced to mere matter and energy. Someone or something outside of time and space had to bring this intricately designed world into existence. Based on the evidence, the most probable answer to that question is God.

From there, we'll look at where we can learn more about this creator God—the Bible. Besides exploring what the Bible is and why it's important, we'll address some of the key questions students ask us about the Bible, including those regarding the historical reliability of the New Testament, as well as why we're convinced that faith in Jesus Christ stands apart from all other religions.

Next, we'll shift our focus to the identity of Jesus Christ. After looking at his ethical teachings, sinless life, miracles, and claims to divinity, we'll parse out the full significance of Jesus's life, death, and resurrection and what this means for us. Finally, we'll end the book discussing what committing your life to Christ looks like, as well as the next steps you can take to grow spiritually and establish a personal relationship with him.

A number of years ago, I got one of the most gut-wrenching phone calls I've ever received. There had been a horrible car accident, and my niece had died. A bright, happy seven-year-old girl taken from us in an instant. I can still feel the heaviness of that grief as I think back to that day.

Within hours, I was on a plane to Madison, Wisconsin, to be with my brother and his family. I vividly remember walking with my brother in a field near his house in the raw aftermath. In that field he poured out his heart about his little girl. Why didn't the babysitter driving my niece see the stop sign? Why did she go right through it at the exact same moment a pickup truck was speeding through that intersection?

How could God let something like this happen?

For anyone who thinks they have a clean or easy or simple rational solution to that excruciating question, they're nuts. The only response I could muster, both then and now, is this: *I do not know.* I don't have an answer for that, and I don't think I ever will. But if there's one thing I do believe in my very depths, it's this: The God who created this world, the God who reveals himself in the Bible, the God who became incarnate and dwelt among us, only to get the snot kicked out of him as he suffered on the cross for our sins—this God is present among us. This God is grieving with us, walking alongside us as we try to make sense of our doubts and disbelief.

The journey ahead won't be without its difficulties. The doubts you're facing won't always easily or quickly go away. But I can promise you that there's hope ahead. The God who walked with my brother and me that evening is the same God walking alongside you right now. This suffering God is more than a fairy tale. This God is bigger than your doubts.

What It's Like Being Cliffe and Stuart Knechtle

It's busy!

When I (Cliffe) first began doing open-air college visits forty-five years ago, things were definitely a lot different than they are now. (TikTok was still just the noise your clock made.) Back when I started, we visited more than thirty universities a year, which basically meant living out of a suitcase for weeks on end during the entire academic year. And not just me either. For that first decade my wife, Sharon, and eventually all three of our boys, came along for nearly every trip as well. Every weekend consisted of hours of driving, foraging through paper maps, and eating meals on the road. Each week, Sharon would gracefully turn whatever living accommodations we were given into a cozy, temporary home for our little family. I loved those years, hectic as they were.

These days, Stuart and I typically visit about twelve to fifteen campuses annually. That still keeps us on the road for a solid portion of the academic year. When we add in travel for interview appearances and preaching invitations, plus our pastoral and counseling duties back in Connecticut, it makes for a pretty full calendar. But we absolutely love it. After all these years, it's still such a thrill to connect with students and share the gospel with them.

Of course, some things never change. The wet and chilly days outside still aren't a lot of fun. We also find specific universities that aren't especially accommodating to our visits. While most institutions are pretty welcoming (we've even had some individuals offer to pay all of our expenses for the week), a few haven't been as friendly, with a couple going as far as to impose limitations on where and even how loudly we could speak.

One thing that has definitely changed over the years is the makeup of our crowds. When I first started, I'd have some days when only a couple of students would stop and chat with me. Sometimes the only person listening to me talk was Sharon! I'd be lying if I said there weren't a few evenings where I went to bed pretty discouraged, wondering if I was really cut out for this. When I did happen to gather a small crowd during those days, the majority of students tended to be agnostics, atheists, or religious skeptics who had no idea who I was. And they didn't hesitate for a second to argue with me. On some occasions, those intense discussions would last hours, with some descending into near shouting matches.

Nowadays, though, by the time we arrive at some college campuses, there's already a group of excited students waiting for us, many of whom have been watching our content for years. Since the pandemic, our crowds have grown significantly. On some visits, it's nearly impossible to fit everyone in the space we're given. Unlike when I first started *Give Me an Answer*, many of the students we talk with now are already Christians. On the one hand, it's wonderful to have deep discussions with believers and help them navigate whatever doubts they're facing. On the other hand, a part of me really misses engaging with non-Christians on a regular basis. They're the people who inspired me to do this in the first place. It's their candid questions that often induced me to grow in my faith and confront my own doubts and skepticisms.

We love what we do. Not a day goes by when we don't feel incredibly grateful for the opportunity we've been given. To be able to share God's love and truth with millions of people, both in person and online, has been an unfathomable blessing. It's been so wonderful to hear from so many people how we've helped them deal not only with doubt and disbelief but also with depression, personal hardships, and divorce. But we know that none of this would be remotely possible without Jesus Christ working in us. Neither Stuart nor I are special by any stretch of the imagination. We're not world-renowned scholars or philosophers. We're not flashy public speakers. There's definitely a lot of content creators out there who are far more skilled at social media than us. We're just two regular guys who love talking about God with college students.

PART 1

WHAT IS THE EVIDENCE FOR GOD?

"I feel like you just believe in God because the Bible told you so."

It was the beginning of the fall semester on the beautiful campus of Yale University. The excited buzz of the incoming freshmen was still present in the air. A new year, brimming with new opportunities for learning and growth. In the moment, however, all Stuart and I could focus on was this student's repeated insistence that our belief in God simply stemmed from our naive trust in "some old book."

"No, sir," I finally retorted. "Flat-out, there's no way any thinking person could start believing in God just because a book told them to . . . not even if that book is the Bible!" He let out a surprised laugh—I'm not sure he expected that answer—before crossing his arms in front of his faded gray T-shirt and staring at me through his clear-rimmed glasses.

"All right, so why do *you* believe in God?"

In the next two chapters, we'll examine what I shared with that young man—namely, the evidence (not proof) for God's existence, compelling clues from the world around us that suggest the reality of a supernatural being. As we'll demonstrate, we can detect the presence of an eternal, all-powerful creator God in the complexity of creation, the universal objectivity of moral absolutes, and the power of human love. All of this evidence, and much more, points to God as the most reasonable explanation for why everything we know, both material and immaterial, exists.

CHAPTER 1

IS GOD REAL?

Is anybody out there?

It's a monumental question nearly all of us will grapple with at some point in life. If you're reading this right now, chances are you have too. The existence of God is a subject that has occupied the minds of philosophers and physicists, mathematicians and historians, pastors and politicians, scientists and celebrities. It's a topic of discussion that consumes high school students and Nobel Prize laureates alike. Nearly every significant thinker in human history has expressed their thoughts on the subject:

> I have concluded the evident existence of God, and that my existence depends entirely on God in all the moments of my life, that I do not think that the human spirit may know anything with greater evidence and certitude. (René Descartes)

> Which is it: Is man one of God's blunders or is God one of man's? (Friedrich Nietzsche)

> If there were no God, there would be no atheists. (G. K. Chesterton)

> I'm an atheist and I thank God for it. (George Bernard Shaw)

> God is most certainly not threatened by science; He made it all possible. (Francis Collins)

> Atheism is not a philosophy; it is not even a view of the world; it is simply an admission of the obvious. (Sam Harris)

And that's just licking the surface. The more you start digging into the question, the further away any sort of answer seems to be. You could spend your entire life trying to digest every single book or article that has been written on the subject and *still* be decades away from reading it all. And that's not even counting the thousands of hours of YouTube debates and podcast interviews on the internet. No wonder so many folks express confusion, uncertainty, pessimism, or doubt when faced with the question "Does God exist?" Where do you even start to untangle it all?

Making this even trickier is how defensive and argumentative people can become when an ideological nerve is hit. It's never easy to deal with disagreement, especially when it's over a subject central to your belief system. But you can't have an honest conversation when every little thing leaves you offended or outraged. Ranting and raving aren't effective ways of navigating complicated questions.

Case in point. One time following a talk at a high school retreat, a young man came up and asked if I could prove to him for absolute certain that God exists. I told him there was no possible way I could make such an argument. He responded by declaring confidently that he could prove that God does not exist. Curious at his self-assurance, I asked him to show me his proof.

Without warning, the young man proclaimed in a loud voice,

"God, if you really exist, when I touch this stone wall, strike me with a bolt of lightning!" After placing his hand on the wall and waiting a few seconds, he turned back to me, a self-assured look on his face. "See, nothing happened. *There is no God.*"

I think most of us would agree that this fellow's argument (if we can call it that) really doesn't settle whether God does or does not exist. But how about when calmer heads prevail, when we take the time to think and listen? Can we prove that God exists? Is there some higher power out there, or are we just aimlessly drifting around the universe all alone on this big blue marble? What sort of evidence is there for the existence of some kind of deity? And does this evidence automatically erase any and all doubts we might have about the reality of God? These are all important questions we must address, but first we need to explore the important distinction between proof and evidence.

What's the Difference Between Proof and Evidence?

Give me 100 percent proof that God exists.

We've heard that line more times than we can count. What often surprises those who demand proof is how freely we admit that we don't have any. *We can't prove that there is a God.* You read that right. There's no fail-safe argument for the existence of God.

Now, that doesn't mean that belief in God is illogical or that there isn't any *evidence* supporting the existence of God. On the contrary, there's a bounty of compelling clues that logically propel us toward God. But possessing ample evidence suggesting that God exists isn't the same thing as having proof.

The distinction between proof and evidence is one that a lot of students struggle to grasp at first. Many of them assume they basically mean the same thing. But that's wrong. Proof demonstrates that a certain fact is 100 percent true and cannot be any other way. You can prove that 2 + 2 = 4 is true; there's no logical way you can get 5 from that equation. You can also logically prove that a square has four equal sides and four 90-degree angles; anything without those qualities isn't a square.

The thing is that proof in the absolute sense is so much rarer than many folks might think. As I (Cliffe) was telling Ed Young during a recent speaking engagement at Fellowship Church, there are very few things in this complex world that we can state with complete certainty. Take the law of gravity, for example. Most people assume that gravity, as a scientific law, is a proven fact. That's because we can observe it working everywhere we go. If I drop a ball here in Connecticut, it'll fall to the ground. And it'll do the same thing in Los Angeles, Munich, and the Sahara Desert. But while we have a wealth of credible and repeatable scientific knowledge regarding how gravity works, we can't say without a doubt that it has been absolutely proven. Scientists don't actually know for certain whether gravity will work the same way tomorrow as it did today. We're tremendously confident it will (most of us would take those odds any day of the week). The loads of evidence we have for gravity backs that up. But 99.99999 percent certainty isn't foolproof. We can't prove gravity. Albert Einstein is reported to have said, "No amount of experimentation can ever prove me right; a single experiment can prove me wrong."

As any biologist or physicist will tell you, science isn't about proofs; *it's about probabilities*. Scientists examine natural processes, collect empirical data, and create theories regarding the patterns they discover. These theories represent the most probable explanation for how physical processes work. They're our closest and most educated guesses regarding the truth. But next to nothing can truly be proven without a shadow of a doubt. As I said to an Oregon State student recently, "I can't begin to prove God because *I can't even prove that you and I are having this conversation*!"

This, of course, doesn't mean that we don't know *anything*. We have a bounty of scientific knowledge in our hands—knowledge that makes our contemporary lives of smartphones, electric cars, and advanced medical treatment possible. But that's evidence-based knowledge, not proof. Unlike proof, *evidence is information that supports the probability of a certain idea or theory*. Evidence represents the building blocks of knowledge. The more convincing evidence we have, the closer we get to understanding something. Everything we believe about reality is built on evidence. This includes not only empirical observations—seeing, touching, or hearing things for ourselves—but also rational thought, as well as knowledge we're given by others who have observed or tested evidence for themselves.

While people often stress the importance of empirical evidence, much of our understanding of reality actually depends on evidence that isn't empirical. When you go to the pharmacist to pick up your monthly prescription, you don't start analyzing it in a lab to make sure it's the right medication. You have to trust that the pharmacist knows what they're doing and that the label on the pill bottle is correct. When you're reading a historical biography about Abraham Lincoln, you don't demand a forensic report confirming he spoke at Gettysburg on November 19, 1863. You have to take the historian who wrote the book as a credible source. When your spouse says they love you, you can't send them into a research facility to confirm the results. You have to trust them, based on who they are and how they've treated you in the past.

You have to have faith.

In popular culture, faith is often defined as belief *without* evidence. However, a better description of faith is belief *based on* evidence. In other words, faith isn't gullible belief lacking any sort of support. *Faith is belief rooted in trust and reasonable knowledge.* Faith bridges the gap between our incomplete evidence and our beliefs. It enables us as human beings to navigate reality in the constant absence of proof.

To explain this distinction between proof, evidence, and faith on college campuses, I often point out that I do not have *definitive proof* that the student whom I'm talking with isn't going to pull a weapon out of their backpack, take my wallet, and run. But I do have several pieces of *evidence* suggesting that they're not going to do that. Campus safety personnel regularly patrol the area. Various university laws prohibit concealed weapons. There are criminal consequences for assault, battery, and theft. In addition, the calm demeanor of the student suggests they're not looking to cause trouble. So I feel I can safely *trust* them. Can I truly *prove* they won't mug me? No, I can't; it is within the realm of possibilities. But *based on the available evidence* and my *trust* in the person I'm talking to, I can have *faith* that they won't harm me.

Contrary to what most people think when they hear the word, faith isn't exclusive to religious folks. Every Jew and Christian, Muslim and Buddhist, agnostic and atheist has faith. We can't empirically test everything in this world. (Can you even imagine how awful life would be if that was the case?) Every time we visit a doctor, read a history book, order a meal, or ask for directions, we'd have to examine the evidence we're given, determine the reliability of our sources, weigh the possibilities, and then make the leap to belief. In a world where proof is a rarity, faith makes belief (and life as we know it) possible.

Faith is even more important when it comes to big philosophical and religious questions of human existence: What is the meaning of life? How do we measure what's right and wrong? How do we make moral judgments? What happens after death? What is the worth of a human being? Is there a God? At the end of the day, the answers to these types of questions can't be determined by pure scientific observation. You can't grasp what the purpose of life is in a research facility.

We can't come up with a chemical equation to test which system of morality works best. While scientific knowledge of our world may help contribute to these discussions in some way, at some point we have to look beyond the empirical to get to an answer.

So the next time someone triumphantly declares that there's no proof for God, don't let that get under your skin. Time-out. There's a lot out there you can't prove. That doesn't mean none of it is real. That kind of scientific fatalism is pure foolishness.

What Evidence Is There for the Existence of God?

So if we can't *prove* God's existence, then what reasonable *evidence* do we have to support belief in God?

Over the past few decades, we've had countless conversations with people about this subject. They've gone in about every direction you could imagine. One student excitedly informed us that the CIA had just proven the existence of God through sleep studies based on Eastern meditation (I'll believe it when I see it). A few times, we've had people dramatically announce that they'd believe in God if we could provide photographic evidence . . . as if you can't fake that (just watch the movie *Forrest Gump*). We've been called gullible idiots for believing in an invisible boogeyman and accused of promoting irrational belief in an immoral deity. We've also been moved by so many who have confided that they believe in God today because of our videos.

Dozens of arguments have been made throughout history supporting the existence of God. To even begin to summarize them all would take this entire book. For the sake of space, we'd like to focus on the five particular pieces of evidence that come up most in our discussions about the existence of God.

The first key piece of evidence, which we'll discuss in more detail in the next chapter, is that the order and design of the universe suggest the existence of a creator. We live in a complex, well-ordered universe where the various physical forces, chemical reactions, and biological events that keep everything working are intricately orchestrated into a cosmic symphony. A statement often attributed to Albert Einstein posits, "The mathematical precision of the universe reveals the mathematical mind of God." The intricate order and fine-tuned design of our universe provide reasonable evidence pushing back against the notion that our universe merely arose by chance. Order does not come from chaos. Intelligent design doesn't just happen out of a cosmic crapshoot.

Another evidentiary point that suggests the existence of some type of God is the amount of densely packed information contained in our DNA. If you and I were walking on the beach and came across erratic squiggly lines in the sand near the water, and you were to ask me what made those lines, it'd be perfectly reasonable for me to respond, "Well, I bet the waves made those lines." But if you and I further down the beach encountered the words "John loves Mary" scrawled in the sand, it'd be totally unreasonable for me to respond that the waves also were responsible for those lines as well. You'd say I'm a dolt. "No, Cliffe, someone *obviously* wrote that in the sand!"

Each cell in our body possesses DNA containing more genetic information than three entire sets of the *Encyclopaedia Britannica*. If you untangled every strand of DNA in a single human cell and lined them up in a row, it would extend more than two meters long. One textbook on molecular biology has compared this to fitting twenty-four miles (!) of fine thread within a tennis ball. The sheer fact that our miniscule cells each contain such an immense amount of organized genetic code points to something more than arbitrary chance; it points to the involvement of a supernatural mind.

Turning our focus from the realm of science, a third piece of evidence for the existence of a personal God is our experience of love.

If there is no God, then reality is comprised of only matter and energy. Nothing more, nothing less. This means, for example, that a kiss is simply the physical contact of two pairs of lips with a reciprocal transmission of carbon dioxide and microbes. Or that taking care of one's son or daughter is merely an evolutionary instinct engrained into our genetic code that is meant to prolong the survival of our species. But neither of these accurately express our experience of reality. None of us in our right minds would describe kissing their romantic partner or being a parent in such a way!

While we can discuss love in terms of biochemical reactions, psychosomatic urges, or animal instincts, by no means can we reduce it solely to these impersonal, mechanical terms. In his book *The Impact of Science on Society*, the British philosopher Bertrand Russell—one of the most well-known atheist thinkers of the twentieth century—expressed this magnificently in response to a question of whether there was any way of overcoming some of the obstacles that stand in the way of human progress:

> What stands in the way? Not physical or technical obstacles, but only the evil passions in human minds: suspicion, fear, lust for power, hatred, intolerance . . .
>
> The root of the matter is a very simple and old-fashioned thing, a thing so simple, that I am almost ashamed to mention it, for fear of the derisive smile with which wise cynics will greet my words. The thing I mean—please forgive me for mentioning it—is love, Christian love, or compassion.

We all have the innate ability to love, to work for the well-being of someone else unmotivated by some external reward. This love can even be extended to others regardless of our emotional state, how difficult the other person is to care for, and the cost of doing so. Such clear evidence that reality is more than just matter and energy suggests the existence of a personal God who imparted personhood to humanity.

A fourth clue that some type of personal God exists is the universal human experience of objective morals or moral absolutes. In order for there to be moral absolutes, there has to be a mind determining what is ultimately good and evil. But if there is no mind prior to the human mind, such morality is a man-made thing dependent on whichever person or group you're talking to and thus is subject to personal biases and preconceptions. In other words, morality is totally relative and situational.

But most of us actually *do* hold that certain things are absolutely wrong. Murder, child abuse, genocide, and other acts of violence are all examples of things that we typically identify as real, universal evils, regardless of who we are and where we came from. In my opinion, the most reasonable explanation for the existence of this is that some type of eternal God defined justice and injustice prior to the existence of human beings. This God then instilled human beings with an objective sense of these moral absolutes, what we might call a conscience. Our consciences reflect God's ability to create and define values of justice and injustice. It is a built-in warning system God gave us to enable us to make moral distinctions between right and wrong, between justice and injustice. If there was no God and everything was morally relative, it wouldn't make any sense why we'd have consciences.

A world dominated by moral relativism is a world fraught by injustice. Take, for instance, the life of Dr. Martin Luther King Jr. On April 12, 1963, Dr. King was thrown into prison following a series of peaceful protests in the city of Birmingham, Alabama. While in prison, Dr. King penned his famous "Letter from a Birmingham Jail," where he argued magnificently that there was a law above that of the Alabama state government—the law of God. And according to the law of God, segregation and racism are absolute evils. This is because all people have been created in the image of God, and all human life has dignity. In a time and place where certain lawmakers and social groups could redefine morality based on their own prejudices and silence human consciences, Dr. King protested that racial violence and discrimination represented objective wrongs anchored in God's absolute moral fabric. What amazing courage and faith he had.

When you look at cultures around the world, it becomes evident that we are often reading off the same moral sheet music. We all know that murder is wrong. We all hold that denigrating life is wrong. Why is this? It is because there are objective moral truths that we all share. There are moral absolutes, created by the eternal God, whose character is good and just.

One final piece of evidence I'd like to bring up here is our trust in human reason. The gift of reason—the ability to think, question, and pursue truth—signals the existence of a higher being who bestowed such ability on us. If our minds are simply the material product of natural selection and chance, then we don't know whether they are an accurate indicator of truth.

The acclaimed Christian philosopher Alvin Plantinga made this exact point in his argument against naturalism—the philosophical belief that nothing supernatural exists and that reality consists of only matter and energy. For the naturalist, evolution as a natural process drives us toward what is useful for survival and reproduction. Our nervous system cares about keeping our bodies fed and free from danger. That's the biological end goal. But rationality isn't a component in that end goal. Natural selection doesn't care about truth. Meaning and purpose aren't part of that equation. From the naturalist perspective, our minds are merely conditioned for survival, regardless of whether the ideas that get us there are true and rational or false and irrational. Naturalism alone cannot explain human reason.

How do we know our perceptions and understanding of the world are truly reliable? If human reason isn't anything more than the result of evolutionary processes, then we don't. However, if human reason derives from the work of a rational creator, it follows that our ability to think rationally is backed by that same supernatural mind. The God who created the knowable universe also created us with the capacity to learn and understand it. Reason cannot come from nonreason.

What About Doubt?

No matter how many convincing signs there may be for God's existence, it is important to acknowledge that no amount of evidence can fully extinguish all the doubts we might experience. Even the most stalwart believers (both Stuart and I included) have moments where belief has been difficult, where the available evidence (ample as it may be) has left us wanting, and where doubt has crept in.

Speaking personally, I'm an empirical individual by nature. If there's something important going on, I don't want to rely on a secondhand report. I want to see it for myself. I want to experience what's happening firsthand with my own eyes and ears. I want to know, based on my human senses, that something is real. The problem is that I can't do this with God. I can't see God or hear God speak audibly or touch him. I can't prove God is real by grabbing God's arm or by taking a video of him. And if I'm being honest, it leaves me with doubt at times. After all, if I can't see God, is he truly real?

The somewhat uncomfortable truth is that doubt often accompanies faith. Because faith is belief based on evidence rather than definitive proof, it follows that there's always room for doubt. *Trust is required.* We don't have all the clear-cut answers to those big questions in life, including whether God exists. And even when we have all the reasonable evidence in front of us, we still may find ourselves in moments when it just doesn't seem like enough. We want a foolproof answer, not (to quote Anselm of Canterbury) faith seeking understanding.

In those moments, it's important to remember that experiencing doubt is not a sin. We all struggle with doubt in this messy world where good and evil, truth and error, right and wrong are so intertwined that it's hard to tell them apart sometimes. Doubt is not weird or wrong in and of itself. The more important issue is what you do with your doubts. Do you become compelled by your doubts to explore your beliefs more rigorously and deeply, to study the relevant evidence more intentionally? Or do you allow your doubts to push you to skepticism, cynicism, or even apathy?

Doubt can be a meaningful motivator that can drive us to nurture and strengthen our faith, but only if we can keep it from becoming the unhealthy center of our worldview. If we allow doubt to become our philosophy of life, we've succumbed to agnosticism for its own sake. Put differently, we've chosen immobility as our mode of transportation. We cannot dwell in our doubts and live in a state of perpetual traction. Doubt ultimately must be demolished. If we choose to never step around the barriers of hyperskepticism, pessimism, or aimless relativism that stand in our way, we'll never get anywhere worth going.

The truth is out there behind the fog of doubt. Don't stop looking.

No intellectual argument can prove with certainty that God exists, despite all the evidence we have that could suggest as much. That's because at the end of the day, belief in the existence of God isn't simply an intellectual hurdle to conquer; *belief in God is ultimately a question of the heart.*

Only a couple weeks before I met the young man at the high school retreat mentioned at the beginning of this chapter, I was at a speaking engagement at the Massachusetts Institute of Technology (MIT), one of the most academically rigorous universities in the country. Afterward, a graduate student in the mathematics department approached us, wondering if we could talk. For over an hour, she interrogated us with a series of deep questions about the existence of God, the person and ministry of Jesus Christ, and his identity as the crucified and resurrected Son of God.

At the conclusion of our discussion, she asked us with great sincerity, "How do I accept Christ?" We proceeded to explain our need for repentance and the profound nature of that decision to believe in Christ. Without hesitation she responded, "I want to accept Christ in my heart." Right there in that moment, the three of us bowed our heads and joined together in prayer, asking Christ to receive our new sister into his arms.

The core problem here isn't an intellectual one. If it was, it would follow that the brilliant MIT-trained mathematician would have had a much more difficult time accepting God's existence than a headstrong teen. Our biggest hurdle to belief in God lies in our human stubbornness to accept that we truly need God. It lies in our lack of humility to admit that we don't have all the answers and that we need God's grace. And this is something that no amount of evidence can fix on its own.

It's been said that it's nearly impossible to receive love with a closed heart. Well, the same principle applies here as well. If you truly want to know whether God exists, you need a heart open to that possibility, a mind willing to consider the evidence beyond the clutches of cynicism. *You need faith.* That might seem like a tall order right now. But don't give up; you're not alone on this journey. There's much more hope ahead of us. Keep going.

CHAPTER 2

DID GOD CREATE THE UNIVERSE?

Nearly every major culture across all of history has tried to formulate some sort of answer to the question "How did we get here?" There are hundreds of creation myths and cosmogonic epics out there, each of them proposing a different answer for how our world came to be. Some of these narratives, such as those from ancient Babylonia and Egypt, view the world as emerging out of some chaotic body of primordial water. According to the old Iroquois traditions, the earth was created when Hawenniyo, the god of light, sent animals down from his island above the clouds to gather soil from the deep waters to place on the back of a giant turtle, thus forming the dry land. Several ancient Hindu texts likewise claim that the world came into being when Brahma, the creator god, planted a seed into a golden womb, out of which emerged the earth.

It's not just ancient people who care about how the world was created. On nearly every campus we visit, we meet students curious about what we believe concerning how our universe came into being.

However, most of the time, their inquiries don't revolve around the specifics of certain ancestral traditions or religious texts dealing with creation. Rather, the central question that they often bring to us is this: "Was our world created by some sort of deity?" As we'll explore in this chapter, there are a lot of reasons why this question is such an important one, and the particular way we answer it says much about the character of the God who created the world.

Why Do We Think the World Was Created by God?

Things just don't happen out of thin air. If you were to wake up one morning to the smell of bacon and eggs cooking in the kitchen, the most reasonable assumption would be that your spouse, parent, or roommate is making breakfast. Cheese omelets and warm coffee don't just randomly materialize. Someone had to take out the ingredients, pull out a frying pan, and prepare the meal. That breakfast had to be made by someone. Postulating that *somebody* was preparing the food is a far more reasonable proposition than the assumption that the food just suddenly appeared out of nowhere.

Our world didn't just emerge out of nowhere either. It had to come from somewhere. *So, then, who or what created the universe?*

There are several different answers that students will give us when this question gets raised. Some simply state that the universe has always existed. Others argue that the universe came to exist by chance through a series of physical processes (such as the Big Bang) that, in a happy coincidence, caused matter and energy to interact in just the right way to cause our universe, planet, and life itself to emerge. Still others admit that while they aren't sure what the exact answer is, they just don't believe our universe consists of anything more than material things, which automatically negates the notion of a divine creator.

So what's the most reasonable answer to this question? Where does the evidence lean? As we've told tens of thousands of students over the years, the concept of an eternal and immaterial creator offers the most plausible explanation for this mystery. There are several reasons why this is the case.

Everything Has a Beginning

First, the world must have a beginning. Causes must precede effects. If something has happened, if something exists, there must be a logical reason behind it. Stuff doesn't just appear out of nowhere; it must have some sort of beginning. The existence of every material thing can be traced to a cause. The last meal you ate can be traced back to the person who made it and then can be traced even further back to the farms that produced its ingredients. All of us can trace our origins back to our parents, who can trace their existence back to their parents and so on. And if we wanted, we could keep tracing these things back further and further to the very beginning of the universe.

But the universe *had* to have a *beginning*. Matter and time and space had to come into existence at some point, be it from a big bang or some other process. But that big bang had to come from somewhere too; it couldn't have just appeared out of nowhere. Something immaterial, atemporal, and outside of space had to be there to bring matter, space, and time into being. But if you're approaching this problem purely from a materialist or atheistic perspective, it's really hard to nail down exactly what this could be.

From our experience, the amount of mental gymnastics needed to solve this problem is often fraught with contradictions and forced solutions. Without acknowledging the existence of some sort of intelligent, uncaused cause behind the origins of the universe, we're more or less forced to resort to the premise that somehow *nothing* caused *something* to happen. And that's a philosophically absurd position. At the end of the day, the most plausible answer is that an immaterial and eternal God, a deity who existed prior to the beginning of time and space, brought our universe into existence. God is the first principle, the first cause, and the eternal creator of the world.

A while ago, I (Cliffe) had a contemplative student comment while discussing this point, "Well, the only reason you think that God is eternal is because the Bible says so." Now hold on there. It's true that the Bible does proclaim God's character as eternal. In Psalm 90:2, for example, the psalmist prays, "Before the mountains were born or you brought forth the whole world, from everlasting to everlasting you are God." Similarly Isaiah 40:28 states, "Do you not know? Have you not heard? The LORD is the everlasting God, the Creator of the ends of the earth."

But the Bible isn't the only place we can infer God's eternality. Rather, as I told this student, I believe that God is eternal because it is the most plausible explanation for the question "What was around before the universe existed?" If God existed before time and space and matter came into being, then it follows that God cannot be reduced to temporal or material forms of being. Before all else existed, there was God. And through God, all that exists came into being.

On a number of campus visits, I've had plenty of skeptical students respond to this with the question, "Okay, but who created God?" This question gives rise to a number of problems, but perhaps the biggest issue stems from its misunderstanding of the idea of God. The very definition of God is "that which is greater than all other things." While everything that has a beginning has a cause, an eternal being does not have a cause—an eternal being does not have a beginning! If something had to cause God, then he would not be eternal. If that were the case, it would contradict the very definition of who God is. In that sense, the question is as unreasonable as asking why there aren't any square circles; it relies on a logical contradiction.

Of course, just because the above evidence is logical doesn't automatically make it easy to comprehend. It's natural for us as human beings to struggle with this notion of an eternal creator because we are creatures bound by time. We experience life as a sequence of moments—yesterday, today, tomorrow. But the God who created the universe is, by definition, beyond time, such that he does not experience a past, present, or future like we do. God is not bound to the creaturely rules that structure our lives as created beings.

Nothing Immaterial Comes from the Material

Last fall while visiting a university in the southwest, I (Stuart) got into a discussion with a philosophy professor who was arguing that atheists can provide perfectly good scientific explanations for the creation of universe without resorting to any mention of God. After rattling off the names of several well-known atheist physicists, the professor proceeded to claim that these authors could use physics and science to offer explanations for the origins of the universe that were just as suitable as those provided by a Christian. According to him, there didn't seem to be anything particularly convincing about the notion of a creator God. Our material world, made up of only matter and energy, didn't need a divine origin.

After pushing him a little to offer me his own views as opposed to name-dropping other thinkers, I responded by pointing out that our world is full of immaterial things that we can't explain by taking a purely scientific or materialist approach. Consciousness, beauty, free will, and even love are all things we cannot detect empirically. We can't see consciousness the way we can perceive an oak tree or a building, nor can we smell or taste free will the same way we do when we're eating our favorite meal. All of these immaterial elements essential to our experience as human beings defy empirical analysis or scientific explanation. But immaterial things can't find their origins in material sources. *Stuff that is made of matter can't produce stuff that isn't made of matter.*

As I told this instructor, this is where God comes in. A purely naturalist view of the world can't explain the origins of consciousness, love, free will, and other immaterial things we experience as human beings; their worldview doesn't leave any conceivable room for them.

I then brought up Richard Dawkins, one of the prominent authors the instructor had cited and arguably the most famous atheist thinker alive today. According to Dawkins, free will is nothing more than an uncomfortable illusion in that our choices are nothing more than the result of evolution and our environment. In other words, free will cannot exist because it is an immaterial reality, and for naturalists like Dawkins, nothing exists outside the material world. This means that everything we do as humans—from scratching our heads and choosing what sandwich we want to eat to loving our children—is nothing more than our genetic code reacting to chemical switches.

Needless to say, our conversation ended rather quickly after that.

The naturalist can't allow free will or consciousness to exist because both of these things require an immaterial creator. The only real option for the naturalist, as Dawkins demonstrates, is to admit that free will and consciousness are imaginary constructs that don't truly exist. And this approach can get messy *fast*. For instance, if free will is only an illusion and all of our choices are determined by our genetic makeup and environmental factors, then every horrific and unthinkable crime ever committed—every instance of murder, abuse, rape, genocide, and unjust political oppression—has been committed by an innocent person who had no choice in the matter. It was the fault of their genetic code, social conditioning, or a combination of the two.

Without the reality of free will, we cannot be held accountable as autonomous moral agents who are able to choose between real good and real evil. Without the immaterial reality of free will, and the immaterial reality of its creator, there is no morality.

A Well-Ordered and Well-Functioning World

Finally, it's important to note that our universe itself reveals evidence that points to the existence of a creator. The order and design of the human body, our planet, and the many creatures that inhabit it are too complex to have arisen by chance. This kind of order and functioning demands an intelligent mind behind it all.

The human body is a remarkable thing. Each of our bodies represents an immensely intricate machine consisting of various interlocking parts that work in tandem to allow life. Take the eye. When we see an image, light hits our cornea (the clear frontal part of the eyes) and passes through our pupil, which controls how much light enters into our eyes. From there, the light is reflected by the lens onto the retina, which takes the image and converts it into electrical signals based on the information it gets from its light-sensitive cells. These signals are then sent up the optic nerves to the brain, which interprets them into images that we can visualize.

Clearly, the eye is an incredibly complex bodily organ. In the past when I've spoken on campuses, I (Cliffe) have often compared the eye to a mousetrap, an analogy most famously used by the American biochemist Michael Behe. A mousetrap is a feat of human engineering. The spring-loaded hammer bar must be attached firmly to the wood platform. The holding bar must be able to be locked in to keep the trap loaded. And the trigger must release the holding bar once the mouse makes contact with it so that the spring will snap the hammer bar down onto the mouse. All of the parts—the spring, the hammer bar, the platform, the holding bar, and the trigger—must be present and in their proper places for the trap to function. If the designer of the mousetrap leaves just one of them out, the mousetrap will never work.

In much the same way, the eye is an irreducibly complex biological system. Without one of its components, our eye would lose all functionality and cease to be a working eye. Every part of the eye has to be in its place for it to actually be an eye. This defies the notion that our eyes are merely the result of evolutionary chance. Any potential evolutionary precursors to the eye would have been missing an eye's essential feature, and thus they wouldn't have been able to achieve the basic function. An eye cannot evolve from something that isn't an eye, just as we can't create a mousetrap without all the proper parts. This means that a purely materialist explanation cannot sufficiently explain the existence of irreducibly complex biological systems such as eyes. Only an intelligent creator can.

The same can be said about a living cell—the basic, self-contained unit of all living things. A cell is an irreducibly complex biological system that needs all of its parts to function. You can't get a cell from nonliving materials evolving step-by-step into a living organism, any more than you could make a mousetrap by having only a trigger and wooden platform. The very existence of an irreducibly complex thing such as a cell points directly to an intelligent creator who designed the cell to be the foundational building block of all life.

It's not just our bodies and cells that point toward the existence of an intelligent creator; the fine-tuned structure of creation itself also pushes back against the idea that the universe arose purely from chance. The physical and molecular constants that structure our universe—be it gravity, the electromagnetic force, or the laws of thermodynamics—are precisely tuned so as to allow for the existence of life. If any of these forces were reduced or strengthened by any degree, our universe, as we know it, would never have existed. Our universe is painstakingly balanced. Can you really tell me that all that is just the product of dumb luck? That somehow we won the cosmic lottery? Not a chance.

So, too, the structure of our solar system points to the design of an intelligent God. For instance, the gravitational field around Jupiter pulls in asteroids headed toward our planet. Without that amazing safety net, there's a high probability we would have already faced extinction. The position of Earth's rotation around the sun also reveals the intentional design of a creator. If our planet were a little closer to the sun, we would all fry to death. If our planet were a little farther from the sun, we would all freeze to death. Our atmosphere on this planet is the perfect cocktail for allowing life to flourish. If there were more oxygen in the air, fires would break out far more frequently. If there were less oxygen, many living creatures, including human beings, wouldn't be able to survive. Clearly the existence of life in our solar system pivots precisely on a razor's edge.

When we take all the evidence into account, it is baffling that some still maintain that the meticulous order and design of our universe, from the smallest cells to the forces that hold our galaxies together, represent nothing more than a lucky draw. It'd be like playing a poker game and watching the same player get dealt a royal flush (a 1 in 649,740 chance) a dozen hands in a row. You wouldn't just shrug and say, "Wow, someone's having a lucky night!" You'd accuse them of cheating because that explanation is the far more logical option. In the same way, our finely tuned universe gestures toward the existence of a creator God, an intelligent supernatural mind. Order and design do not get dealt out of chaos by chance.

What Does This Tell Us About God?

While there is more plausible evidence we could cite, the above summary offers a sufficient picture to demonstrate why the existence of a divine creator is the most plausible explanation for the existence of the universe. Only an eternal creator could have possibly been the uncaused causer who brought time, space, and the material world into existence out of nothing. Only a spiritual, immaterial creator could have brought the immaterial aspects of our humanity—free will, consciousness, and love, among others—into reality. Only an intelligent creator could have finely balanced the forces structuring our universe into a life-supporting world capable of sustaining our existence.

All that being said, what might this tell us about this God who created the world? For one thing, this evidence suggests that the God who created this universe did so with incredible care and attention to detail. For our remarkably complex world to be little more than a random lucky coincidence grossly overlooks the intentionality that went into designing our universe. Our world was created as the optimal place to sustain living creatures. This is exactly what we see described in Genesis 1, where God creates the world as a good place where all creatures, humans included, may be fruitful and fill the earth. Creation is a purposeful place, and so, too, each of us has been created with a purpose by this God.

Second, this evidence reveals that the God who created this universe did so with the intention that its inhabitants exercise free will and moral choice. Our world cannot be reduced to mere matter and energy. If we are nothing more than pure matter, then immaterial things like consciousness, free will, and souls would never have existed as well. As I (Stuart) recently talked about with a student at Harvard, the result of this would be a world where human choice—including our ability to choose right or wrong—would not be possible, as our every move would be determined by our evolutionary biology in conjunction with our environment. This would leave us with a world without justice or culpability, one where even the worst behaviors and crimes are simply the predetermined results of one's genes and upbringing. The fact that we live in a world where right and wrong, justice and injustice, are persisting fixtures reflects back on a God who wants us to act justly and love mercy (Micah 6:8). Justice is not the product of our imagination; justice is not voted on by an elitist culture. Justice flows from the character of God the creator.

Finally, the fact that God the creator must have existed before time and space and matter speaks to God's divine characteristics. If the most reasonable explanation for the existence of this world is the work of an intelligent divine being, then that being must be an eternal and immaterial being who exists outside our universe and above our full comprehension. If we go out of our way to praise a chef who crafts a culinary masterpiece, a composer who writes a beautiful symphony, or the architect who designs a breathtaking skyscraper, how much more should we praise this God for the immense and incomprehensible work he has done in creating this universe!

The reason we are here is that something eternal and immaterial, existing before space and time and matter, had to create the universe. Existence can't come from nonexistence. Something doesn't just come from nothing. There must be some uncaused cause that explains how the universe came to be.

In this chapter, we presented some of the evidence demonstrating that this entity, by definition, must be God. As we demonstrated, the world we live in is far too elaborate, complex, and finely tuned simply to have arisen by sheer chance. And the immaterial things that make us truly human and give life purpose and meaning—consciousness, free will, and love—cannot be explained by a purely materialist or naturalist understanding of the universe. Such essential components of our humanity point to the existence of God.

In the end, the discussion here boils down to one central issue: Do we believe that an intelligent God created this fine-tuned universe with intention and meaning, or is life nothing more than a purposeless cosmic accident? Despite how compelling the evidence presented in this chapter may be, at the end of the day, belief in God as the creator requires a step of faith. As we saw in the last chapter, faith is neither about having every answer nailed down nor about unsubstantiated belief. Faith is belief based on evidence. And no matter how reasonable and powerful such evidence may be, we do not have proof that God created the world, nor do we have any clear idea exactly how God did this.

The origins of our universe are, and may always be, a mystery to us. But in our grappling with such challenging mysteries, we can discover fresh understanding. In the midst of such moments of doubt, we can find life-giving faith that shapes our lives and transforms the way we see the world around us.

Where Did the "Knechtle Stance" Come From?

You can imagine my reaction the first time I (Stuart) came across a social media clip of a pair of guys impersonating my dad's stance. Legs wide apart, backs hunched slightly forward, hands on their knees. The impression was uncanny. It definitely got a laugh out of me. Of course, I thought this would be just a one-off joke. I mean, come on, there's no way that my dad's public speaking stance could possibly become a "thing." Cliffe Knechtle, my Oxford-wearing father who avoids technology at all costs, going viral? No way.

Man, was I wrong.

I can't even begin to count how many "Knechtle Stance" homages I've seen over the past couple years. There have been montage videos of Cliffe dropping his mid-debate pose on various campus visits. There have been hundreds of clips of folks mimicking his stance and other mannerisms, sometimes even to the same background music we've used on our social media content. Many of them are captioned with phrases such as "POV: You try to debate God with

Cliffe," "You know Cliffe's 'bout to start cooking when he hits this look," or even just "The Gospel Stance." Needless to say, we've occasionally leaned into the sensation with a couple of videos of our own. Guess you can say the stance is here to stay.

People have often asked about what started the stance. Is it just a hilarious quirk? Is Cliffe bracing himself to make a big point? Is it a display of judgment or aggression? Funny enough, it's none of the above. The reason behind it is actually quite simple. During most of our campus visits, we're on our feet from the moment we arrive on campus in the late morning until we head out in the evening. By the time three o'clock rolls around, we can definitely start to feel it. My dad's lower back starts to get particularly sore. To relieve some of the pressure on those muscles and focus more attentively on the conversation in front of him, he'll often widen his legs, bend his knees a bit, and brace himself on his legs with his arms. Hence the origins of the famous "Knechtle Stance."

Little did I know when I started working with my dad that I'd emulate him in the posture department. It was 2018. We were visiting UConn one blustery afternoon when an atheist student began to bombard me with questions, declaring with gusto that the Bible was oppressive and we were just there to get some social media clicks. For nearly an hour we went back and forth as the crowd around us started attracting more spectators, many of them curious what this young woman was getting so worked up over. By this point, I was more than ready for a breather but didn't want to end our conversation prematurely. So without even thinking about it, I stretched out my sore legs far beyond the width of my shoulders (pretty much a full-on split) in the hope of getting a smidge of relief.

A few days later, we posted the UConn footage online, along with a couple of shorter clips from the visit, including the clip of my passionate debate with the animated student. Before I knew it, that snippet had garnered *more than a million views*. Curious about why this clip had become so popular, I began scanning the comments, only to find that most of them weren't about the content of my argument or the subject matter itself; *they were about my crazy-wide stance*. "Power pose unleashed." "Why's bro standing like that lol?" "Gotta get into that Cliffe stance."

Like father, like son I guess.

It's been a ton of fun connecting with folks from all across the world over something as outlandish as our stance. If it's true that imitation is the sincerest form of flattery, we appreciate the love. But as we've both said, what ultimately matters isn't fame or flattery but rather promoting relationships that bring people closer to God. More than anything, we want God to use our campus visits, interviews, and online content to reach people struggling with doubt and disbelief. We want to spark conversations that compel students to examine the evidence for the reliability of Jesus Christ. We want to bring good news to a broken world. And if somehow, in some strange way, God uses a couple silly memes to get us closer to this goal, we're game.

Keep those "Knechtle Stance" videos coming. We'll be watching.

PART 2

WHY SHOULD I TRUST WHAT THE BIBLE SAYS?

Have you ever been to a concert that left you in awe? Maybe it was a singer-songwriter with a guitar in a grungy coffee shop. Maybe it was your favorite pop star belting out tunes to a sold-out arena. Either way, by the end of the show, maybe you felt like you had an almost personal connection with the artist, like you truly understood who they are.

The thing is, though, you've likely never met that person or spent time talking with just them. You might know *about* that artist, and their music may resonate with you, but do you *really* know them *personally*, like their friends or family do? No, that's a totally different kind of relationship.

In the first part of this book, we took a careful look at what we can learn about the great cosmic artist from his artwork. In this second part, we're going to shift focus to the artist himself. But where should we look to learn more about God? Where does God speak to us? The answer is the Bible. For the next few chapters, we'll explain what the Bible is, why it's important, and whether the evidence points to the New Testament as being historically reliable. We'll also address some of questions we frequently get about the Bible, as well as why we're convinced that the Bible, as opposed to some other religious texts or traditions, gives us a reliable glimpse into who God is through Jesus Christ, the incarnate Son of God.

CHAPTER 3

WHAT IS THE BIBLE AND WHY DOES IT MATTER?

It's hard to believe that the bestselling book of all time is also one of the least read, but it's the truth. It has been estimated that more than five *billion* Bibles have been printed and sold throughout history. This book can be found on every continent, appearing in hundreds of different languages. Yet a 2024 study by the American Bible Society observes that only 38 percent of all North Americans open up their Bible on their own at least three times *a year*. Several other surveys also revealed that a majority of Americans (self-professed Christians included!) have little to no understanding of what the Bible is, what it actually says, how to read it, and even why it matters in the first place. Put differently, even though we *own* a lot of Bibles (and keep buying more of them), many of us aren't really opening them. *We're still a biblical illiterate society.*

When we visit university campuses and churches and conduct podcast interviews, we receive a lot of questions about the Bible and its interpretation. Over the years, we've met many people who, being completely unfamiliar with the Bible, genuinely want to know more about it. We've had countless discussions with well-meaning skeptics who wonder how the Bible relates to modern scientific theory and whether its miraculous claims are nothing more than mere myths. We've also had plenty of intense conversations with folks who are critical of what they perceive to be significant ethical problems with the Bible, such as its apparent acceptance of slavery, its allegedly oppressive view of women, and its depiction of genocide, along with its relationship to various other contemporary cultural issues. Finally, we've had no shortage of Christians approach us who are wrestling with serious doubts about their faith due to their confusion about the Bible. After all, if the Bible is nothing more than an antiquated storybook from the distant past, as many people say, then can we really trust what it says about God? Does it have any real bearing on our lives today?

In this chapter, we're going to begin to break down some of those misunderstandings and doubts about the Bible. First, we're going to offer a basic description of what the Bible is. Then, we'll take a look at what Christians believe about the Bible. Finally, we'll explore what it means to interpret the Bible and why it's so important to do so correctly.

What Is the Bible Anyhow?

Whenever you pick up a copy of the Bible (or pull it up on your smartphone), you're looking at a text written by dozens of different authors over the course of hundreds of years. The Bible isn't so much a book as it is an entire library, or anthology, spanning different periods of time, ancient languages, and empires.

Our modern Christian Bibles contain sixty-six different writings (often called books). Originally, most of these texts were written and circulated as separate documents. Only later, following the invention of the codex (the ancient ancestor of our modern book) in the first century AD, were many of these writings first gathered together into one bound collection. Today, these texts are organized into two major sections—the Old Testament and the New Testament.

The Old Testament consists of thirty-nine different books composed by various authors in ancient Hebrew over the course of several centuries (roughly 1000–200 BC). All of these books were written prior to the life of Jesus in the first century AD, hence the name "Old Testament." The books collected in the Old Testament draw from several different genres of writing and deal with several different topics. The first five books of the Old Testament (known as the Pentateuch) describe God's creation of the world, his selection of the Israelites as his chosen people and his promise to take care of them, the escape of the Israelites from slavery in Egypt (known as the exodus), and their journey to the land promised to them by God. The next twelve books, often called the "historical books," chronicle how the Israelites settled in the land promised to them by God, established a monarchy, eventually were conquered by neighboring empires and brought into exile, and then were returned by God to their homeland. The next five books consist of wisdom writings and hymns praising God, and the final seventeen books of the Old Testament contain the words of the Israelite prophets.

During the first century AD, a Jewish man named Jesus living in the land of Israel (which was then a province of the Roman Empire called Judea) started a movement based on his interpretation of the Jewish Scriptures (that is, the Old Testament). This Jesus claimed to be the Messiah (Hebrew for "anointed one," translated into Greek as "Christ"), taught in parables, preached about God's coming kingdom, and performed healings and miracles.

Due to the uproar surrounding his message and ministry, Jesus was ultimately crucified by the Roman government around AD

30–33. Soon after Jesus's death, however, his followers proclaimed that he had been raised from the dead and began to preach this good news across the entire Roman Empire, converting both Jews and non-Jews to the movement. Eventually, some of these first-century followers began to write down accounts in ancient Greek (the common language of the ancient Mediterranean world at that time) about the miraculous life and teachings of Jesus, as well as about the acts and theological beliefs of this early movement. Over time, these writings were collected together into what we now call the New Testament.

Like the Old Testament, the New Testament is not so much a single work inasmuch as it is a library of twenty-seven different texts of different genres composed by different authors during the second half of the first century AD. The first four writings in the New Testament—Matthew, Mark, Luke, and John—are known as the Gospels (which means "good news"). The Gospels were composed a few decades after Jesus's death either by disciples of Jesus or those who knew them, as attested by early second-century Christian writers like Papias of Hierapolis. These writings are our primary sources for the life, teachings, miracles, death, and resurrection of Jesus Christ. The book of Acts, which was written by Luke as the sequel to his gospel, continues this historical narrative by describing how the early followers of Jesus brought the message of his death and resurrection across the Roman world.

The next thirteen books of the New Testament consist of a series of letters (also known as epistles) attributed to the apostle Paul, one of the early converts of the Jesus movement. Paul established Christian communities across the Mediterranean from the mid-40s until the mid-60s AD. During that time, he sent letters to these different communities in which he examines a wide array of theological topics about who Jesus was, why his death and resurrection matter, and how early communities of believers in Jesus should live their lives. The next eight books consist of letters attributed to other prominent figures of the early church (Peter, James, John, and Jude). Like Paul's epistles, these letters also engage several different theological topics having to do with the life and identity of Jesus Christ, alongside other practical issues faced by the early Christian movement. The last work of the New Testament is the book of Revelation, which describes a series of apocalyptic visions that foretell the future victory of the kingdom of Jesus Christ in his second coming.

The frequent use of the words and teachings contained in the Old and New Testaments by early Christian churches motivated early believers to make numerous manuscript copies of the Bible to help instruct other Christian communities (a topic we'll deal with in the next chapter as well). Some of these Christian scribes even translated the Bible into other popular ancient languages to help missionaries spread the message of Jesus across the world. During the first several centuries of the Christian movement, the Bible was translated into Latin, Syriac (a dialect of Aramaic), Coptic (an ancient form of Egyptian), Armenian, Georgian, Old Slavic, Gothic, and Ge'ez (ancient Ethiopian).

By the end of the Renaissance, several English translations of the Old and New Testament had been created. The most famous was the 1611 King James Version, named after the king of England who commissioned and funded the translation. For many years, the King James Version was the dominant translation of the English Bible, and as such it deeply impacted English speakers around the world. However, while the King James Version is certainly a wonderful translation that has a rich place in the Christian tradition and Western culture as a whole, this doesn't mean it's the *only* good or valid translation of the Bible. Today we have more than one hundred different English Bibles in print, each of which—be it the New International Version, the Revised Standard Version, the New Living Translation, or the New King James Version—represents the work of a cohort of scholars who, looking back at the original Hebrew and Greek manuscripts, seek to provide an accurate rendering of those ancient languages using the English spoken by people today.

The Bible is the most translated book in the entire world. In many ways, this reflects the universal nature of the Bible's message. The Bible is God's good news for everyone—for all nations and all people of all ages across our globe.

Why Is the Bible So Important for Christians?

"Why are Christians so obsessed with the Bible?"

It's a question we've heard plenty of times on campus visits. To some degree, we get why people ask it. After all, how is it possible that these old texts written so long ago by people living in a world so different from ours (no electricity, no modern medicine, no Instagram) could have anything meaningful to say to us today? When we combine this with the fact that people (Christians included) are becoming increasingly less literate when it comes to reading and understanding the Bible, it shouldn't surprise us at all that so many folks ask us questions such as these:

- Isn't the Bible simply some sort of bleak rule book that Christians have to follow?
- Doesn't the Bible just tell a bunch of old stories?
- Why should I even try to read such a confusing book? What's the payoff?

In the following chapters, we'll run through a number of specific reasons why the Bible matters for us today. But for the time being, we put forth three of the most significant explanations for the Bible's importance for Christians.

First, the Bible is important for Christians because *it reveals more about the character of the God who created the universe.* Imagine standing at the Grand Canyon at sunset, marveling at its immense beauty. Or think about the last time you looked deep into the night's sky and saw all the many stars and galaxies. In those moments when the majesty, beauty, and complexity of our universe are on full display, we come to the authentic realization that we are far from the biggest things out there. We begin to encounter the God who created this world. And it's when we come to grasp the reality of a creator God that the Bible steps in and tells us *who* exactly this God is.

As we demonstrated in the first part of this book, there is evidence for God's existence in creation. Through human reason and experience, we can arrive at the logical conclusion that it is rationale to believe that our fine-tuned and irreducibly complex universe was brought to being by an eternal, spiritual God. But although we can gather some basic ideas about the character of this God by scientifically observing the intricate order of our world, we can't truly come to know this God beyond surface level just doing that alone. In the same way, you can't personally know an artist by simply looking at one of their paintings or a builder by simply walking through one of his houses. If you want to cultivate a real relationship with an artist or builder, you need to spend time with them and listen to what they say about themselves.

The Bible is just that—it is the special way the God who created the universe speaks to us about his character beyond the material witness of his creation. The famous church father Augustine pointed to how the book of Scripture complements the words of the book of nature. The Bible reveals God's identity to us through the words of the biblical authors.

It is through the Bible that God, the cosmic artist and builder, opens himself up and reveals who he truly is. Through the Bible, we encounter an everlasting God (Isaiah 40:28) who knows all things (Psalm 139:1–4) and is always present (139:7–12). Through the Bible, we learn that God is faithful (1 Corinthians 1:9) and loving (1 John 4:7–10) and works for the good of those who love him (Romans 8:28). Throughout the Bible, we discover a compassionate and gracious God (Psalm 103:8–12) who loves justice (Micah 6:8) and mercy (Psalm 86:15–16).

Finally, through the Bible we also learn that God revealed himself to us through Jesus Christ, the Son of God. We can't decipher any of this about God simply by looking into the evening sky, examining the wonders of the human body, or wrestling with various logical arguments for God's existence. Reason and human experience alone cannot generate a life-giving relationship with any being. It is only through the divine revelation of the Bible that we can come to know on a personal level the God who crafted creation.

Second, the Bible is important for Christians because *it tells the story of what God has done in history.* One of the central claims of the entire Bible is that the God who created the universe did not simply sit back after finishing his labors and let the world run itself. The God of the Old and New Testaments isn't a disinterested and detached deity who lingers in the background. Rather, what we find in the Bible is a personal God who strives to cultivate a good and loving relationship with humanity and seeks their flourishing. We find a God who, through Jesus Christ, lived among humanity and brought love, grace, and the news of salvation to us despite our sin.

When we open the Old and New Testaments, we can detect a clear, overarching message that weaves its way like a through line across all the biblical writings. Because of the meticulous work of faithful human scribes down through ages, we can read in the Bible about how the eternal God created a good world that quickly became marred by human disobedience and sin. But God did not give up on human beings. Instead, this God chose to bless all of humanity through the people of Israel.

Over the centuries, this God communicated with his chosen people through various prophets who called for them to be faithful to God and trust his divine plan of rescue for this world. According to the New Testament, this God became fully revealed to all humankind through the person of Jesus Christ, who demonstrated firsthand God's love for all of creation and God's power over sin and death through Jesus's crucifixion and resurrection. At no point does the Bible indicate that this story takes place in some fantasy world or alternative reality different from our own. On the contrary, the biblical authors insist that their testimony of God's work and revelation through Jesus Christ describes events that happened within history. Accordingly, the biblical writings display the same literary characteristics as the writings of other ancient historians (a topic we'll cover in the next chapter). That's what makes the Bible so powerful: It speaks to God's transformative activity in history. It recounts what God has actually done in our world in view of God's plan for our future. In that sense, we might say that while creation speaks to the *reality* of God, the Bible speaks to God's *historical relationship* with all humanity.

Third, the Bible is important for Christians because *it gives us principles that can bring us fulfillment in this life*. The Bible doesn't just tell us *who* God is and *what* God has done in history; it also tells us *how* God designed us to live as human beings. As we stated in chapter 1, one of the pieces of evidence supporting the reality of God is the existence of objective morality. Before the world came into being, God determined absolute good and evil and then instilled humanity with an innate sense of that morality. Without God, morality is nothing more than a relative human construct, a subjective sense of right and wrong dependent on the desires of the individual. In that sense, the Bible is the place where the God who established objective morality fleshes out what exactly it means to live a flourishing life of justice, mercy, and love.

Take, for instance, Genesis 1:27–28, which highlights God's creation of human beings in his image. What does it mean to be created in God's image? For one thing, it means that all humans possess innate dignity and infinite worth because they are created in God's image. One aspect of this is that, much like the God who created them, human beings are made to be in relationships. Human beings are not designed to be solitary creatures—even God himself declares this (Genesis 2:18). Rather, we are made to cultivate healthy families and friendships, communities and cultures. Human flourishing is inherently relational.

Unfortunately, the Bible also reveals that our God-given identity as relational beings has been polluted. Our relationships with our parents and children, our neighbors and coworkers, our Facebook friends and even complete strangers, have all experienced the distrust, disunity, and destruction caused by sin. We cause hurt instead of healing, anger instead of affection. We seek our own selfish benefit at the expense of the well-being of others. We let down those who we love. And the same can be said about our relationship with God, despite his many promises to us.

But the Bible doesn't say that all is lost in this regard. Despite the polluting power of sin, we can still seek out loving relationships of trust with both our fellow humans and with God. And the Bible offers wisdom regarding how we can achieve this. Take Philippians 2:5–11, where the apostle Paul models how we as humans should have relationship with one another by referring to the mindset of Jesus Christ, "who, being in very nature God, did not consider equality with God something to be used to his own advantage; rather, he made himself nothing by taking the very nature of a servant, being made in human likeness. And being found in appearance as a man, he humbled himself by becoming obedient to death—even death on a cross!" According to Paul, our relationships with one another should mimic the self-sacrificing love of Jesus, valuing the well-being of others over our own.

The practical wisdom of the Bible relates to nearly every aspect of our lives. As 2 Timothy 3:16–17 summarizes it, "All Scripture is God-breathed and is useful for teaching, rebuking, correcting and training in righteousness, so that the servant of God may be thoroughly equipped for every good work." The Bible anchors its moral instruction in the eternal word of a benevolent God in contrast to the fleeting opinions of mere mortals. It preserves the ethical instructions of Jesus, who, in addition to being the eternal Son of God, is also one of the most acclaimed moral teachers in the history of the world (as we'll talk more about later).

As God's special word to us, the Bible reveals *who* God is, *what* God has done in history, and *how* God has designed us to live. In other words, the Bible answers the deep questions about our place and purpose in this world, questions that human reason and experience cannot answer on their own. This is why the Bible is so important for Christians. The Bible isn't some sort of textual Magic 8 Ball that you can shake and get an answer for all the little dilemmas of life. It isn't a fairy tale detached from human history. It is where the eternal God of creation speaks to us.

How Should We Read the Bible?

Before we look more closely at the content of the Bible and especially the New Testament, we must first address a topic that often comes up when we discuss the Bible—the issue of biblical interpretation. The Bible isn't an enchanted document that just fell from heaven and lays everything out straightforward with no complications. Like any writing composed by human hands, the Bible cannot be read in a conceptual vacuum. As noted earlier in this chapter, the Bible was written by people who lived a long time ago in cultural contexts much different from our own. So to understand what God is really saying to us through the Bible, we need to first understand how to detect God's truth through its words. And that requires interpretation.

I've had a number of students over the years push me on this topic. "Aren't you just stacking the deck and interpreting the Bible to say whatever you want?" asked one University of North Carolina student recently on a campus visit. "Isn't interpretation just a matter of your own opinion?" I responded that if we were simply twisting the biblical text to find convenient linguistic loopholes that fit my opinion, that would be *mis*interpretation.

Good biblical interpretation doesn't play those manipulative language games. It doesn't conform itself to one's biases or intellectual goals, noble or ignoble as they may be. It instead relies on the same critical tools we use when we read any text to get to the truth. Good biblical interpretation doesn't force meaning on the text; rather, it uncovers and draws forth its true meaning by taking into account the literary genre, social and historical background, context, and linguistic features of the Bible. To interpret the Bible means taking into full account *all* the issues surrounding the text. In that sense, as I've often told students, to interpret the Bible properly, you need to use the same principles you'd employ for interpreting any text, be it a historical document, a piece of poetry, or a news article.

Take, for instance, the issue of literary genre. The Bible, as we already noted, is a collection of different writings composed by different authors at different times for different reasons. This means we can't always read one passage of the Bible the same way we'd read another. For example, when Psalm 23 famously proclaims that "the LORD is my shepherd" who "makes me lie down in green pastures," it wouldn't make sense to read this as saying that God is a literal shepherd forcing the psalmist to sprawl out in a meadow. That's because Psalm 23 is a hymn that uses metaphorical language to describe God's gracious care and protection. In much the same way, you can't pick up the gospel of Matthew, whose literary features clearly indicate its literary genre as an ancient biography, and read it the same way you'd read the *Iliad*. Literary genre gives us an interpretive basis for understanding how a text was meant to be read. Ignoring genre will cause us to misunderstand the true meaning behind the text.

Another factor to always consider is that the books of the Bible were not originally written to you and me. The book of Exodus, for example, was written to the ancient Israelites to remind them of God's deliverance of their people from slavery in Egypt. The prophetic book of Jeremiah was composed for the people living in Jerusalem who were facing the impending threat of the Babylonian Empire in mind. Paul's letter to the Romans was sent to first-century Christians living in Rome. None of these texts were written to twenty-first-century Westerners. But that doesn't mean these texts weren't written *for* us. The distinction here is that although the biblical writings were originally intended to be read by a certain group of people, God's Word nevertheless possesses significant meaning and insight for those reading it today. So although the words of Jeremiah 29:11—"'For I know the plans I have for you,' declares the LORD, 'plans to prosper you and not to harm you, plans to give you hope and a future'"—were originally addressed to the displaced Jewish exiles brought to Babylon, they can still provide comfort for readers today. But this also means that when we read the biblical text, we cannot ignore questions about who wrote the text, the reasons they originally wrote it, the audience they were writing to, and the historical context of their writing. The words of Jeremiah 29:11 only find their full significance when they are read with their original purpose in mind.

Still another interpretive issue lies in taking the text out of its original context. As I told one student on a recent university visit, you can't read *Macbeth* and take one random line out of the play, such as "fair is foul, and foul is fair," and say, "See, Shakespeare was a moral relativist." No, you have to read in context. In the same way, you can't rip one line out of the Bible and say, "Well, this is what the Bible says on the subject."

For instance, in Luke 14:26, Jesus proclaims, "If anyone comes to me and does not hate father and mother, wife and children, brothers and sisters . . . such a person cannot be my disciple." Does that mean that Jesus says we should hate our parents, siblings, and children? Is Jesus *anti-family*? Well, it sounds that way on its own. But when you read this statement in light of Jesus's broader teaching in Luke 14 about the absolute devotion required of his disciples; his acceptance of the Torah, including the commandment to honor one's father and mother; and Jesus's teachings elsewhere, it seems obvious that he is using hyperbole here to make a point. Jesus isn't saying you need to despise your family to follow him, but rather that your love for Jesus should supersede that of your immediate family (see also Matthew 10:37). But when you take this saying out of context, these important details become obscured and lead to misinterpretation.

Of course, interpretation isn't always clear-cut and easy. The Bible is a complex document, one that has undergone centuries of interpretation. You can go on the internet right now and find dozens and dozens of massive commentaries by well-read scholars on every book of the Bible, each one offering its own interpretation of what the text says (rarely contradictory, but with nuances of similar conclusions). Scriptural interpretation is a complex, ongoing process, one that Christians believe is guided by the Holy Spirit. Sometimes we have to wrestle with the Bible to understand what God is speaking to us there. But such wrestling is futile if we fail to recognize how the Bible should be interpreted and instead engage in frivolous language games.

If creation is where we encounter evidence pointing to the reality of the eternal, spiritual cosmic artist behind the existence of our universe, the Bible is where we learn who that artist is, how his creative power has shaped the world, and what it means for us today. Where reason and experience find themselves grasping for words, the Bible provides us a third form of knowledge—divine revelation. This is why the Bible is so important for Christians today, and why learning how to interpret the Bible fluently is so crucial for those seeking to demolish the crippling doubts standing in their way. After all, if we don't know how to read God's Word and find truth in it, how will we be equipped to face the misinterpretation, cynicism, and hyperskepticism of others? How will our faith be able to stand in the midst of such misgivings? How will we be able to escape our disbelief?

That being said, by no means should we reduce the importance of the Bible solely to apologetics. Perhaps the most powerful reason to read the Bible is simply to hear from God and grow in relationship with him. So many days, I (Cliffe) find myself reading the Bible not because I need more philosophical ammunition to confront some atheist podcaster; I read it because I need God's wisdom in the face of life's hardships, guidance and insight to confront a looming problem, or comfort from reminders of God's promises to us. In those moments, I know the only way to confront my concerns, fears, and doubts is to open my heart to the creator and allow his word to speak to me.

CHAPTER 4

CAN WE TRUST WHAT THE NEW TESTAMENT SAYS?

It was another beautiful day at the University of Texas in Austin. As we were speaking to the lingering crowd beneath the warmth of the fading afternoon sun, a young man stepped forward and earnestly asked, "Why should I believe what the New Testament says about Jesus? Why trust the Bible as the word of God?"

Taking a couple of steps back, I (Cliffe) looked him in the eyes and calmly retorted, "Well, you can't trust that the Bible is the word of God. You don't believe that!" Almost instantly, his expression changed from one of guarded skepticism to one of baffled curiosity. This definitely wasn't the answer he expected.

"I can't prove the Bible is God's Word," I continued, "because I can't show you that *any* book is inspired by God, regardless of whether or not I'm personally convinced it is. But what I can show you is that the New Testament Gospels are historically reliable."

Over the next several minutes, I walked him through four tests we should give to any historical text in order to gauge its reliability. After that, I asked him to read all four of the gospels and apply the same analytical tests. "See if they get a passing grade," I said. He nodded, silently accepting the challenge. As he walked away, I silently prayed that he'd take up my proposed experiment in good faith, hoping that perhaps he would come out victorious in the face of his doubts.

Can we really trust what the New Testament writings say? It's something we're asked almost every time we step onto university campuses. In my opinion, there are few questions more important for Christians to ask. As we noted earlier, the gospels of Matthew, Mark, Luke, and John are our primary source of information about Jesus Christ. It is through these texts, written in the last few decades of the first century AD, that we learn about the ministry, miracles, and teachings of Jesus, as well as his crucifixion and resurrection. All of Christianity pivots on the testimony of the four gospels.

But if the Gospels and the other sections of the New Testament aren't historically reliable and fail to offer an accurate account of the life, death, and resurrection of Jesus, then, to echo the words of the apostle Paul, all of Christianity is mere "foolishness" (1 Corinthians 1:18). But how do we test whether the New Testament is trustworthy? How, in the face of skepticism and doubt, can we find certainty that what each gospel reports about Jesus is historically accurate and not pure fiction?

Why Is It Important to Test the Reliability of the New Testament?

Many folks are pretty surprised to find out that I (Cliffe) am a pretty skeptical individual. I have to admit that I need to see and corroborate the evidence before coming to a conclusion because I don't want to be hoodwinked. As I constantly tell students, if we blindly accept everything that people tell us, there's a good chance we're going to get ripped off. Which is partially why I can relate to those who wrestle with uncertainty about Christianity. I've spent my entire life wrestling with these same doubts and seeking answers to many of the same questions they ask me, and it's because I'm a skeptic too.

We need to be skeptical because the unfortunate reality is that we live in a broken world full of fake news, conspiracy theories, and countless internet scams. We have to be at least somewhat skeptical when truth and falsehood, good and evil, often coexist in a tangled web that can quickly entrap us. None of us can afford to be naive or gullible when there's so much on the line. Luckily, we don't have to just drift along, accepting every idea that comes our way. Each of us was given a brilliant, rational mind that we can (and should) use to the fullest. We shouldn't be afraid to dig deep for the truth and ask questions; we were created to do exactly that!

It's because I'm a skeptic that I find intellectual honesty to be so important. It is crucial to base our beliefs on reliable and convincing evidence, especially when it comes to historical knowledge. As any historian worth their weight will tell you, good historical inquiry requires healthy skepticism, one that neither blindly rejects nor blindly accepts something as fact. We can't go back in time and see for ourselves how the pyramids were built, who painted the *Mona Lisa*, or what happened during the War of 1812. Those events already happened, and they won't happen again. The best any historian can do is figure out whether we can rely on what eyewitnesses who lived back then had to say about that person, place, or event. We need to investigate what the evidence tells us, test whether it is credible, and then decide to what degree we can trust our sources.

For instance, none of us can personally verify that George Washington was a real person. None of us have seen him firsthand, much less attended his inauguration or took a photograph of him. But we can investigate different eyewitness accounts of his life, inspect the reliability of these witnesses, assess the relationship between these sources, and corroborate them using historical artifacts related to events in Washington's life. Based on the results of these tests, we can determine that our best and most reliable evidence demonstrates that Washington was a real person who fought in the Revolutionary War and was elected as the first president of the United States—those are accurate historical statements. The same tests can also reveal that, contrary to some accounts, Washington did not have wooden teeth and never refused to lie to his father about chopping down a cherry tree. Those statements lack reliable evidentiary support.

As a skeptic, I take a similar approach to the New Testament. If I'm going to believe what the Gospels say, I need to first determine whether I can trust what they say. I need to test whether they are historically reliable. Why would I want to follow Jesus Christ if he's just a made-up character? That'd be foolish! If the Gospels really do offer an accurate historical portrait of Jesus, there should be credible evidence indicating as much—evidence that can endure rigorous historical examination. This is why I have no reservations about encouraging fellow skeptics to embrace intellectual honesty and to read the Gospels and test for themselves whether they're historically reliable; I believe the evidence should speak for itself.

What Evidence Is There That the New Testament Is Reliable?

So how can we know the New Testament Gospels are historically accurate? What sort of questions do we need to ask? Over the years, we have found four particular tests to be especially helpful when it comes to addressing skepticism and guiding Christians through their doubts about the Bible.

Literary Style and Genre

Good interpretation of any piece of literature requires knowing which genre of writing it is. You won't enjoy a poem if you read it the same way you read a newspaper, and you won't make heads nor tails of a science textbook if you approach it the same way you would the *Lord of the Rings.* The literary style and genre of a piece of writing frame how a text should be understood. To put it another way, genre and literary style are intentional clues left by the author to let us know whether we should interpret a text as epic prose or a parable, mythology or a memoir, a research paper or a self-help manual.

Luckily for us, the gospel writers left clues pointing to how we should read them. The Gospels are *historical narratives about the life of Jesus of Nazareth.* They are first-century *biographies.*

"But, Cliffe, how can we know that the gospel writers intended these texts to be read as historical narratives? How can we be certain they're not like other myths?" That's a good question I hear a lot when talking about the historicity of the Bible. If you want an answer to that, again, look at the clues in the text. Observe, for instance, how the beginning of the gospel of Luke emphasizes the role of eyewitness testimony:

> Many have undertaken to draw up an account of the things that have been fulfilled among us, just as they were handed down to us by those who from the first were eyewitnesses and servants of the word. With this in mind, since I myself have carefully investigated everything from the beginning, I too decided to write an orderly account for you, most excellent Theophilus, so that you may know the certainty of the things you have been taught. (Luke 1:1–4)

Does this sound like something you'd read in Homer's *Odyssey*, the Assyrian *Epic of Gilgamesh*, or *Harry Potter*? Definitely not. Myths don't proclaim themselves to be based on eyewitness accounts or careful historical investigation. Myths don't inform their audiences that their goal is to make sure they "may know the certainty of the things you have been taught." That's something historical narratives do. It's a clear sign that Luke wants his readers to interpret his gospel as a historical biography of Jesus Christ, not a fictional story.

The gospel of Luke isn't alone in this regard. The gospel of John concludes by identifying its author as a disciple of Jesus, an eyewitness who "testifies to these things and who wrote them down. We know that his testimony is true" (John 21:24; see also 1 John 1:1).

We find other statements of eyewitness testimony elsewhere in the New Testament. Arguably the most notable one is found in Paul's first letter to the Corinthians:

> For I handed on to you as of first importance what I in turn had received: that Christ died for our sins in accordance with the scriptures and that he was buried and that he was raised on the third day in accordance with the scriptures and that he appeared to Cephas [Peter], then to the twelve. Then he appeared to more than five hundred brothers and sisters at one time, most of whom are still alive, though some have died. Then he appeared to James, then to all the apostles. Last of all, as to one untimely born, he appeared also to me. (1 Corinthians 15:3–8 NRSVue)

We'll discuss this passage in more detail later in the book. For now, however, notice the language that Paul uses here. The compact prose, logical progression, and emphasis on eyewitness testimony read more like a witness statement than what we'd see in a Greek myth. As Paul highlights here for his readers, the news of Jesus Christ's death and resurrection isn't just baseless gossip. Paul points to hundreds of people—some of whom are still alive at the time he is writing—that corroborate reports that Jesus was crucified, buried, and appeared again on the third day. This includes well-known figures in the early church (Peter, James, the twelve disciples, Paul himself).

Several other literary features of the New Testament Gospels also point to their status as historical narratives. They do not cast the events involving Jesus in the imaginative or folkloric language found in other ancient myths. Rather, the gospel writers often employ succinct, matter-of-fact rhetoric when describing the life and teachings of Jesus. They focus on naming *where* Jesus was, *who* was with him, *what* he did and said, and *when* he did it. There are no extensive mythic elaborations, no lengthy poetic stanzas to enthrall the audience. Just the bare facts: At this place, at this time, and in front of these people Jesus did this.

It's also important to note that this literary style is not unique to the New Testament Gospels. Over the past several decades, scholars have increasingly noted linguistic and stylistic similarities between the Gospels and other ancient biographies, such as those written by well-known Greco-Roman historians like Plutarch, Tacitus, and Xenophon. Greco-Roman biographies of famous emperors, military heroes, political leaders, and philosophers typically proclaim to offer an organized portrait of their respective subject's lives, based on reliable sources, as do each of the New Testament Gospels (think back to Luke 1). Moreover, much like the Gospels, these ancient biographies also describe key events concerning the birth, teachings, moral character, and death of their subjects, using detail-focused language clearly different from the epic prose of ancient myths. These similarities only further highlight the literary intention of the gospel writers—namely, to offer an accurate and reliable historical account of the life, death, and resurrection of Jesus.

The Gospels don't read like a fairy tale. There's no clichéd "once upon a time in the land of Nod" opening. There are no damsels in distress to be rescued, no mythic beasts to be conquered. While many Christians may recognize the name of C. S. Lewis, far fewer realize that he was an Oxford-educated expert in Norse and Greek mythology. In his book *Christian Reflections*, Lewis writes regarding the Gospels, "I have been reading poems, romances, vision-literature, legends, and myths all my life. I know what they are like. I know none of them are like this. . . . The reader who doesn't see this simply has not learned how to read." I would happen to agree.

External Evidence

If the New Testament Gospels were written as biographical accounts of the life of Jesus, then we should be able to corroborate some of their specific details with other historical and archaeological evidence. We can't accept a source as credible if it doesn't even get the basic historical details right. We wouldn't trust a biography of Abraham Lincoln that mentions him taking a zeppelin to the land of Oz, right? Of course not! In the same way, the Gospels cannot be deemed historically reliable if they depict Jesus going to made-up places like Atlantis or meeting made-up people like Hercules. The concrete details given in the Gospels must correlate with verified historical and archaeological knowledge. Otherwise, they fail the test.

The Gospels preserve a considerable amount of specific details about where Jesus went, who he talked to, and when he lived. They state that Jesus was born in Bethlehem, raised in Nazareth, and spent his last week in Jerusalem. All four gospels also depict Jesus being baptized by John the Baptist in the Jordan River. They likewise mention Jesus teaching in a number of cities and towns across first-century Palestine. For instance, all four of the gospels depict Jesus teaching in a synagogue and performing miracles in the fishing village of Capernaum, a town about twenty-five miles away from Nazareth on the northern coast of the Sea of Galilee. Archaeologists have even discovered the remains of the first-century synagogue in Capernaum where Jesus likely taught (Mark 1:21–28). Jesus doesn't visit imaginary locations concocted by the gospel authors; he isn't gallivanting around Wonderland. The Gospels discuss *real places* mentioned in other ancient sources that archaeologists have confirmed were inhabited during the lifetime of Jesus.

The same can be said for various political figures mentioned in the Gospels. For instance, when we were recently discussing this very subject on YouTuber Jack Neel's podcast, I (Cliffe) brought up an excellent example of this from the gospel of Luke:

> In the fifteenth year of the reign of Tiberius Caesar, Pontius Pilate being governor of Judea, and Herod being tetrarch of Galilee, and his brother Philip tetrarch of the region of Ituraea and Trachonitis, and Lysanias tetrarch of Abilene, during the high priesthood of Annas and Caiaphas, the word of God came to John the son of Zechariah in the wilderness. (Luke 3:1–2 ESV)

Now, I'll be the first to admit that this type of passage used to put me to sleep. I mean, who really cares who was in charge of what way back when? But as I told Jack, what makes Luke 3:1–2 so important is the fact that these intersecting details reveal just how meticulous a historian Luke is. All of these political figures mentioned here—from the Roman emperor Tiberius down to the most insignificant of tetrarchs—are verified historical individuals. Not only that, but just as Luke says, ancient inscriptions and evidence from other ancient Roman sources confirm that the reigns of each of the people overlap during the fifteenth year of Tiberius Caesar's rule. Luke was spot-on here.

We can find even more historical corroboration in the Gospels when we turn to the archaeological record. Take, for example, the mention of the pool in Bethesda in John 5, where Jesus heals a paralytic man lying near the pool. According to John 5:2, this large pool located near Jerusalem was surrounded by "five covered colonnades" (freestanding rows of columns supporting a roof). This detail puzzled scholars, as the wording suggests that this pool had an unprecedented five sides. Most of them assumed that John's gospel got this detail wrong. However, near the Church of St. Anne in Jerusalem, archaeologists later discovered a pair of rectangular pools dating to the time of Jesus that were surrounded on each side by a colonnade, with a fifth colonnade separating the two pools. John had it right!

Even more interesting, the same thing can be said for the Pool of Siloam mentioned in John 9. Until recently, some scholars believed that the Pool of Siloam was made up by John, as there was no archaeological research confirming that such a site existed. However, in 2005, a group of excavators accidently unearthed a massive pool that was more than two hundred feet in length near the exact place where ancient Christian writers believed the Siloam pool may have been located. Again, John got it right.

Now, some of you might be saying, "That's all fine and good, Cliffe and Stuart, but none of this confirms that Jesus was a real historical person. Sure, maybe the gospel writers knew something about the local landscape of first-century Palestine. And yeah, maybe they correctly identified the people in charge during Jesus's day. But none of that proves that Jesus really existed. Couldn't the Gospels just be a well-researched fairy tale?"

Well, that's a plausible theory if the Gospels are our only source of knowledge about Jesus Christ. But the truth is that they aren't. The Jewish historian Josephus in his *Antiquities* (18.3.3), which he wrote around AD 94, notes that during the reign of Pontius Pilate a certain wise teacher named Jesus did wonderful deeds, attracted considerable attention, and was crucified. Josephus later also mentions the stoning of "James, the brother of Jesus who is called Christ" (*Antiquities* 20.9.1).

Josephus isn't the only ancient writer to mention Jesus either. Writing around AD 116, the Roman historian Tacitus in his *Annals* (15.44) describes how the Roman emperor Nero blamed the Christians for the Great Fire of Rome and had them executed. Tacitus goes on to explain that these Christians were named after "Christus," who suffered under the reign of Pilate during the rule of Tiberius Caesar.

Another possible mention of Christ may be found in the writings of the second-century-AD Roman historian Suetonius.

While Josephus, Tacitus, and Suetonius certainly don't tell us nearly as much about Jesus as the Gospels do, at the very minimum they historically corroborate that Jesus was not the mere invention of the New Testament authors. In fact, you'd be hard-pressed to find a serious historian, classicist, or biblical scholar who doesn't believe that Jesus was a historical person who was crucified by the Romans, died, and was reported by his followers to have appeared to them following his death. Although those scholars may certainly dispute whether we can say that Jesus actually rose from the dead (a topic we'll deal with later in this book), at the bare minimum they can agree that the earliest Christ followers who wrote the New Testament writings weren't making Jesus up. Jesus was, without a doubt, a real person, not a mythical figure.

So does the external evidence from archaeology and other ancient sources support the historical reliability of the New Testament? As I (Stuart) said to one student recently, "Take a tour of the Holy Land. Notice how often any tour guide—whether Jewish, Christian, Muslim, or even atheist—will reference or cite a passage from the New Testament." That's because so many of the significant ancient sites we've excavated are named in the Bible. You can literally open the Gospels as a map and trace the very steps of Jesus across Palestine. And you can do the same thing with the apostle Paul through the book of Acts and his letters. In that sense, it's not just that the Gospels are corroborated by archaeological evidence; they actually can help inform our archaeological knowledge of the ancient world.

Internal Consistency

We've met all sorts of folks from all walks of life on our campus visits. But even Stuart and I were taken aback during a recent visit to Texas State University when a figure wearing a neon-green, full-body spandex suit beneath a blue T-shirt and white athletic shorts suddenly materialized out of the crowd. *This has to be a prank*, I thought to myself. *There's no way this guy is serious.* As it turned out, I was wrong. Over the next thirty minutes, we had an incredibly fruitful discussion with our green friend, one characterized by deep intellectual honesty, mutual respect, and a parting embrace.

One of the first questions our alien-like discussion partner asked was how we can be certain that the gospel writers give an accurate account of the life of Jesus. "Well," I responded to him, "let me just say that my three granddaughters would get a kick out of what you're wearing right now. Tonight I'm going to call them and tell them I had the privilege of talking to a green man and describe what you looked like and how our talk went. But I'm sure Stuart is going to call them tonight and describe what he saw and experienced too. Now do you think our descriptions will be exactly the same?"

"Well, probably not," he responded, shaking his head.

"Yeah, I might mention how we shook hands when you arrived, whereas Stuart won't. Or maybe Stuart in his description will mention your blue shirt, whereas I won't say what color it was. They're not going to be identical descriptions. But that doesn't mean we're contradicting each other. It just means we have different perspectives that accurately describe the same event. We can say the same thing about the Gospels. Matthew has a unique perspective. So do Mark, Luke, and John. They don't need to be identical because no two historical accounts, if they're genuine, are identical. What's important is that they're *internally consistent*."

So what do I mean by *internal consistency* of the Gospels? I mean that while Matthew, Mark, Luke, and John each articulate different theological points, emphasize certain elements of Jesus's life and ministry more thoroughly than others, and even choose not to include specific details found in the other three gospels, overall they exhibit no major contradictions that suggest confusion or historical unreliability.

Put more simply, the Gospels are accurate historical accounts of Jesus's life told from their own selective perspectives.

For example, let's say you and I are standing on a street corner when suddenly a red convertible slams on its breaks before crashing into a gray SUV driving through the intersection. When the police arrive on the scene, you might give a report that reads, "I heard the screech of tires behind me before seeing the red sports car hit the side of the SUV in the intersection." But let's say my report reads, "I saw the convertible speed toward the intersection, heard the collision, and then turned around to see the convertible embedded into the gray SUV." These accounts clearly describe the same event; they're internally consistent. Yes, your account may reflect a different perspective of the event (you saw the crash actually happen, whereas I only heard it), use different language (you called it a sports car, whereas I identified it as a convertible), and even include details that I didn't notice or include in my report (such as the screech of the tires or the color of the car). But that doesn't mean your accident report is accurate and mine isn't. Nor does it mean your account outright contradicts mine.

We see something similar with the Gospels. Take the different description each one gives about the women who visited the empty tomb—an example that quite a few folks will reference as a "contradiction." All four gospels (Matthew 28; Mark 16; Luke 24; John 20) state that Mary Magdalene came to the site on the morning of the third day and saw that Jesus's tomb was empty. But Matthew, Mark, and Luke report that "Mary the mother of James" was also there. Mark also states a woman named Salome was there, and Luke includes a woman named Joanna, as well as other nameless women.

Now, do the Gospels offer different details here? Yes, they do. But do they contradict one another? Does John, for instance, state that Mary Magdalene was the *only* woman at the tomb? Or does Mark emphasize that Joanna *wasn't* at the tomb or explicitly claim there were exactly *three* women at the tomb? Not at all. All four gospels are consistent in their report that the first people to encounter the empty tomb were women. The fact that some gospels mention more specific names than others simply reflects the choice of the evangelists rather than a barefaced contradiction.

The same can be said for a lot of other alleged "contradictions" in the Gospels. For instance, the visitation of the Magi, Herod the Great's vindictive slaughter of the male babies of Bethlehem, and Jesus's subsequent flight to Egypt with Mary and Joseph are only mentioned in Matthew 2. Does that mean the other gospels contradict Matthew? Not one bit. It just means the other gospels don't take the time to deal with that aspect of Jesus's life. Notice that Mark, Luke, and John never claim that these events *didn't* happen. Nor do they contain any evidence that would render those events impossible, such as Jesus being born in Alexandria and not Bethlehem. Do the four gospels differ here? Yes, they're coming at Jesus's life from different angles. But that doesn't mean Matthew's perspective is right and the others are wrong, or vice versa. At the end of the day, the Gospels remain internally consistent.

What is important to remember is that each gospel offers a *selective* account of the life of Jesus. Their authors had to choose which details to include and which to exclude. And while their accounts are certainly *consistent*, none of them are *comprehensive*. The gospel of John concludes as much: "Jesus did many other things as well. If every one of them were written down, I suppose that even the whole world would not have room for the books that would be written" (21:25).

Manuscript Evidence

One final test relates to the manuscript evidence for the New Testament. Every once in a while, a student will come up and say something like, "The New Testament is nearly two thousand years old. How do we know for sure that someone hasn't changed it at some point in its history?" In some cases, folks have even gone so far as to argue that they can't trust *anything* the Gospels say about Jesus simply because we don't have the original New Testament manuscripts.

Let me start by saying that such hyperskepticism is not only unproductive but also fatally reductionistic when it comes to historical knowledge. It's one thing to be skeptical that we can know for certain that the Bibles we possess today accurately represent what the New Testament authors originally wrote. That's a valid question if we're going to test the historical reliability of the Gospels. However, to be so cynical to say that we need the original manuscripts or else the New Testament has no historical weight is downright incredulous. We have no manuscripts containing *even a single sentence* from Aristotle's writings until several centuries after his death, and no complete copies of any of his works until the early medieval period. Does that mean we can't trust anything we know about Aristotle? So, too, the earliest copy of Suetonius's *The Twelve Caesars*—one of our primary historical sources about Julius Caesar, Augustus, and many of the Roman emperors—dates from the early ninth century, nearly eight hundred years *after* Suetonius wrote this work. Does that mean we know nothing about the Roman emperors?

As you can see, the problem with this hyperskeptical approach is that it quickly makes us feel like we can't trust almost any of our ancient sources. The truth is that we have no original copies of pretty much any culturally significant ancient text. Papyri manuscripts decay. Parchment manuscripts are damaged. Only under the right conditions can such documents last long enough to be discovered and recorded. More often than not, we have to rely on copies (or copies of copies) produced by later scribes. The demand that we can only trust the original manuscripts thus holds a standard of knowledge that pretty much no ancient text, biblical or otherwise, can truly satisfy.

That being said, the question still remains whether we can trust that our New Testament writings are accurate representations of the original documents. After all, if we have two different ancient manuscripts of the Gospels that say radically different things about Jesus, it's going to be hard to determine what is historically accurate and what isn't.

Here are the facts. We possess more than 5,800 manuscripts of the New Testament writings in the original Greek. Of these, more than 250 date from within five centuries of Jesus's death, including four that date as early as the mid-second century AD. This is an incredibly impressive number when we consider that we have only fifty such manuscript fragments that contain *any* portion of Plato's various dialogues. In fact, the New Testament has the highest manuscript attestation of any ancient Greek writing, period. More than Homer's *Odyssey*. More than Plato's writings.

Even more impressive is the fact that we know of around ten thousand Latin copies of the New Testament along with more than 9,300 copies written in Syriac, Coptic, Armenian, and several other ancient languages. Adding even more to this wealth are the tens of thousands of additional quotations of the New Testament found in the writings of early Christian figures such as Clement of Rome, Justin Martyr, and Tertullian, who lived from the second to the fourth centuries AD. From their biblical quotations alone, we could nearly reconstruct an entire copy of the New Testament even without all the other biblical manuscripts we possess.

Of course, having a lot of manuscript copies of an ancient text doesn't automatically mean they all say the same thing. As many critics are quick to point out, there are hundreds of thousands of variants—perhaps as many as four hundred thousand—across these different manuscripts. Indeed, no two New Testament manuscripts are exactly alike. But just how problematic are these variants? The answer is that they are far less problematic than some folks make them out to be.

To begin with, the vast majority of these variants do not change the central narrative or message of the text. Some manuscripts may possess the same words but in different order, perhaps placing the verb before the noun instead of after it. Other manuscripts may contain slight spelling variations of certain personal names or place names. Some manuscripts contain trivial typos, such as a scribe forgetting a vowel in a lengthy verb or accidentally copying a word twice. Other manuscripts may contain minor grammatical variations, such as using a dative noun instead of an accusative. Altogether, these rather insignificant disparities and blunders account for *more than 99 percent* of all New Testament variants. Hardly the smoking gun some would make it out to be.

Now, are there at least some significant textual variants in the New Testament? Yes, there are. But this isn't breaking news for anyone who studies the Bible. Most of these are well-documented and have been known for centuries. It has long been recognized, for instance, that the ending of Mark 16 and John 7:53–8:11 aren't found in our earliest New Testament manuscripts and were likely added by later scribes. In fact, most biblical translations today say as much in a footnote. It's not some dirty secret; there's no controversy here. It's just historical fact.

Most of the variants deemed "significant" are actually quite inconsequential in the grand scheme of things. Take Matthew 21:12. While some Greek manuscripts read, "Jesus entered the temple," others read, "Jesus entered the temple *of God*." Is this a variant? Yes. Two whole words are added in some manuscripts. Does it change the meaning of the text? Not really. How about Mark 5:21, which mentions that Jesus crossed the Sea of Galilee. Some manuscripts read, "When Jesus had crossed again to the other side," whereas others read, "When Jesus had crossed again *in the boat* to the other side." Is one version of this verse longer than the other? Clearly it is. But does this variant lead to a radical change in the meaning of the text? Of course not! At the end of the day, the message remains clear, despite scribal discrepancies.

So can we trust that the New Testament manuscripts we possess accurately transmit what the biblical authors saw and recorded about

Jesus Christ? Without question we can. I'd venture to say we can trust the accuracy of the text of the New Testament more so than any other ancient document due to its extensive ancient manuscript witnesses and the nearly infinitesimal level of overlap displayed by these documents.

Stuart and I were back in Austin. It had been nearly a year since we last visited the University of Texas campus. It only took a few minutes for a group of students to trickle over to us once we established our spot in the shade. Suddenly, in the midst of the crowd, I recognized a familiar face weaving his way through the sea of people.

"Hey, Cliffe, do you remember me?" It was the young man I had met the year before. I was shocked. I thought for sure I'd never see the guy again—that's just the reality of traveling from one massive college campus to another across the country. I greeted him warmly and asked how he was doing.

"I'm doing great," he responded, smiling the whole time. "I just wanted to let you know that I took up your challenge. I read all four gospels simply as history, like you told me to do. I applied your tests to them too. And I realized that the historical evidence pointing to Jesus truly is reliable. So I've put my faith in him now."

Wow. Incredible.

If there's one lesson we can take away from this encouraging anecdote, it's this: We can't help others combat doubt purely by telling them they're dead wrong. Parroting over and over again that the Bible is reliable simply because it's the Word of God isn't going to persuade folks who don't accept that as factual. True as it may be for Christians, it's a nearly impenetrable nonstarter when it comes to having an impactful conversation with someone who doesn't share that view. If, as we saw in chapter 1, faith is belief rooted in reason and knowledge, then we can't demolish skepticism merely by talking past it. *We need to give people whatever available evidence we have that directly addresses their doubts.*

Navigating doubt is a multistep process, one that requires evidence and encouragement, discussion and understanding, reflection and prayer. Doubt needs to be faced head-on. It won't disappear just because someone says, "God says so." I wasn't any more able to prove to that young man that the Bible is the Word of God than he was willing to concede such a monumental point in the first place. But when confronted firsthand with the compelling evidence for the historical reliability of the portrayal of Jesus in the Gospels, that young man was able to challenge his doubts and, through the work of the Holy Spirit, come to faith in Christ. All that is to say that you can't face doubt lying down. Get up and seek out answers. You won't regret it.

CHAPTER 5

ISN'T THE BIBLE PROBLEMATIC?

As we said in chapter 3, one of the goals of this section of the book has been to deconstruct some of the misunderstandings and doubts people express about the Bible. For Christians, the Bible is how God speaks to us, reveals who he is and what he has done in history, and provides principles for living a flourishing life. However, as we've said countless times, we can't prove that the Bible is the Word of God to someone who hasn't already come to that reality by faith. We can only offer well-reasoned evidence to counteract the doubts that prevent someone from accepting Jesus Christ as Lord and Savior. It is only then, once someone has demolished those nagging doubts that keep them from trusting Jesus Christ, that they can go on to follow Jesus's example and accept the Scriptures as God's Word.

In the last chapter, we addressed one of those doubts—namely, whether the New Testament is historically reliable. Although we address this topic frequently in our campus visits, it's definitely not the only issue students bring up regarding the Bible. So in this chapter we're going to take a look at some of the other questions we've encountered in the last several years. Some of them piggyback off our previous discussion of the historical reliability of the Bible. Others deal with perceived ethical problems that many find offensive about the Bible in today's culture.

Such complex questions are important to address because they get at whether we can honestly claim that the Bible remains relevant for us today. But as we hope to show here, although these are doubts worth wrestling with, they are also doubts that can be defeated through reasonable reflection and the right evidence.

Couldn't the New Testament Authors Have Just Made Stuff Up?

"How do we know that the biblical writers weren't just making stuff up?"

We hear this counterpoint all the time in response to our evidence for the historical reliability of the New Testament. And at first glance, it's a pretty daunting critique. How, for example, can we be sure that Paul's claim that five hundred people saw Jesus Christ appear to them following his crucifixion and death (1 Corinthians 15:6) isn't any different from one of us reporting that we know five hundred people who have seen the Easter Bunny in real life? How can we know that what the Gospels report concerning Jesus's miracles and resurrection aren't just some fantastical flourishes added by the gospel writers to their otherwise historical treatments of his life? (For more on this one, see chapters 8–9.) Could Christianity really just be an ancient conspiracy theory that somehow survived into modernity?

We can take a number of different angles when addressing such questions. One of the approaches we often start with is the counterquestion concerning what the New Testament authors would have gained from lying about something like this. As we see in the New Testament and in the writings of the early church fathers, many of Jesus's earliest followers experienced familial rejection, social ostracization, economic hardships, persecution, and even death due to their beliefs. In fact, quite a few of Jesus's twelve disciples—our earliest eyewitnesses to Jesus's life—were either tortured to death or executed. So was Paul. Persecution, oppression, and death aren't exactly great motivation for creating a lie or defending it. On the flip side, if these guys just came together after Jesus died and said, "Hey, let's start telling people we saw Jesus alive," you have to think that the threat of being stoned, speared, or crucified would have silenced them pretty quickly. No one in their right mind would die for something they know is a lie.

Another problem arises when we realize that the New Testament writings don't stray from providing potentially embarrassing details that no person would have included if they were trying to create a convincing lie. For example, why would the gospel authors make up the fact that the first people to see Jesus resurrected from the dead were *women*? In the ancient world, women were viewed as having less reliable testimony than men had. According to some ancient Jewish rabbis, women shouldn't be allowed to give eyewitness testimony in a trial, since their testimony was inadmissible. For the gospel authors to say that the first eyewitnesses of Jesus's post-resurrection appearances were women actually would have *jeopardized* their credibility for many ancient readers! If they truly wanted to make their "conspiracy" persuasive, they easily could have had some of Jesus's male followers showing up to the empty tomb first to avoid the reliability problem.

The same can be said for many other seemingly humiliating details included in the Gospels. What, for instance, would *all four* gospels authors have to gain from stating that Peter, Jesus's closest disciple, disowned him three times or that the other fearful disciples abandoned Jesus following his arrest? Not exactly a good look for them. Or why would the book of Acts note that the early movement's most revered missionary, Paul, actually *persecuted* Christians at one point in his life? Or why depict Jesus crucified like a common criminal?

None of these scandalous details would have helped Jesus's followers attract people to the Christian movement. On the contrary, such embarrassing details would likely have hindered that task. However, if the Gospels were written as accurate historical accounts of Jesus's life, death, and resurrection based on eyewitness testimony, it makes sense why such embarrassing details would have been included. Good historical writing doesn't shy away from messiness or attempt to whitewash reality; it presents a careful and orderly account of things (Luke 1:1–3).

So could the New Testament authors have been lying about Jesus? Sure, it's possible. We could say the same thing about any ancient historical writer and allow our hyperskepticism to reduce all our historical knowledge to zilch. But perhaps the more fruitful and logical question is why the gospel authors would have gone through so much trouble to fabricate such a fantastical story that would only get them killed, especially one riddled with degrading and counterproductive details that make them look like cowards and their leader like a criminal. The most logical answer is that they believed it was true.

Why Were Some Books Excluded from the New Testament?

At almost every campus we visit, we meet at least one student who tells us that there are lots of ancient texts about Jesus that aren't found in the New Testament. Do any of these "mysterious" writings contain things we should know about Jesus? Why were they excluded from the New Testament? Is this evidence of some kind of early church campaign that sought to suppress certain information about Jesus? Needless to say, the answers to these questions aren't as exciting as some folks might hope.

The existence of other ancient texts about Jesus isn't exactly breaking news for scholars. It's long been known that dozens of ancient writings tell stories about Jesus or his apostles, discuss aspects of his teachings, or make theological claims about who Jesus is. These are often known as the New Testament Apocrypha. Some of these works, such as the Gospel of Peter or the Gospel of Nicodemus, are written in the style of the New Testament Gospels. Other works, such as the Acts of Andrew or the Acts of John, mimic the book of Acts. Still other works, such as the Apocalypse of Paul, contain symbolic visions similar to Revelation.

So why aren't any of these writings included in the New Testament, especially when so many of them are attributed to people associated with Jesus? It's here that students already suspicious about Christianity begin to spout off a handful of bizarre details found in these writings and assert that we're ignoring these important "historical" sources. Some even go as far as to claim that the New Testament is the result of a widespread church conspiracy that took place at a fourth- or fifth-century church council.

The problem is that we have no evidence supporting this perspective. For one thing, scholars are unanimous that *all* of these New Testament apocryphal works, supposedly authored by Peter, John, and other close followers of Jesus, are falsely attributed to these figures (also known as pseudepigrapha). Most of these texts were written in the second, third, and fourth centuries, long after all the apostles and earliest Christians had died, and many of them build on events found in the canonical gospels, inferring they were written *after* the New Testament writings were well-known.

Moreover, even though these nonbiblical writings adopt some of the literary characteristics of the New Testament writings, they also contain far more imaginative language than the four gospels and a lot of outrageous or far-fetched details you'd never see in any ancient historical narrative. For example, the apocryphal mid-second-century Gospel of Peter depicts a massive Jesus exiting the tomb with his head above the heavens alongside a talking cross. The late-second-century Infancy Gospel of Thomas depicts the toddler Jesus bringing clay birds to life, striking Mary and Joseph blind for correcting him, and even slaying a child who mistreats him. These texts read far more like tall tales or an early form of fan fiction than they do an ancient biography.

Some of the other works found in the New Testament Apocrypha contain ideas associated with Gnosticism, an ancient Christian philosophy that emphasized secret knowledge (Greek, *gnosis*) as the pathway to salvation and taught that the physical body and material existence were the flawed creation of an evil god. As a result, many Gnostics, contrary to what we find in the four New Testament gospels, denied that Jesus Christ was embodied or died on a cross. As a result, Gnosticism was denounced early on by Christians, as its teachings contradicted the historical information contained in the canonical gospels. While the gnostic gospels and treatises may adopt certain ideas found in the New Testament, they often twist them into unrecognizable forms, merging them with esoteric ideas found in the Platonic thought of the day.

Early Christians recognized these differences between these apocryphal or gnostic works and the twenty-seven writings that became part of the New Testament canon (Greek, *kanōn*, meaning "rule, standard"). The main tests used by early Christians to determine what made it into the New Testament canon are these:

- Can we confirm that this text was written by an eyewitness of Jesus or someone who knew eyewitnesses?
- Does this text contain ideas and information that match what we find in other texts written by early witnesses to Jesus,

as well as what we find in the teachings of the Old Testament, which Jesus accepted as Scripture?
- Do other churches and Christian communities also accept these texts as Scripture?

Note that these criteria don't exclude writings based on whether someone liked them or not. Nor do they rely solely on the power of a pope or a secretive group of bishops. Contrary to what some students claim, no papal decree or single church council listed once and for all the official books of the New Testament.

The key principle here is *worldwide consistency*. This is why the Gospel of Peter, for example, isn't included in the New Testament. It was written too late to actually be composed by Peter; its imaginative account of Jesus's life does not correlate with what we find in the authentic gospels; and many early churches never accepted it as authoritative. There is no mystery here, no hidden agendas. Our New Testament is the result of the worldwide church's organic acknowledgment that these specific books were clearly distinct from the other texts in circulation.

Now, this doesn't mean there was unanimous agreement right away on what books were canonical. The official canonization of the New Testament was a long process. Some early Christian communities, for example, accepted the Letters of Clement as Scripture. Others excluded books like Hebrews or Revelation. We even see this in our earliest complete manuscripts of the New Testament. But what is important to realize is that even in the second century AD, there was a general recognition among Christian communities across the ancient world that the gospels of Matthew, Mark, Luke, and John, alongside the letters of Paul, were uniquely authentic and authoritative. We can be completely confident that our New Testament contains the closest and most reliable witnesses to Jesus Christ and the beliefs of the early church.

Does the Bible Promote Slavery?

"I can't trust the Bible," one student, a US veteran, fiercely protested, "because God promotes slavery there." We've had a lot of heated conversation partners over the years, but few of them could rival his outrage. As I (Cliffe) reached to shake his hand and thank him for his service for our country, he snatched it back. "I'm not letting you shake my hand in the middle of what I'm saying," he yelled. You could have cut the tension with a knife.

The question of the relationship between the Bible and slavery has become a hot-button issue of late, one we've encountered more and more frequently both on campus visits and in interviews. We know it's a really tough question, one we still wrestle with. As I recently recounted to Graham Stephan and Jack Selby on their *The Iced Coffee Hour* podcast, I remember being cornered early in my career by a few graduate students asking why the Bible never explicitly condemns slavery. I had to admit to them that I hadn't really given it much thought at that point. So I spent a lot of time talking with biblical scholars who were far more well-read than I was, gleaning whatever wisdom they had to offer.

After years of reflection and earnest discussion, I've come to realize that no one can deny that several Old Testament passages, such as Exodus 21 and Leviticus 25, contain laws having to do with the practice of slavery. This is absolutely true. But it is important to put these laws into context and recognize that *instruction* does not mean *approval* and that *regulation* does not mean *endorsement*. Just because the Old Testament contains instruction about how one should treat slaves doesn't mean God approved of the practice any more than we can say that God endorses polygamy, divorce, or other unlawful practices mentioned in the Bible.

The Old Testament law was written specifically for the nation of Israel, who lived during a time where slavery was universally rampant.

It was an inescapable and unjust reality that affected every nation across the ancient Near East, including Israel. The Old Testament never declares that slavery is good or offers divine endorsement. Rather, we see in the Old Testament an effort to help the Israelites navigate their corrupt cultural environment within the restrictive economic and social constructs of their day. It is God pushing the Israelites a step in the right direction against the culture of their day. So to say the Bible is proslavery is as ludicrous as saying the Bible is also prodivorce just because it offers instruction about the practice of divorce.

It's also crucial to note that the theocratic law of Israel does not apply to us. Nowhere in the Gospels does Jesus declare that the Israelite legal system remains true today. While Jesus does declare that he came not to abolish the law but to fulfill it (Matthew 5:17), this applied to the moral law of God, not the theocratic law of Israel. Similarly, in Acts 15, we see the apostles declare to non-Jewish followers of Jesus that the only Jewish laws they must follow are avoiding food sacrificed to idols and fleeing from sexual immorality. That's it. Notice that no instructions about slavery are found on this list. Those laws stopped being relevant; they no longer applied.

Of course, the practice of slavery did not end during Jesus's day. Much like it was in the ancient Near East, slavery in the Roman Empire was a fundamental social and economic institution. Around one-third of all people living in the empire were slaves of one form or another. Some were uneducated laborers or servants; others were educated scribes, accountants, and even physicians. It was an unfortunate reality of that day, one that could not be escaped.

So when Paul instructs slaves to obey their masters (Ephesians 6:5), it doesn't mean he believed slavery was a good thing or endorsed its practice. Rather, what we see here is Paul navigating the injustice of slavery within the social constructs of his day. Yes, Paul here instructs those who are slaves to respect their masters and treat them as they would Christ. But this also echoes the challenge that Paul issues to the master of the slave a few verses later (v. 9). Both slave and master are to treat each other as they would Christ. This is reminiscent of Paul's words in Galatians 3:28: "There is neither Jew nor Gentile, neither slave nor free, nor is there male and female, for you are all one in Christ Jesus." According to Paul, all people, regardless of social status, are unified in Christ. That doesn't sound like someone endorsing slavery. In his brief letter to Philemon, Paul lives this out when he tells the slave owner, Philemon, not to treat his runaway slave, Onesimus, harshly but instead to accept him as a fellow brother in Christ. That's a radical, countercultural statement in a world where slavery was the prevailing norm.

Slavery is a gross injustice. It was wrong in the ancient world, and it remains wrong today, because it is a sinful rejection of the inherent worth each of us possesses as God's creation. It's true the Bible never outright expresses this condemnation, which doesn't mean the biblical writings don't take meaningful steps toward curbing this awful practice within their cultural contexts. Nor does it mean the Bible endorses slavery. After all, if the Bible is proslavery, then why is one of the greatest miracles ever performed by God—the parting of the Red Sea—performed to *free* an entire nation of slaves? If the Bible is proslavery, then why did so many prominent abolitionists, such as William Wilberforce and Frederick Douglass, embrace Christianity? The God who created all of humanity in his divine image never intended for his image bearers to enslave one another. That's not God; that's human sinfulness.

Is the Bible Sexist?

About a year ago, we were invited to appear on Alex O'Connor's podcast, *Within Reason*. Alex is a prominent atheist YouTuber who has interviewed figures ranging from Sam Harris and Richard Dawkins to Jordan Peterson and Ben Shapiro. For nearly three hours, the three of us had a cordial and stimulating conversation on a variety of topics. One subject that Alex seemed especially keen to talk about was the treatment of women in the Bible and whether the New Testament authors, most notably Paul, viewed women as inferior.

In particular, Alex had two texts he wanted to discuss. The first was 1 Corinthians 14:34–35:

> Women should remain silent in the churches. They are not allowed to speak, but must be in submission, as the law says. If they want to inquire about something, they should ask their own husbands at home; for it is disgraceful for a woman to speak in the church.

It didn't surprise us that Alex cited this text. We've had a fair number of students over the years ask us whether Paul is being misogynistic here. When these verses are taken out of context, it seems like he is. However, it is only after we situate this passage within its broader context that we can truly understand what Paul is really trying to say.

First, it's crucial to acknowledge that the early Christian movement was known for supporting women and giving them more opportunities for active participation than they typically experienced in other social circles of the Roman Empire. We see this with Jesus, who broke social norms by including women, such as Mary and Martha, among his closest followers and even appeared first to women after his resurrection. Early Christian communities followed suit by including women as members and empowering them to take on leadership roles in worship and other ministry functions. Acts 16:14–15, for example, tells of a merchant woman named Lydia who let Paul stay as a guest at her home and later hosted a house church. In Acts 18:18–28, we learn of Aquila and his wife, Priscilla, who accompanied

Paul in his mission and together taught the Jewish intellectual Apollos about Jesus Christ.

We can also note that the New Testament emphasizes in several places the importance of financially tending to the needs of widows (Acts 6:1; 1 Timothy 5:16). All that is to say, the early church supported women and gave them freedoms they did not previously possess. The early Christian movement embraced women as being equal in Christ (Galatians 3:28), a countercultural shift from the oppressive treatment of women in the broader Roman world.

Once we understand that women were given a refreshing degree of freedom within the early church, we can begin to make sense of 1 Corinthians 14. As I (Stuart) told Alex, 1 Corinthians 14:35–36 occurs within a section of Paul's letter where he's addressing the disorganized worship practices of the Corinthian church. One of those issues was the fact that women who embraced their newfound freedom to participate in worship had apparently become unruly and caused services to fall into chaos. In turn, many of these women were trying to teach, just like Priscilla did, but lacked enough education to do so sufficiently. So when we look more closely at this text, the problem wasn't that women shouldn't be teaching or participating in the church. If it had been, then why would Paul in the same letter have instructed women to cover their heads when praying or prophesying (1 Corinthians 11:2–16)—activities done in the context of worship. Rather, the issue lies in whether the ways they were contributing to the community were fruitful or disruptive. Paul wasn't anti-women; he was just opposed to disorderly worship.

The second text Alex mentioned was 1 Timothy 2, where Paul stated several seemingly troublesome things about women, including that they should dress modestly and learn in full submission, that he didn't permit a woman to teach or assume authority over a man, and that a woman would be saved through childbirth. Like 1 Corinthians 14:34–35, this passage sounds pretty rough if you rip it out of context.

Again, it is only once we locate this passage within its historical environment that what Paul is actually doing here becomes clear.

Paul's first letter to Timothy was written to his younger colleague who was establishing a church in Ephesus. Like the church in Corinth, the church in Ephesus seemed to have struggled with women who, in embracing their newfound freedom in the Christian church, were causing disruption in worship or were requiring further instruction in the gospel before being equipped to teach. So here again, we need to read Paul's instructions in light of this ongoing issue.

What made Timothy's situation in Ephesus trickier than what the Corinthian church was experiencing was a crisis of sexuality. Ephesus was one of the larger cities in the Roman Empire and had a prolific number of brothels and bathhouses. Ephesus also housed a massive temple dedicated to Diana of Ephesus, a Roman fertility goddess, which was served by female cult prostitutes (Acts 19). This temple was even considered one of the seven wonders of the ancient world. So it seems likely, as some biblical scholars have noted, that when some of these former temple prostitutes and brothel workers joined the Christian movement, they struggled to adapt to their new way of life. So when Paul told Timothy that women should avoid fancy clothing or jewelry and not speak out against their Christian brothers, he was likely addressing issues that had to do with the proper integration of these women into the community rather than offering instructions on how to treat women in general.

Something similar can be said regarding Paul's statement in 1 Timothy 2 that women are saved by childbirth. As we noted earlier in this chapter, one of the early challenges that faced the Christian movement was the rise of Gnosticism and its understanding of the physical body as evil and flawed. For many Gnostics, this meant that having sex, getting pregnant, and giving birth were bad things because they resulted in the imprisonment of a soul in the dirty material body of a baby. It seems likely that Paul here was addressing just that issue, declaring to women being influenced by gnostic ideas that they shouldn't disregard the good bodies God gave them.

It surprises some feminists who approach us and say, "I'm sick of the sexism in our culture," when we respond, "Yeah, we're right with you." It surprises them even more when we tell them we believe women are equal to men *because of* the Bible, not *in spite of* Scripture. When God created humanity (both male and female) in Genesis, he created both in his image. Not just the men. All people have value because they are image bearers of God; men and women alike are one in Christ. This is what the early church believed, taught, and acted out through the support and freedom they gave to women. And this is what Christians today should practice as well.

Does the Bible Endorse Genocide?

"I would condemn the God of your Bible as an immoral, tyrannical monster." It's been more than two decades since a Florida International University professor declared this in the middle of our animated conversation about the way God is portrayed in the Old Testament. Ever since I (Cliffe) began doing campus ministry more than forty years ago, lots of folks have asked me why the God of the Old Testament seems so much more wrathful and angrier than the God of the New Testament—a topic I addressed in my first book. More recently, however, I've had an increasing number of people question why the Old Testament has God telling the Israelites to slaughter the Canaanites before entering the promised land. Isn't that genocide? Does this mean the Bible condones this horrific practice? How could a good God do such a thing?

As I told the FIU professor, we need to remember that the goodness of the biblical God is represented in two ways: (1) love for and forgiveness of repentant sinners and (2) his judgment of injustice. You must have both. If God only forgives, then the unrepentant Hitlers and Stalins and murderers of the world get a free pass, and that's not justice. But if God only punishes, then there's no hope for any of us. We're all hopeless sinners. God's love and justice, forgiveness and punishment, are two sides of the same coin.

In the Old Testament, God sent the Israelites to conquer Canaan as a punishment for the depraved behavior of the Canaanites. The Canaanites were a wicked people (Deuteronomy 9:4–5) who worshiped idols (12:3) and practiced cultic prostitution and child sacrifice (Leviticus 18:21, 24; Deuteronomy 12:31). The conquest wasn't a case of God commanding the Israelites to massacre an innocent people; it was a case of God using the Israelites to judge a people who, for several centuries, had refused to turn from their sinful and unjust ways. God doesn't call for the massacre of the Canaanites simply because they weren't Israelites, which would be genocide. The problem lay in the collective wickedness of the Canaanites, not their ethnic identity.

Another issue that often gets ignored is the use of hyperbolic language in passages that tell the story of the conquest of the Canaanites. This is especially common in Joshua, where a common theme is the way the Israelites utterly destroyed entire cities, their inhabitants, and their possessions. However, in Judges, these same nations still exist and even fight back against the Israelites. As some scholars have also suggested, it seems likely that the Israelites did not carry out a wholesale slaughter of all the Canaanite inhabitants.

Finally, we can't talk about the punishment of the Canaanites for their wicked ways without pointing to God's punishment of the Israelites for *their* wickedness. Throughout the Old Testament, prophets such as Amos, Isaiah, and Jeremiah warn the Israelites that if they do not turn from their wicked deeds—their worship of other gods, mistreatment of the poor, adopting of unjust Canaanite practices—they will experience God's judgment too. Sure enough, just as it did with the Canaanites, the Bible also shares how Israel was brutally conquered by the Assyrians and Babylonians, who destroyed their cities, massacred their people, and even took some of the Israelites into exile. And the Bible insists that it was God who did this to Israel because they did not repent, despite having had ample opportunity to do so. This demonstrates that God in the Old Testament doesn't restrict his punishment to some ethnic groups and not others. God's goodness, both his forgiveness and mercy as well as his punishment of injustice, is universal in scope. God doesn't favor one ethnic group or type of person over another.

One of my (Cliffe's) favorite quotes about the Bible has long been attributed to Mark Twain: "Some people are troubled by the things in the Bible they can't understand. The things that trouble me are the things I can understand." On the fundamentals, the Bible can often be quite simple and clear. But it also contains a lot of weighty side issues, some of them very important ones, which even well-meaning and intelligent Christians strongly disagree about. And that's not surprising. The Bible is an incredibly complex document, a library of texts written over a millennium of history by dozens of people who lived in a world much different from ours, spoke different languages from the ones we speak, and encountered challenges that many of us have never experienced firsthand. Even the most seasoned biblical scholars, equipped with immense historical knowledge and an expertise in ancient languages, would admit as much.

It shouldn't shock us, then, when our attempts to answer these questions don't totally extinguish our worries, when our efforts to make sense of difficult texts don't arrive at the kind of conclusive answers we'd like to hear. This is especially the case with some of the topics we've covered in this chapter.

Both of us still struggle over these truly difficult subjects in Scripture. We don't know and understand everything. We have doubts just like everyone else; our faith runs up against challenges too. But that doesn't mean we toss our hands up, stop searching for answers, and succumb to cynicism. We keep asking intellectually honest questions, even when the solutions they offer aren't convenient or comfortable. We continue wrestling with our doubts alongside the students we talk with each week. We keep our eyes on God's Word and pray for understanding in the midst of our confusion. I truly encourage you to do the same. Don't give up.

CHAPTER 6

BUT WHAT ABOUT OTHER RELIGIONS?

"I just don't think anything is ever going to change your mind," the University of South Carolina student retorted as she slowly pushed back a strand of sandy brown hair behind her ear before placing her hand back into her olive-colored sweatshirt. "I mean, I know several people from several different religions who are all just as sure as you are that theirs is the correct one and that all the other ones are false." She shrugged, pausing for a few seconds as the spring breeze whistled through the red cedars dangling above us. Looking back at us, she spoke again, her voice firm and clear yet tinted with uncertainty, "They can't all be right, *can they*?"

Talk about a tough question.

As we stated earlier, our goal in the second part of the book is to turn our focus from the evidence for the existence of creator God, whom we experience in nature and encounter through rational thought, to the question of who this God is and where we can learn more about this God. That brought us to the Bible, the place where God reveals himself through his acts in history and through the life of Jesus Christ, the Son of God (something we'll discuss in more detail in part 3). In the last several chapters, we've examined what the Bible is, where it came from, and what Christians believe about it. We've also wrestled with the historical reliability of the New Testament and its biographical account of the life of Jesus, as well as with a number of other pressing historical, cultural, and ethical questions about the Bible.

What we haven't addressed yet, however, is what this all means when it comes to other world religions. If the Bible is the special place where the God who made the world speaks to us, does that mean this God *doesn't* speak through the Islamic Quran, the Pāli Canon of Theravada Buddhism, or the four Vedas of Hinduism? Is Christianity the *only way* to come to know God? *Are other religious traditions just plain false?*

If you've had questions like these, you're not alone. Chances are that many of you have coworkers and neighbors, friends and family members, who are Jewish, Muslim, Buddhist, or Hindu, or even just believe in an ill-defined "higher spiritual power." It's what makes this much more than just a casual topic for philosophical or theological debate; it is a deeply personal issue with profound, real-world consequences. So how should we understand what other religions have to say in relationship to what the Bible proclaims about God? Is there something that makes Christianity truly distinct? Or do all religions, despite their differences, end up in the same place? Let's begin with the last question.

But Aren't All Religions Just the Same?

Our world is full of a diverse array of religious traditions—we don't even know how many there actually are—with estimates ranging from four thousand to ten thousand different religions. Some religions, such as Christianity, Islam, and Hinduism, have more than a billion adherents, with followers living on every continent. Other traditions may only have a few thousand followers centralized in one geographical region. Each of them has their own beliefs, sacred texts or teachings, key figures, ritual practices, worship styles, and communal structures. But are they really that different? Aren't they more or less just doing the same thing?

Perhaps you've heard the popular parable about a group of blind men who happened upon a massive, mysterious animal. After touching the creature, the first man exclaimed, "I think it must be some kind of a thick and strong snake."

The second fellow responded, "No, not at all. It's a gigantic type of bird. Didn't you feel its massive wings?"

"You're crazy," another blind man yelled, shaking his head. "With those thick, tree-trunk legs? It's *clearly* some kind of a hippopotamus."

"H-h-h-how are you not absolutely terrified?" The fourth guy barely got the words out due to his stuttering. "Those two massive teeth are definitely those of a dragon or some other monster!"

For the rest of the afternoon, the four blind men continued to argue about who was right. The conversation eventually descended into bitter and senseless screaming. *The other guys clearly must have been touching some other animal*, they each thought to themselves as they bickered back and forth. *There's no way they know what they're talking about. They're dead wrong!*

If you haven't figured it out yet, that peculiar animal was an elephant. *All four men were touching the exact same elephant*, albeit its different parts. As the first man grasped the trunk, the second was feeling its flappy ears. While the third man hugged the legs of the beast, the fourth man was shaking in his boots as his hands grazed its tusks.

This parable often gets referenced in discussions of the worldview of religious pluralism. Unlike religious pluralism *as a social virtue* (one where people accept those of other religious traditions and peacefully coexist with them), religious pluralism *as a worldview* maintains that, much like the four blind men, every religion has a grasp of who God is. They're all getting at the same thing. And while religious traditions may differ in the way they perceive who God is, the specific things they believe about God, and the way they worship God, each of them ultimately points to the exact same higher power. At the end of the day, according to a pluralistic worldview, we're all touching the same elephant. So what's the point of fighting over who's right or wrong?

Sounds wonderful at first glance. We can all agree that fighting is an awful thing. Religious differences should never be the cause of war, persecution, discrimination, bigotry, or other acts of violence. That's sin, pure and simple. Regardless of what religion we may (or may not) subscribe to, we believe all of us have been created in God's image. We all have inherent value and worth. Anyone who uses religion as a justification for cruelty is morally wrong.

That being said, just because we all have equal value as human beings doesn't mean that all religions worship the same God and are, more or less, just slight variations of each other. There's more to it than that.

Now, that's not to say there aren't similarities between various religious traditions. Across almost all world religions, we see rituals performed, worship conducted, and holy sites visited. Almost all religions embrace certain stories or texts as being especially authoritative or sacred, acclaim particular sages or legendary founders as foundational figures, and commemorate specific days of the year. The same can be said for their shared emphasis on ethical behavior. Some specific teachings can even exhibit similarities. For example, most major world religions have some variation of the Golden Rule: "Do to others as you would have them do to you." And not surprisingly, you will find kind, gracious, and devout people in every religious tradition.

But how significant are these similarities? Not as significant as those religious pluralism adherents would like you to believe. Just because many religions have a few features in common doesn't make them the same thing. You wouldn't say your toaster, electric car, and laptop are just slightly different versions of the same thing, since they're all machines made of metal that require electricity. Of course not! One of them you toast bread in; one of them you drive; one of them you check emails on. They're *radically* different things. A few surface-level points of resemblance don't change that.

The same thing can be said about religion. In fact, many of the similarities listed previously are so broad that they're shared by groups that aren't religions. Your family has certain traditions and rules that everyone follows, specific places you all like to visit, and particular days, like birthdays and anniversaries, that you celebrate. Does that mean you've started a brand-new religion? Definitely not.

Additional problems with certain expressions of religious pluralism arise when we look more closely at what different religions believe. Take belief in the divine, for example. Nearly every religion holds some sort of belief in the existence of a higher spiritual power. But that's where the similarities end. Hinduism allows for belief in many gods, as does Japanese Shinto. Adherents of Bahá'í believe in an unknown divine essence. Buddhism doesn't require belief in any god, as Siddhartha Buddha barely said anything about any specific deity. Judaism and Islam are monotheistic religions, as is Sikhism. Christianity is also monotheistic, but maintains that God is a Trinity—one deity in three persons: Father, Son, and Holy Spirit.

None of those are minor theological discrepancies that can be glossed over. Try asking a Mahayana Buddhist how they'd feel about singing hymns in a Roman Catholic church about Jesus Christ. Or asking an Orthodox Jew whether they're fine with worshiping Vishnu, Shakti, or Shiva? After all, they're all the same deity, right? Believe me, you'd get quite the bewildered looks.

And that's just scratching the surface. Key Hindu notions of *saṃsāra* (the endless cycle of death and rebirth), karma, and reincarnation don't translate into Shia Islam. Jewish *halakhah* (religious law) and *kashrut* (dietary laws) don't fit within Jainism. You don't see United Methodists reciting the Four Noble Truths of Buddhism on Sunday morning or practicing tantric meditation. Each of these concepts and practices fits within the particular worldview of their respective religious tradition. Claiming that they're essentially similar makes no more sense than mixing four boxes of puzzle pieces together and assuming that somehow they'll all meld together into one unified picture.

We can't just water down all of the world's religions to one essential core that everyone can accept. Even on the most basic level, they contradict one another in drastic ways. We can't ignore that fact, which is why we don't see followers of other religions conceding that the theological beliefs, practices, sacred texts, and customs specific to their own traditions are just surface-level, subjective preferences that really don't matter. If those religious differences truly didn't matter, we wouldn't find so many religions around today. If all religions are just particular variations of the same thing, so many folks out there wouldn't be trying to convert people to *their* specific belief systems or proclaiming that *their* traditions are special.

Contrary to the old adage, not all roads lead to Rome. While we believe all religions do share some broad characteristics, to go so far as to say that the remaining differences don't matter is not only ridiculous but also quite insulting. All religions don't point to the same God, and if you don't believe us, ask the next religious person you run into what they think about that. What sort of nerve would I (Cliffe) have, for example, if I told one of my Jewish or Hindu acquaintances that we're all just "touching the same elephant," and so their distinctive beliefs and practices aren't very important in the grand scheme of things? That's not enlightened; it's disrespectful.

So Why Christianity and Not Some Other Religion?

Religions aren't like a plate at Thanksgiving dinner that you can indiscriminately fill with whatever entrees and sides you want until it's nearly overflowing. Every religion makes specific *truth claims* about God, the world, and our identity as human beings. The truth claims of Hinduism are different from those of Islam, which are different from those of Taoism, which are different from those of Christianity. And these truth claims cannot be mixed together, switched out interchangeably, or stacked on top of the others. You can't just take the Buddhist notion of Nirvana (the ultimate state of salvific escape from one's desires and suffering) and organically transplant it into Islam. Nor can you take Muhammad and turn him into a bodhisattva. It doesn't work that way, and it's audacious to think it does.

There are contradictions and disagreements among all religious truth claims, with many theological ideas and practices that don't translate from one to the other. You can't intellectually disregard the incompatibilities; they're as clear as day. You're comparing apples to oranges, not a red apple to a green one. All this is to say that religious pluralism doesn't work as a worldview. In fact, *religious pluralism as a worldview is itself a particular truth claim*, which makes it no different from any other religion.

Not every perspective can be right. It's either *all* religions are wrong, or there must be *one* religion that's right, and all the others contradict it. You can't ignore or whitewash the truth.

As I (Cliffe) have told many students over the years, the truth is the truth, regardless of who says it. Just because someone might be a committed Christian, Muslim, Buddhist, or atheist doesn't mean that what they believe is automatically true. It doesn't matter how sincere or authentic my beliefs may be. It doesn't matter how emotionally attached I am to them. It doesn't even matter that my beliefs give me happiness and fulfillment. If what I believe contradicts what is true, if the evidence doesn't support it, *then I'm wrong*. There's no way around that reality. Truth isn't an illusion or something we can manipulate and distort to support our desires and fantasies. Truth matters, especially when it comes to something as important as what we believe.

So why Christianity? Why am I convinced by Christianity's truth claims? Why have I put my faith in Christianity over against some other religion? What evidence do I need to fall back on when I'm experiencing my own doubts? (And trust me, I do have doubts.)

First of all, as I've told many folks over the years, I don't put my faith in Christianity; *I put my faith in Jesus Christ*. Those who hold positions of political, social, and cultural power have often used Christianity to justify many awful things throughout history—the Crusades, the Spanish Inquisition, the Salem witch trials, the persecution of European Jews, slavery, and many other acts of violence. Like any human institution or belief system (religious ones included), Christianity has been abused by people for sinful purposes. Christianity is not perfect, because the human beings who call themselves Christians are not perfect either. I would *never* put my faith in Christianity. So the really important question for me isn't, "Why is Christianity the best religion?" but rather, "Why should I trust Jesus Christ?" That's the one question that ultimately matters.

Having made that clarification, I believe and trust in Jesus Christ because of what the Bible says about him. I follow the evidence. And the biographical evidence we have for Jesus as found in the New Testament (as we'll discuss in more detail in the next part of this book) leads me to *four reasons I find Jesus to be trustworthy and reliable*—reasons powerful enough to rely on in the moments when I experience doubt and uncertainty.

First, *Jesus was an unprecedented ethical teacher*, a moral genius who astonished listeners and inspired people to change their lives.

When people heard Jesus teach, they universally recognized his authority (Matthew 7:28–29). If you don't believe me, read his Sermon on the Mount in Matthew 5–7 (which we'll discuss in chapter 7). As Gandhi once famously said, "If I had to face only the Sermon on the Mount and my own interpretation of it, I should not hesitate to say 'Oh yes, I am a Christian.'"

Second, not only was Jesus a great moral teacher, but unlike us, he lived his life as a flawless and sinless example of his teachings (1 John 3:5). *Jesus lived a morally perfect life*—a profoundly admirable thing from my perspective, especially as someone who has failed time and time again to live that way. Jesus didn't just offer virtuous lip service; he wasn't a hypocrite. He genuinely lived the good life we strive to live.

Third, when Jesus was crucified, he didn't harbor bitterness or hatred toward his enemies; *he forgave them*. While dying an excruciating death on the cross, Jesus easily could have cursed those who put him up there. I wouldn't have blamed him. But he didn't. No, instead he exclaimed, "Father, forgive them, for they do not know what they are doing" (Luke 23:34). If that kind of response doesn't demand respect and admiration, I don't know what does.

Fourth, according to the four gospels, when Jesus was crucified, it didn't end there. *Jesus was raised from the dead*, and through his death and resurrection he freely extends forgiveness and eternal life to all of us. I don't know about you, but if I were to meet someone who was raised from the dead, I'd listen very carefully to what they have to say. We'll unpack this in more detail later, but for now, it's important to stress just how monumental this act of self-sacrificial grace is. It is, without question, one of the truly unique aspects about the Christian faith, something that differentiates it from all other religions.

During a conference at Cambridge University on comparative religion, C. S. Lewis wandered into a room where a group of esteemed philosophers, historians, and scholars of religion were debating which aspect of the Christian faith truly distinguished it from all other religions. Various suggestions were offered, only to be shot down by one expert after another who came up with a parallel from another tradition. Finally, Lewis piped up, "Oh, that's easy. It's *grace.*" Sure enough, after some discussion, a consensus was reached that he was right: Grace is the most unique thing about Christianity.

You see, every religion offers some path to salvation, divine favor, or a good afterlife. But nearly all of them claim that, in one way or another, you have to do a lifetime of hard work to reach that end goal—be it hours of rigorous meditation or achieving enlightenment, performing ethical deeds or removing bad karma, maintaining ritual purity or faithfully following certain laws or covenants. But that's not the case when it comes to Christianity and its allegiance to Jesus Christ. Only Jesus Christ, the crucified and risen Son of God, makes God's love truly unconditional for those who accept it. Only Jesus Christ freely presents us with forgiveness, despite our many imperfections, forgiveness he gave even to those who sentenced him to death, as he prayed from the cross, "Father, forgive them, for they do not know what they are doing" (Luke 23:34). Only Jesus Christ, through his death and resurrection, can offer humanity eternal life, no strings attached, even though none of us have earned it. That's what makes Christianity powerfully different from all other religions. That's what gives Christianity a liberating sense of meaning unparalleled in any other religion or worldview. It's not about the work we have done; it's about the grace we have been given.

It was the power of God's grace that first swayed me to choose Christ over all other religions and worldviews. I grew up in a suburb of New York City surrounded by wealth and materialism, a world in which stock portfolios and bank accounts were the gods people worshiped. As I got older, I began to encounter the religion of hedonism among my friends, who worshiped the gods of drink, sex, and drugs. I also was confronted with the option of atheism, the belief that there is no greater power or order to the world beyond the material.

All of this left me searching for meaning, for something more. I began to examine all those options as clearly and objectively as I could, trying to discern what I believed. I also began to look at the evidence for God's existence and exploring various religions through the same critical lens, scrutinizing their truth claims and navigating the many doubts I had—doubts that included Jesus Christ. I read the New Testament gospels of Matthew, Mark, Luke, and John, tested the evidence presented there, and pondered whether this Jesus fellow was credible. Over a long period of time, I started to become convinced by the truth claims of the Christian faith. I began to realize how exceptional Jesus Christ was as a teacher, an ethical model, and the resurrected Son of God. It was then that it hit me: It wasn't enough simply to believe that Jesus Christ was who he said he was; I needed to *follow* him too. I needed to be in relationship with him, to live out the truth claims he made, and to accept his grace and the promise of eternal life he extended to me.

I've never looked back.

Does That Mean Non-Christians Will Go to Hell?

"So I asked a pretty religious person, someone who's really close to me, what happens to people who don't believe in Jesus but are still extremely religious. Maybe they worship Allah, or they're Buddhist or something else. *Are those people going to hell?* Are they doomed for the rest of eternity?"

Stuart and I could tell by the somber tone of Logan Paul's voice that this topic bothered him. The entire *Impaulsive* space grew surprisingly quiet as he finished speaking, which was especially noticeable, given the laughter and vibrant conversation that had filled the space minutes before. I could empathize with Logan. It's a gut-wrenching question for me as well, one that has always sat heavy on my heart, and that hasn't changed over the past four and a half decades I've been doing campus ministry.

I've had a lot of conversations with folks who flat-out struggle with this. Some express outrage that a supposedly benevolent God could condemn good, well-meaning people to hell. Others feel confused about why a loving God seems to be dangling eternal punishment over us so as to force us to love him. Still others admit their painful doubts as they talk about loved ones and family members who don't believe in Jesus. *What's going to happen to them?*

Part of the difficulty with this topic lies in the fact that we don't know much about hell. The Bible isn't always clear on the topic, and the last time I checked, there weren't any photos. Yes, Jesus talks about it in the Bible, so we can trust that hell is a real place. But in the few times he describes hell, he seems to be speaking symbolically more than literally. After all, how can a place filled with blazing fire (Matthew 5:22) also be a place of darkness (8:12)? It doesn't make sense.

Rather, I think Jesus is using a metaphor here to point to truth, much like he does when he declares, "I am the bread of life" (John 6:35). So I'm quick to discount the cartoonish images of hell as a fiery underground lair ruled by a red-horned devil with a pointed tail and a pitchfork who is stabbing people with hot pokers for eternity. The famous Italian Dante Alighieri was a superb writer, but the horrific description of hell found in his poem *Divine Comedy*, so central to the way our culture imagines this place, surely takes some creative liberties.

More than anything, hell is, in its essence, total separation from God. As I said in my response to Logan's question, the only reason anyone goes to hell is that they have chosen to live their life separated from God. If I consciously choose to reject Jesus Christ and distance myself from him as far away as possible, then being in heaven with him goes against my will. God isn't going to drag anyone kicking and screaming into his presence when they've spent their whole life proclaiming that they don't believe those truth claims or don't want a relationship with him. Being in hell is our decision, not God's. G. K. Chesterton is thought to have said, "Hell is God's great compliment to the reality of human freedom and the dignity of human choice." A person doesn't end up in hell simply because they skipped church too many times, had an affair, or cheated on their taxes. Rejecting Jesus is their free choice.

In the words of Frank Sinatra, they did it their way.

"But, Cliffe," Logan interjected following my initial response, "doesn't that just isolate such a large portion of the world's population who will never hear about Jesus?"

That's another tough question that stirs my heart, and unfortunately, it's one I don't have a definite answer for. Jesus famously claims in John 14:6, "I am the way and the truth and the life. No one comes to the Father except through me." Clearly, Jesus is saying that if someone chooses separation from God, they will not experience eternal life. But the Bible never addresses God's plan for those who haven't had a chance to choose or not choose Jesus Christ because they've never been given the choice in the first place. What happens to someone who lives in a place where the gospel will never reach them? What if they live in a culture that suppresses their freedom to decide in the first place? What if they suffered a traumatic brain injury early in life and now lack the mental capacity to make such a choice? Would it be fair for God to consign all of these folks to hell?

Here are a few thoughts on this challenging topic. First, I believe that God is just. Moses proclaims that our faithful God is "upright and just" (Deuteronomy 32:4). Psalm 89:14 likewise declares, "Righteousness and justice are the foundation of [God's] throne." God is far more just and impartial than you or I could ever hope to be. While I can't read God's mind and declare with certainty how he would answer these grueling questions, I *can* say that a just God would not offer an unjust solution.

Second, I don't believe anyone blindly slips and slides their way into hell. Through his death and resurrection, Jesus Christ blocked the path to hell, offering us grace, forgiveness, and eternal life, despite our sinful ways. No one is headed for hell unless they contort and crawl their way around Jesus, refusing his extended hand and expressly rejecting him. No one is going to hell unless they're hell-bent on getting away from God.

Third, the New Testament reveals that some of the people we'll see in heaven actually lived before Jesus and never got the opportunity we have to hear the gospel. According to Hebrews 11, Abraham, Moses, David, and many others who responded positively to God prior to the earthly life of Jesus Christ will receive the same promises we do. If God freely extends grace to those individuals in the past who never knew who Jesus Christ was, it stands to reason that God will extend grace to those living today as well.

All that being said, the mysterious power of God's grace and the sacrifice of Jesus will always be far too great for us to understand. I know I've done wrong in my life and haven't earned any sort of heavenly afterlife. I'm a dirty, rotten sinner, just like everyone else, and that's why I need Christ. Without Christ's death and resurrection, nothing is blocking my path to hell; no one is reaching out to me in love and forgiveness for my numbskull ways. God's grace is the only reason I'll be in heaven. But while I can tell you what my choice is, I cannot judge anyone else's decision about their relationship with Christ, nor can I make a judgment about who will be in hell. That's way beyond my knowledge and comprehension.

But What About Tolerance?

By this point in the chapter, some of you may be thinking, *Okay, Cliffe and Stuart, I see what you're saying here. But doesn't that feel a little intolerant, closed-minded, or judgy? It just feels like you're vilifying all other religions except for the one you guys follow, or like you're claiming that only Christianity is worth caring about. Is that true?*

Let us first say that it's important to remember that Christianity isn't the only religion that makes exclusive truth claims. *All religions have truth claims.* All traditions make explicit, authoritative statements about God, the world around us, and our identity as human beings. Those statements not only assert what is *true* but also infer what *isn't true.* When Islam claims that Muhammad is the last and greatest prophet sent by God, it is also stating that no other religion possesses a prophet greater than Muhammad. When Judaism emphasizes the Torah as *the* sacred scripture, it's also claiming that the Hindu Vedas are not *the* sacred scripture. So if you're going to say that Christianity is closed-minded or intolerant because it has exclusive truth claims that distinguish it from other traditions, you have to be fair and include nearly every other religion in the world in that critique as well.

Second, a big problem lies in our misconceptions of what tolerance looks like. So often I've seen students presume that tolerance entails accepting whatever someone says as valid and true. According to this view, if you happen to meet someone of a different religion and they begin to tell you about what they believe, you have no right to declare to them that they're wrong or actively question aspects of their beliefs. You need to accept what they believe as *their truth* and find *agreement* with them. It's not your place to tell them you disagree. To do so would be narrow-minded. You have your religion, they have theirs, and both can be true. Let me just say, that's not tolerance or enlightenment; that's being brainless. Tolerance doesn't mean conceding to someone else's beliefs by silencing or stifling your own. Nor does it require finding agreement on every possible front with someone before having a civil or fruitful discussion. *Tolerance involves continuing to love someone and respect them in the midst of disagreement.* It means being able to walk away from a debate with a handshake or a hug, leaving your animosity at the door. It means never forgetting that the folks you don't see eye to eye with are fellow human beings who, just like you, possess inherent worth and significance as part of God's creation.

Contrary to what some people may think about Christians, Stuart and I both deeply value the virtue of tolerance. In fact, it's pretty hard to grow and flourish as a human being without it. For example, let's say Stuart and I were invited to appear on the podcast of an avowed atheist. If we headed in there with guns blazing and aggressively attacked his character and accused him of being an immoral, godless nihilist, it would be an absolutely awful and unbearable interview to listen to. It would be not only embarrassing for us but utterly uninformative for anyone genuinely interested in the discussion. Or we could go into the interview and simply nod along the whole time and agree with whatever he said and intentionally avoid making any truth claims that might offend his views in the hope of not seeming narrow-minded. It would likely be a far less polemical interview but certainly wouldn't be particularly edifying either.

However, let's say instead that we arrived at the interview and took what the atheist said seriously, offered our own critical points in response, and gave him space to do the same. No vicious name-calling or personal attacks, but also no softballs or passive concessions. Well, that sounds like an engaging conversation, one I'm sure both of us would have learned something from (and I'm guessing some of you would have too). It doesn't mean any of us would have switched religious affiliations; we would undoubtedly still disagree about a lot of things. But I think we would've all come away with a slightly new perspective about the beliefs of others and even our own. We'd all grow from the experience.

Tolerance isn't an intellectually lazy attribute. It involves more than just casually telling someone they're right without giving their ideas serious attention. If I truly respect the people I disagree with, I will listen to them closely, make the effort to investigate and honor where they're coming from, and then explain my disagreement with their beliefs, all the while remembering that this person is not an impersonal debate robot but a real human being created in God's image. And I hope they will extend the same courtesy and kindness to me!

True tolerance doesn't apathetically accept everything that comes its way and ignore contradictions, blatant falsehoods, or unevidenced claims. It's surprising that the same students who claim we're intolerant or narrow-minded and unwilling to respect other people's beliefs will later admit they've never taken the time or effort to learn about anyone else's beliefs but their own. Talk about being narrow-minded!

And so we encourage everyone we meet to explore these things for themselves. Take ownership of your beliefs and doubts. Go study another religion. Listen and learn from your friends or neighbors who come from a tradition different from your own. Figure out exactly why you disagree with someone rather than just make assumptions or guesses. After all, it's hard to exercise respectful and compassionate tolerance if you can't genuinely articulate why your beliefs differ from theirs.

Finally, we should strive to be tolerant because God calls us to be tolerant. In a culture that radically disagreed with Jesus—even to the point of crucifying him—he still loved every person he encountered to the extent that he died to provide forgiveness and eternal life. This same radical type of love should be the foundation of our interaction with people we disagree with. But again, as Jesus demonstrated, loving and respecting those we disagree with doesn't mean disregarding the truth. As Dorothy Sayers once put it:

> In the world it calls itself tolerance; but in hell it is called despair. . . . It is the sin that believes in nothing, cares for nothing,

> seeks to know nothing, interferes with nothing, enjoys nothing, loves nothing, hates nothing, finds purpose in nothing, lives for nothing, and remains alive only because there is nothing it would die for.

This is the kind of sloppy tolerance that many in our world embrace. It's cheap, easy, and lacks substance. True tolerance, however, is a daring thing. It requires intellectual work, serious listening, and radical love. But as we know from experience, it is well worth the effort.

The Noble Eightfold Path of Buddhism is not a polite suggestion. The Quran of Islam doesn't leave room for any prophets greater than Muhammad. Jesus did not say, "I am *one of* the ways and *one of* the truths and *one of* the lives." When it comes to religious truth claims, you can't have your cake (and several other cakes) and eat it too. That's why it's so important to put in the work, investigate the evidence, and determine which traditions pass the test. It's not always an easy task, nor is it always an enjoyable one. But it is an important one.

Of course, it doesn't mean we'll always have all the answers. While speaking one time on the plaza at Stanford University, I (Cliffe) encountered an intense student who asked one excellent question after another. It was an honor to have such a rigorous discussion with this skeptic. After finishing the dialogue, I was talking with a group of people when suddenly someone touched me on the back. I turned around to find that young man standing behind me. This time, however, his look had changed from one of engaged curiosity to troubling sadness. "My grandma does not believe in Jesus," he told me quietly. "If I accept Christ, it means I believe my grandma will go to hell. This is unacceptable to me." It was a moment that remains penetrating and painful even today.

I knew he wanted a satisfying or easy answer, but I didn't have one. I gently told him that neither of us knew what was transpiring in his grandmother's soul, nor can we comprehend the extent and power of God's grace. Such matters were definitely outside of my very limited expertise. But I also encouraged him to reach out to his grandmother and tell her the truth about Jesus, offering him whatever support and advice I could give. As the young man walked away, I felt a deep respect and love for him. I prayed that God would help him confront his grandmother's disbelief, that the same unique and powerful grace that swayed my heart decades earlier would move hers as well.

I don't know yet what happened to this young man and his grandmother, and maybe I never will. But I do know that the God who created this universe, the God of the Bible, loves both of them very much and is waiting with open arms to offer forgiveness and peace for them as well as for everyone else who seeks it. Out of the pits of doubt and the trenches of despair, this loving God stands and calls to each of us. All we need to do is follow his voice.

What Motivated Stuart to Follow in Cliffe's Footsteps?

Some of you may be surprised to know that for a long time, I (Stuart) really wasn't interested in the whole campus evangelism thing. Throughout high school and most of college, I was planning to pursue a marketing or a sports-related career, or maybe even go to law school and become a lawyer. Don't get me wrong, I respected what my dad did and had many fond memories as a kid traveling with him, my mom, and my brothers from university to university across the country. But what he did never particularly interested me as a career. More often than not, when that prospect crossed my mind, I'd think to myself, *No way would I ever do that.*

It was during my senior year at Gordon College in Wenham, Massachusetts, however, that God started to shatter those preoccupations and ambitions. Like many other schools, Gordon College would host prospective students and their parents every year on campus visits. They recruited current undergrads to tell these groups about their intellectual and spiritual experience at the school (Gordon is a nondenominational Christian college). Somehow (I'm not entirely sure why) I ended up being selected as one of those representatives that year.

At first, I wasn't too wild about this new opportunity. I was told I was doing a great job, that I was articulate and personable, and that I made visitors feel welcomed and well-informed, but I still didn't really enjoy it. Soon, people from the college who heard me talk during these visits asked if I'd be willing to talk at student chapel about my personal relationship with God, which eventually led to invitations to speak at a few evening church services in the area. Over time, I began to warm up to the public speaking and had even developed a deep interest in learning more about theology and Christian apologetics. I began reading whatever books I could get my hands on. But I still was pretty hesitant about going into any type of ministry. Sure, theology was super interesting, and I really did like talking to people about God and sharing about my faith experience, but actually becoming a *pastor*? That was a tough pill to swallow.

Things changed early in the spring semester. One afternoon, I was talking with a group of friends about our next steps after graduation. When it became my turn to share, I admitted I didn't know what my plan was. I was surprised when they asked why I hadn't thought about applying to seminary. After all, they argued, I was already preaching at church services and spending my evenings and weekends reading theological books. What was the hang-up? I can't say their advice fell on receptive ears at first. Me? Doing public ministry *like my dad*? No way. Seminary, hmm, more like *cemetery*, if you asked me. Once again, God began to break down my walls of hesitation, and by the time final exams came along, my application to seminary had been accepted.

I immediately loved seminary. During my three years there, I learned an enormous amount not only about the Bible, theology, and preaching but also about myself. I realized that I very much enjoyed pastoral counseling and other aspects of ministry. I began to recognize that God had called me to do this kind of work and that he had equipped me with the gifts and interests to do that well. For the first time, I truly felt I had found my real purpose, landing in a place with plenty of room for spiritual growth.

After completing seminary, I got a job working at my dad's church alongside my brother Rob. At first, I set my focus solely on being the best teacher, counselor, and pastor I could be. When my dad hit the road to speak with college students and film videos for *Give Me an Answer*, I'd stay behind. That was his thing, not mine. Eventually, though, a couple of people began asking when I was going to start joining him on his trips. As we began to explore the potential of social media as a useful tool to reach more people, I began to feel like maybe this was exactly what God was preparing me to do with my life.

After a little more (futile) foot-dragging, I finally conceded in 2015 and visited my first campus, Southern Connecticut State University, with my dad. I still remember it vividly—it didn't go well *at all.* I felt like a total bust, like nothing that I said to that group of two dozen students made any sense whatsoever. On the drive home, my dad—being the thoughtful and encouraging parent he is—didn't let me beat up on myself. He offered some constructive criticism and affirmed that I had the necessary knowledge and gifts to do this. I walked away that day with a whole new level of respect for my dad.

Since then, I've visited more than a hundred and fifty colleges with my dad and have had thousands of awesome conversations with people about their beliefs, doubts, and personal faith journeys. Having been a part of *Give Me an Answer* prior to its explosion into the social media stratosphere, I can say that I truly cherish where God has brought this ministry over the past decade and how he is using it to reach people across the globe. I wouldn't want to be doing anything else with my life.

PART 3

WHAT DOES THE BIBLE SAY ABOUT JESUS CHRIST?

If someone claims to be able to walk on water or identifies themselves as God incarnate, we would definitely invite them to get psychiatric treatment. Who in their right mind would say such things? But when we look at the New Testament account of the life of Jesus Christ, that's what we see. So what makes Jesus's claims any different?

According to the reliable eyewitness testimony presented in the four gospels, Jesus Christ was not a ranting lunatic. He was someone never before seen by the world—an ethical genius who lived out his high moral principles to the fullest as the only human being in history to have never sinned. Jesus performed powerful miracles that improved people's lives and pointed to his identity as the Son of God. Most miraculous of all, when Jesus died on the cross for our sins, he didn't stay dead. He was raised from the dead and in the process extended the promise of forgiveness, salvation, and hope to all of us.

Unlike the promises of redemption and enlightenment found in all other religious traditions, the promise of Jesus Christ isn't something we need to earn; it's freely given through God's grace.

In part 3, we will examine in greater detail all these aspects of the person of Jesus Christ. We'll analyze the biographical details about Jesus found in the Gospels, from his ethical teachings and miracles to his resurrection and identity as God incarnate. The evidence of what Jesus taught and how he lived, died, and rose from the dead should help us understand whether or not Jesus's claims are any different. If, in fact, the evidence suggests he died and came back to life, we should listen carefully to what he has to say.

CHAPTER 7

WAS JESUS AN ETHICAL GENIUS?

Who is Jesus Christ?

There's a lot of disagreement and, at times, confusion around that question. Was he an extraordinary miracle worker and healer? An ancient sage or philosopher? A political rabble-rouser? The perfect human being? The incarnate Son of God? Maybe he was nothing more than a mere charlatan or a quack. Could he have been an alien from another planet? (Yes, we've actually heard that one before.) Perhaps he wasn't any of those things. The answers just keep coming.

Without a doubt, the most common answer we get to the question of Jesus's identity is that he was a great ethical teacher. Nearly everyone—even those who have never picked up a Bible or who strictly doubt other truth claims about Jesus—accepts this without flinching. While it's not uncommon to encounter individuals who may express disbelief about Jesus's divinity, miracles, or resurrection, it's quite rare to run into someone who seriously thinks Jesus was a flat-out unethical person.

In this chapter, we're going to dive deeper into Jesus's ethical teachings and extraordinary sinless life in the New Testament. After first explaining why it's so important to see that Jesus was an outstanding moral teacher, we'll look at what the Bible tells us about his moral teachings. Most notably, we'll examine in detail the Sermon on the Mount, which has been called by philosophers, ethicists, and theologians alike one of the most brilliant moral teachings in all of human history.

Why Does It Matter That Jesus Was an Ethical Genius?

As mentioned in chapter 7, there are four reasons we find the truth claims of Jesus Christ to be most convincing over those of other religions. One of those reasons is that Jesus Christ was an unprecedented ethical teacher. However, not everyone sees this as being an important piece of evidence, at least not at first. "Aren't Jesus's claims to be God or his resurrection a bigger deal than his moral teachings?" one student asked me (Cliffe) at the University of Arizona a few years back. "Shouldn't those things overshadow Jesus's role as an ethical teacher?"

To be sure, Jesus's identity as the Son of God and the reality of his death and resurrection (which we'll discuss later in this book) are central aspects of the Christian message. Without those things, there would be no Christianity. But that doesn't mean his moral teachings don't matter. If anything, Jesus's exceptional ethical instructions further highlight his miraculous deeds and make his message even more credible.

It'd be tough to accept the truth claims expressed in the New Testament about Jesus Christ if his teachings were unethical or misled people. If you found out, for instance, that Stuart and I were instructing folks how to embezzle money, cheat on their spouses, and abuse their children, you wouldn't trust anything we told you. (In fact, if that was the case, we wouldn't blame you if you put this book down right now.) Self-serving or destructive teachings are a clear warning that something doesn't add up.

We've seen this in many cult movements—like Jonestown, Heaven's Gate, or the Children of God—whose charismatic leaders used their teachings to manipulate people for money, sex, and power. Nobody feels they can safely trust someone who misleads them or pushes them toward sin, especially those who claim to have authority. How much more would this apply to someone who claimed to be God incarnate?

The moral teachings of Jesus Christ deeply matter. His *ethical genius* displays wisdom and truth, mercy and self-sacrificial love—the types of virtues that frustrate the greedy, power hungry, and wicked. Such exceptional teachings show that what the New Testament says about Jesus should be taken seriously. His extraordinarily high ethical standards authenticate his equally remarkable claims to be the Son of God. His teachings point back to the all-benevolent and all-powerful creator who designed this world with absolute moral truth and instilled in each of us a conscience to guide us toward that truth (as we saw in chapter 1). In short, Jesus taught the things we'd expect an entirely good, loving, and all-powerful God to teach. His character is consistent.

Conversely, if Jesus Christ wasn't an ethically outstanding teacher, then who would ever be inspired to follow him, especially to their death? That wouldn't add up. If Jesus just passed down a harebrained collection of random sayings, who in their right mind would say, *Wow, this guy must be God*? If Jesus's Sermon on the Mount amounted to little more than "Do whatever feels good to you because it really doesn't matter," or "Seek first yourself and your own well-being," then how could anyone trust Jesus's claims to divinity or the miraculous reports of his resurrection? You can't separate what a person says and does from who they are. Exceptional people do exceptional things, and if the New Testament truth claims about Jesus are true—that he is the sinless Son of God who performed miracles, was crucified for the forgiveness of our sins, and was raised from the dead to bring us new life and hope—then we should expect his moral teachings to follow suit.

As Jesus himself said, a good tree will bear good fruit (Matthew 7:18). The credibility of the evidence for Jesus's truth claims, as presented in the New Testament, would be greatly diminished if his moral teachings weren't powerful and convincing.

What Do You Mean That Jesus Lived a Sinless Life?

The Greek word translated "sin" in the New Testament is *hamartia*. It derives from a verb that means "to miss the mark," like an arrow that misses a target. Sin is where our actions don't hit the target, where we miss the spot we've aimed at.

Some people believe sin is simply breaking the commands set out in the Bible. While the Bible does give us ethical guidance and principles to live by, there's more to sin than that. Sin is our human tendency to let our desires and selfishness distract us and lead us to harm others and ourselves. Sin is idolatry. It is taking good gifts God has given us and putting them in a position to be worshiped. As a pastor, I (Stuart) meet with more than a few people who have caused great harm by taking good things and turning them into hyperdesires. A spouse whose addiction to work is breaking their family apart. A high school student whose rejection letter from a university pushes them over the deep end. Men and women who have been caught in a web of dishonesty in the pursuit of money or pleasure. Temptation is a sober reality we all face. No human being is immune to sin.

It's not enough that Jesus was a brilliant ethical thinker. Being able to articulate amazing moral principles or maxims is one thing, but to live them out is a completely different story. That's where the rubber meets the road. All of us, Cliffe and I included, have tried and failed in that department, and we know we're not alone. How many of the greatest ethical thinkers and philosophical minds in history have had a checkered record when it comes to their own actions? Hypocrisy is an easy trap to fall into for every one of us.

One time when we were speaking at MIT, I (Cliffe) asked the large group of students, "Who here has lived a life without sin?" No one moved. That is, until one energetic student shot his hand up in the air. "Me! I've lived a morally perfect life and have never sinned." He barely got the words out before a loud burst of laughter filled the air. Even the avowed atheists in the crowd joined in the hysterics. Why? Because it was clearly a ridiculous thing for the student to say. Even the most brazen moral relativists would shy away from claiming that they've lived a perfect life, that every action and choice they've ever made has been spot-on.

Jesus was an ethical genius not only because his teachings were unprecedented but also because he lived out those teachings to perfection. Jesus was able to live a sinless life because he was more than just merely human; Jesus was also fully God. This truth is stated throughout the New Testament. According to New Testament authors, in Jesus "is no sin" (1 John 3:5). First Peter 2:22 calls believers to follow after Jesus's perfect example, for "he committed no sin, and no deceit was found in his mouth." In John 8:46, Jesus said to his enemies, "Can any of you prove me guilty of sin?" You'd think that Jesus's enemies would be the first in line to list off Jesus's missteps and sins. But no one said anything, because there were no sins to list. The historical witness of the New Testament shows that Jesus wasn't full of hot air. He walked the walk and talked the talk.

Now, to say that Jesus lived a sinless life doesn't mean Jesus wasn't capable of sinning. That'd be a hollow victory. While Jesus was fully God, he was also fully man, which meant that like any of us, he could have sinned at any time. But he didn't. That's the difference. We see this in Matthew 4:1–11, where Jesus, after fasting for forty days and nights in the wilderness, is confronted by Satan, who tries to tempt him with food to meet his physical needs, with a challenge to show his power and glory, and with an appeal to gain worldly power and recognition. Those were real temptations, desires that most of us would have followed. But Jesus didn't. Using words from the Old Testament as his rebuttal, Jesus did what no human being could ever do—resist the unrelenting pressure of sin. He broke the pattern of sin that has defined humanity since the fall in Eden. In the words of Hebrews 4:15, "For we do not have a high priest who is unable to sympathize with our weaknesses, but one who in every respect has been tempted as we are, yet without sin" (ESV).

"But couldn't Jesus have sinned when no one was looking?" a University of Arizona student asked during a recent visit there. "The New Testament doesn't tell us *everything* about Jesus's life." I responded, "Sure, it's totally possible. But does it really seem likely when we look at the evidence?"

Most biblical scholars believe that the four gospels preserve about three years of eyewitness testimony concerning Jesus's life. This is how long Jesus's disciples—his closest eyewitnesses and the sources behind Matthew, Mark, Luke, and John—spent with him. As I told the student, three years is about the same amount of time you'll live with your college roommate (assuming you actually like them enough to room with them for that long). By the end of that time, I think you'll have gotten to know your roommate pretty well, better than almost anyone else. Do you think after those three years, you'll be able to say without any hesitation, "Yeah, I never saw them sin once. Never cheated on an exam or lied. Never mistreated anyone. Never acted out of anger or selfishness. They're the perfect person." Even if you love your roommate dearly and they're your best friend, there's no way you can say that with a straight face. After all, most of us can't make it for *three hours* without sinning, much less three years.

Neither Stuart nor I could claim anything remotely close to that about *anyone* in our lives, be it our closest friends, our kids, or even our wives. Three years is a pretty substantial sample. If Jesus lived without sinning for those three years under intense public scrutiny, it's pretty safe to say that Jesus lived his entire life in the same sinless manner.

Obviously, living a perfect life is an extraordinary thing in and of itself. No one else but Jesus can truly claim that, be it Siddhartha Gautama (the Buddha), Mother Teresa, or any Nobel Peace Prize winner. But why is it so important to know that Jesus lived a perfect life? According to the apostle Paul, we have been reconciled with God through Jesus Christ because "God made him who had no sin to be sin for us, so that in him we might become the righteousness of God" (2 Corinthians 5:21). As we'll discuss in greater detail later, the perfect life of Jesus Christ was necessary in order to restore and redeem our woefully imperfect lives. The words of Jesus in Mark 10:45 make this clear: "The Son of Man did not come to be served, but to serve, and to give his life as a ransom for many."

The sinlessness of Jesus Christ and the way he lived out all of his ethical teachings without error or misstep tell us that his truth claims are credible, his promises are reliable, and his message is trustworthy. I hope we will decide to trust the words of a sinless person.

What Did Jesus Teach?

Just be a good person.

Don't sin or you'll go to hell.

Everybody love everybody.

Give away all your money.

If you ask a random person off the street to summarize Jesus's ethical teachings, these are the kind of answers you're likely to get. While most people recognize that Jesus was a morally outstanding man, far fewer can articulate what exactly made his teachings so special. The problem is that so many people haven't read closely what Jesus actually teaches.

When we meet students who are curious about Jesus's ethical teachings, I (Cliffe) always point them to the Sermon on the Mount (Matthew 5–7). The Sermon on the Mount is one of the most powerful ethical messages ever preached. It displays in full color the moral genius of Jesus. But don't take my word for it. Robert Coles, emeritus professor of psychology at Harvard University, once said that all of his teachings on ethics over the years point back to the Sermon on the Mount. President Franklin Roosevelt echoed that sentiment: "I doubt if there is any problem in the world today—social, political, or economic—that would not find happy solution if approached in the spirit of the Sermon on the Mount."

So what makes the Sermon on the Mount so powerful? I could easily devote this whole book to analyzing it verse by verse and unpacking its incredible wisdom. I cannot stress it enough: Go read it for yourself. Because our space is limited, I'll focus solely on the first section of the Sermon on the Mount, known as the Beatitudes. The name "beatitudes" derives from the Latin adjective *beatus*, which means "happy" or "fortunate." This section is called the Beatitudes because it contains a series of Jesus's sayings in which he describes certain types of ethical people as "blessed."

Beatitude 1: Being Poor in Spirit

Jesus begins the Sermon on the Mount with the words, "Blessed are the poor in spirit, for theirs is the kingdom of heaven" (Matthew 5:3). To be poor in spirit consists of acknowledging my spiritual bankruptcy before God. It means to grasp that there is no way I can earn heaven. I need to throw myself totally upon Christ. I need God to give me the forgiveness and eternal life I do not deserve. This attitude strikes at the heart of religion. For most religions, a happy afterlife is reserved for good people alone. Enlightenment is saved for the wise and diligent. Liberation from suffering can only be gained through diligence and discipline. Eternal life is something you have to put in the effort to achieve.

The problem is that I *don't* and never could measure up to Jesus's high standard of moral perfection. I can't achieve eternal life because I'm a miserable sinner who needs help. This awareness of my need for help is the definition of what it means to be poor in spirit. In Luke 18:10–14, Jesus tells a parable that illuminates what it means to be poor in spirit:

> "Two men went up to the temple to pray, one a Pharisee and the other a tax collector. The Pharisee stood by himself and prayed: 'God, I thank you that I am not like other people—robbers, evildoers, adulterers—or even like this tax collector. I fast twice a week and give a tenth of all I get.'
>
> "But the tax collector stood at a distance. He would not even look up to heaven, but beat his breast and said, 'God, have mercy on me, a sinner.'
>
> "I tell you that this man, rather than the other, went home justified before God. For all those who exalt themselves will be humbled, and those who humble themselves will be exalted."

The Pharisee, a religious leader esteemed among the Jewish people, boasted in his accomplishments. He wanted everyone to hear his prayer, to see how pious he was. In contrast, the tax collector, a man hated by the people of Jesus's day, humbly admitted his sinfulness. He sought mercy, knowing full well that he could never truly achieve anything even remotely close to ethical perfection.

That is what it means to be poor in spirit—to admit our bankruptcy before God in the currency that gets us to heaven. The poor in spirit realize that, without God's intervention, we are on our way to hell, regardless of whatever good deeds we can muster. As we'll talk about in the next chapter, this is where the cross of Jesus Christ comes into play.

Beatitude 2: Mourning Sin and Brokenness

The next beatitude Jesus gives is this: "Blessed are those who mourn, for they will be comforted" (Matthew 5:4). How ironic it is that Jesus teaches that real blessedness is found when we mourn and then receive God's comfort. We live in a world so fragmented that we sometimes become entirely desensitized. Every single day, we watch or read news reports about famines, wars, acts of social injustice, and crime after heinous crime. Such atrocities are standard fare at this point. We've become so calloused to it we forget that things aren't the way they are supposed to be. We just shrug our shoulders and live with it.

Jesus pushes back against this callousness toward sin. He doesn't want us to be insulated to the tragedy of sin. *He wants us to mourn sin.* Mourning is a genuine acknowledgment at our very core that our world is full of brokenness. To be incapable of mourning is to be incapable of loving. It means we have become totally insensitive to and complacent about the suffering that infects this world. We need to mourn. We need to be open about the presence of injustice and evil. We must also mourn our own sinful actions. As James 4:7–10 puts it, we should all submit ourselves to God, lament our sinful ways, and humble ourselves before God.

But we must not mourn as those who have no hope. As Jesus teaches, God comforts us by giving us hope for the future. God is still working even in the wreckage and carnage of this world. His kingdom is coming. At the end of human history, God will do away with the old and make all things new. God gives us hope by offering forgiveness. He comforts us by giving us his presence and by assuring us he is at work in the midst of the mess.

Beatitude 3: Being Meek

In the Roman world, honor, reputation, and brute force were king. Subservience to anyone was viewed as a universal negative. Power was something to be exploited whenever and wherever possible. Meekness was not valued; any ancient Roman would tell you the meek never prosper. So when Jesus says, "Blessed are the meek, for they will inherit the earth" (Matthew 5:5), he is making an extreme countercultural claim. For Jesus, though, to be *meek* does not mean to be *weak*. It means to radically give yourself to others, serving and loving one another without selfish ambition or pride.

Jesus displayed what it means to be meek. When Jesus became incarnate, he placed his power under the control of God the Father. He took on the nature of a human being. Even more amazing, despite being the Son of God, Jesus still served others, even when it was far beneath him to do so. He didn't hold his status or power over their heads.

Take John 13, where Jesus kneels and washes his disciples' feet. In a world where travel involved walking miles of dirt trails, feet were constantly filthy. Foot washing was considered a servant's job in Jesus's day, something far beneath any person of significance. No wonder Simon Peter protested Jesus's request to wash his feet. How could he allow the Son of God to do something so disgusting? But after Jesus had finished washing their feet, he put on his clothes and went to his place at the supper. He told his disciples this:

> "Do you understand what I have done for you?" he asked them. "You call me 'Teacher' and 'Lord,' and rightly so, for that is what I am. Now that I, your Lord and Teacher, have washed your feet,

> you also should wash one another's feet. I have set you an example that you should do as I have done for you. Very truly I tell you, no servant is greater than his master, nor is a messenger greater than the one who sent him. Now that you know these things, you will be blessed if you do them." (John 13:12–17)

Jesus modeled the meekness we must show one another. He ate with sinners and tax collectors. He healed beggars and social outcasts. He spent time with women and lepers. Jesus did not mingle with the wealthy; he did not hobnob with the politically powerful. The Son of God gave his time and love to those whom society considered to be losers and the scum of the earth.

The irony of this beatitude is that those who give up power and pride for the sake of others will inherit the earth. The world is not for those who take it by force; it is for those who give themselves for others. As Jesus says in Matthew 20:16, "So the last will be first, and the first will be last."

Beatitude 4: Hungering and Thirsting for Righteousness

In Matthew 5:6, Jesus declares, "Blessed are those who hunger and thirst for righteousness, for they will be filled." We try to manage our metaphorical hunger and thirst through many ways. We can fill ourselves with sweet pleasure. We can gorge ourselves on fatty wealth. We can drink ourselves drunk with power and status. Those things may momentarily satisfy us, but they'll never truly fill us. We'll find ourselves always wanting more. Only God's righteousness can truly fill us.

Fulfillment and satisfaction come from living in God's love and doing life his way. Moral integrity and living in right relationship with God are the healthy foods that truly nourish us. This is why the psalmist writes in Psalm 90:14, "Satisfy us in the morning with your unfailing love, that we may sing for joy and be glad all our days." Jesus points out that real fulfillment and satisfaction, real blessedness, come from putting God at the center of our lives, allowing him to change our motives and ambitions, and then doing life his way. A life built purely on our own feelings and selfish wants is a life out of control. It is no better than consuming endless junk food. Only when we seek out God's will can we travel the path to true fulfillment and satisfaction.

Beatitude 5: Being Merciful

Abraham Lincoln once said, "I have always found that mercy bears richer fruits than strict justice." Mercy is a response to injustice or need that lets compassion speak louder than suffering or punishment. That's what makes mercy so difficult.

In his fifth beatitude, Jesus says, "Blessed are the merciful, for they will be shown mercy" (Matthew 5:7). In Luke 10:25–37 (ESV), Jesus depicts this attitude in his parable of the good Samaritan. Perhaps not coincidentally, Jesus tells this parable to a lawyer, who is the type of person who would have cared deeply about the implementation of just punishment and recompense:

> Jesus replied, "A man was going down from Jerusalem to Jericho, and he fell among robbers, who stripped him and beat him and departed, leaving him half dead. Now by chance a priest was going down that road, and when he saw him he passed by on the other side. So likewise a Levite, when he came to the place and saw him, passed by on the other side. But a Samaritan, as he journeyed, came to where he was, and when he saw him, he had compassion. He went to him and bound up his wounds, pouring on oil and wine. Then he set him on his own animal and brought him to an inn and took care of him. And the next day he took out two denarii and gave them to the innkeeper, saying, 'Take care of him, and whatever more you spend, I will repay you when I come back.' Which of

> these three, do you think, proved to be a neighbor to the man who fell among the robbers?" [The lawyer] said, "The one who showed him mercy." And Jesus said to him, "You go, and do likewise."

During Jesus's day, the Samaritans were an ethnic group hated by the Jews; the conflict between the two groups dated back centuries. By making the Samaritan the hero, Jesus highlights the boundary-breaking power of mercy. The priest and the Levite, two reputable social figures, failed to show compassion to the beaten man. They probably asked themselves, *What will happen to me if I stop to help this fellow? Maybe the people who beat him up will beat me up.* But the Samaritan asked a different question: *What will happen to this fellow if I do not stop to help him?* And so he stopped and showed him mercy.

If there is no God, it makes perfect sense to avoid messy situations that require an attitude of mercy. Showing compassion to others is risky. It can put our time, energy, finances, psychological well-being, and reputations on the line. But if there is a God who gave us the gift of life, who commands us to love one another, and if God loves us so much that he gave his own Son to die on a cross to pay the penalty for our wrongdoing, then it is totally reasonable to dedicate our lives to showing compassion to others. Love is not simply a feeling; it is a decision to action.

Mercy also involves forgiveness. Forgiveness is at the center of what Christianity is all about. To forgive involves absorbing the pain and absolving the debt of another. It is a costly endeavor as powerfully pictured in the cross of Jesus Christ. The cross is a clear statement that God is merciful and gracious. It is the costliest of payments for the costliest of debts—the sins of all humanity. A Christian is someone who has accepted responsibility for their wrongdoing and has turned to Christ for forgiveness. Once we accept this forgiveness, it is mandatory for us to extend this same mercy to those who have wronged us.

Instead of seeking revenge, we are called to forgive. I (Cliffe) will be the first to say that doing so can feel horrible. Real forgiveness, if we've been hurt badly, is never easy. It's hard to love our enemies. It's hard to show mercy to those who have cut us off at our knees. Luckily, we have Jesus as our model. The one who died a painful death on a cross for our sins did not hesitate to proclaim in his agony, "Father, forgive them, for they do not know what they are doing" (Luke 23:34). If Jesus could lavish such mercy on us, the least we can do is pour out this same mercy on others.

Beatitude 6: Being Pure in Heart

We don't talk much about purity these days. So when we hear Jesus say, "Blessed are the pure in heart, for they will see God" (Matthew 5:8), it can be difficult to fully grasp what he's declaring. During the time of Jesus, purity was an important concept. Jews who entered the temple to worship God had to follow a number of ritual laws to ensure that they were prepared to be in God's presence. They had to avoid contact with impure things such as dead bodies. They had to eat a proper diet. They had to wash themselves in a ritual bath known as a *mikvah*. All of these rituals were intended to make their bodies pure before God's holiness. Any impure person who entered God's presence risked provoking God's wrath or being overwhelmed by his holiness.

Purity matters to Jesus too, but it's purity of the *heart* that truly matters, not the body. For Jesus, what makes someone pure depends on the quality of their inner person. We can't fake purity with outward actions. It must come from within. Jesus teaches exactly this in Matthew 23:25–26: "Woe to you, teachers of the law and Pharisees, you hypocrites! You clean the outside of the cup and dish, but inside they are full of greed and self-indulgence. Blind Pharisee! First clean the inside of the cup and dish, and then the outside also will be clean."

The Pharisees were among the key authoritative figures in Jesus's day when it came to purity law. They were the experts who knew what people had to do to prepare themselves to go into God's presence. So when Jesus said the Pharisees cleaned only the outside of the cup but not the inside, he was declaring that they cared far more about appearances and performance than true purity from within. A person can look clean on the outside yet still have a dirty heart.

A pure heart seeks to overcome the influences of selfish desire and sin. It strives to forge healthy and genuine relationships with God and with others without becoming distracted by insincerity and deceit. Hypocrisy and deception are unacceptable to the pure in heart. It can be tempting to weave a web of lies to make ourselves look like we have it all together, to post misleading pictures of ourselves on social media, boast about false accomplishments, or hide our failures and sins behind closed doors. But just because the outside of our cup is clean doesn't mean the inside is. This is what makes this beatitude so powerful. A pure body may allow a person to enter God's temple, but only those with a pure heart can truly see God.

Purity of heart is a lifelong project. It is an endeavor that forces us to give up our insecurities and moral shortcomings. And if you're like me, you'll be dragged kicking and screaming into it, because it's not easy to give up our crutches. But it's all worth it because it will allow us to see God in a more intimate way, to know him more personally.

Beatitude 7: Being a Peacemaker

Jesus's statement "Blessed are the peacemakers, for they will be called children of God" (Matthew 5:9) is the only place in the New Testament where the Greek word *eirenopoios* ("peacemakers") is used. The notion of peace, known as *shalom* in Hebrew, is a key idea in the Old Testament. Unlike our modern conception of peace, *shalom* goes deeper than simply avoiding conflict and getting along with one another. *Shalom* means wholeness and completeness. A world of *shalom* is one in which strife and animosity do not exist, where God's image bearers value one another as his creation. *Shalom* isn't just a temporary ceasefire; it is the harmonious way life was created to be. It's the amazing moment when the way we organize and conduct our lives correlates with God's good order.

Why did Jesus die on the cross? To bring the *shalom* that would restore the relationship between humanity and God. To mend what was broken. We, too, have been called by Jesus to bring *shalom* to the world. We live in a time rife with conflict. Every day we witness the world-destroying effects of selfishness, greed, anger, and hatred. From international wars and political combat to communal disunity and families torn apart by arguments and disagreements, our planet longs for wholeness again. The cross offers this wholeness. It enables each of us to become adopted as God's children. Let that sink in. God wants to call us his sons and daughters. But this kind of family cannot be defined by conflict and hatred. In order for us to have genuine peace, we have to be willing to bridge the gaps that divide us.

True peace is about more than grinning and bearing pain. *Shalom* takes more than just ignoring hurt. We must be willing to both apologize to and forgive our fellow humans. We must be willing to do the difficult work of working through our disagreements. We must be willing to see one another as Jesus Christ sees us. In that sense, the peacemakers are more than conflict resolvers; they are those who bring our broken world back in line with the way God first created it.

Beatitudes 8 and 9: Experiencing Persecution

The final two beatitudes, which are interconnected, appear in Matthew 5:10–12. There Jesus says, "Blessed are those who are persecuted because of righteousness, for theirs is the kingdom of heaven. Blessed are you when people insult you, persecute you and falsely say all kinds of evil against you because of me. Rejoice and be glad, because great is your reward in heaven, for in the same way, they persecuted the prophets who were before you."

The building up of God's kingdom will always have detractors. The early church experienced this firsthand. Quite a few of the first apostles who followed Jesus—including Peter, James, Paul, and Thomas—were martyred for their faith in Christ. The Romans viewed many of their emperors as gods. Coins depicting the emperors often claimed as much. Jesus's followers refused to proclaim that Caesar was Lord, insisting that Jesus Christ was Lord, and some paid the ultimate price for that refusal. They rejected the Roman deities worshiped by their surrounding culture and faced social discrimination, mistreatment, imprisonment, and even death as a result. The second-century Christian author Tertullian wrote, "The blood of the martyrs is the seed of the church" (*Apologeticum* 50).

Just because Roman persecution of Christians officially ended at the beginning of the fourth century doesn't mean followers of Jesus have had it easy ever since. It is harrowing to know that more people have died globally for their faith in Christ in the twentieth century than in all the preceding nineteen centuries. Although it's unlikely many of us living in the West will be pressed to die for our belief in Christ, it doesn't mean we won't receive some raised eyebrows or be the subject of stereotyping or cultural ridicule. As the apostle Paul said, the cross of Christ is a stumbling block and foolishness for many (1 Corinthians 1:23). It's why taking the initiative to wrestle with your doubts and allowing those uncertainties to propel you to seek growth and understanding is so important. At some point, you will face people who will call into question your trust in Jesus Christ. We can tell you from experience that some of them will be genuinely curious about the evidence that led you to belief. Others will ask because they're struggling with their faith and need encouragement. And unfortunately, a few are out to demolish your faith and prove you wrong.

But notice that Jesus doesn't encourage us to get even. He doesn't proclaim, "When you're insulted, strike them right back. Have that good-feeling gotcha moment!" In a radical departure from the way the world does things, Jesus says to turn the other cheek (Matthew 5:38–42). He calls us to respect those who have done us dirty:

> You have heard that it was said, "You shall love your neighbor and hate your enemy." But I say to you, Love your enemies and pray for those who persecute you, so that you may be sons of your Father who is in heaven. For he makes his sun rise on the evil and on the good, and sends rain on the just and on the unjust. For if you love those who love you, what reward do you have? Do not even the tax collectors do the same? (Matthew 5:43–46 ESV)

I'll admit this can be incredibly hard for me (Cliffe) to do. I'm prone to hate my enemy; I can be pretty stubborn and proud sometimes. But when I stop and look at our world and watch the amount of animosity that spews from its political, cultural, racial, social, and economic conflicts, it hits me that something needs to change in all of us, me included. It's tragic to see good people just start outright hating each other because of their differences. That's not the way things should be. Jesus calls us to break that vicious cycle of violence and find joy in the radical grace and mercy of Christ's heavenly kingdom. Revenge and indignation are cheap trinkets compared to the rich reward of heaven.

The Beatitudes only scrape the surface of the genius of Jesus's ethical teaching, both in the Sermon on the Mount and across the entire New Testament as well. During his life, Gandhi also professed profound appreciation of the Sermon on the Mount: "I have regarded Jesus of Nazareth as one amongst the mighty teachers that the world has had. . . . I shall say to the . . . Hindus . . . that your lives will be incomplete unless you reverently study the teachings of Jesus." The Beatitudes offer a crystal clear description of what it means to follow Jesus as Savior and Lord.

Jesus Christ had a truly ethical mind the likes of which the world has never seen. But just as astonishing as the content of Jesus's moral principles is how faultlessly he lived out those teachings. Jesus was no hypocrite; he lived a life without sin, the type of life we all wish we could live. Yet remarkably, Jesus does not judge us for our faults and shortcomings. He doesn't hang over our heads the inability to live up to his high moral principles. His gracious promise of eternal life is always freely given, never earned. That's the good news of Jesus Christ.

In a heartfelt moment we shared with our friend George Janko on his show, he captured just how beautiful and utterly unbelievable this promise is. Recalling how his life has changed since starting *The George Janko Show* and becoming serious about his belief in Christ, George admitted feeling like a fraud sometimes, especially when fans thank him for changing their lives. "I'm ashamed of myself," he confided. "I keep trying to push people in the right directions that I'm trying to go toward, but I'm failing at it myself. And yet they're looking at me like I'm killing it."

We've both been there too. Perhaps the apostle Paul said it best: "For I have the desire to do what is good, but I cannot carry it out. For I do not do the good I want to do, but the evil I do not want to do—this I keep on doing" (Romans 7:18–19). But in the eyes of God, we are not our sin. When we don't measure up, the grace of Jesus Christ tilts the scales in our favor. As George put it so well, "You're never going to be perfect. You're always going to fail God. But because of Jesus Christ, you're still going to be good enough to go to heaven." That's good news if we've ever heard it.

CHAPTER 8

DID JESUS REALLY PERFORM MIRACLES?

It was a dreary November day, the air soggy with a steady drizzle. Winter coats and umbrellas peppered the walkways as the splash of shallow puddles echoed between buildings. Not exactly an ideal afternoon for outdoor campus ministry. It's not easy to have a serious discussion about the existence of God when everyone is muffling their shivers just to get a word out! But it blows me (Cliffe) away that so many students, even after all these years, will still leave their warm dorms and brave the elements to participate in these honest conversations. I'm grateful for each of them.

On this particular day, a religion studies major approached me and stated that while she believed Jesus Christ was a historical person, she wasn't convinced any longer that he was God incarnate. When I asked her why, she responded that it was because she didn't believe his miracles actually happened. For the next several minutes, our conversation jumped from one topic to the next before finally circling back around. "I don't believe Jesus is God because I don't believe in the supernatural," she stated as she pulled her burgundy cardigan tightly around her shoulders before crossing her arms. "It's fantastical and magical. *It just doesn't seem possible.*"

Accepting that Jesus was an influential ethical teacher and an all-around "good guy" isn't a huge stretch for most folks, as we saw in the previous chapter. That's a pretty low-risk claim. Plenty of my atheist friends have said as much without batting an eye. But when it comes to whether Jesus Christ performed miracles—well, that's a different story. In many ways, this is where the proverbial rubber hits the road and people are forced to confront the reality of whether Jesus truly is the Son of God. Not surprisingly, this is also where doubt starts creeping in for many believers. How could Jesus have done all those wondrous things recorded in the New Testament? Why don't we see miracles like that today? How can we even know stuff like that happened so long ago in the first place?

Such doubts can feel earth-shattering when someone first encounters them, cutting to the very core of their faith. Dozens of people have approached us and admitted that they stopped believing in Jesus because they felt so overwhelmed by the constant hum of suspicion surrounding his miracles. They surrendered to the power of skepticism. "How could anyone even begin to prove something like that?" one former Christian lamented to us. "Nobody really believes supernatural things happen today. I think our culture has outgrown stuff like that." It's no wonder people struggle to demolish such doubts when they're faced day in and day out with the constant message that Jesus's miracles are nothing more than feel-good fables made up hundreds of years ago.

For the rest of this chapter, we'll wrestle with the intimidating doubts surrounding Jesus's miracles. After first explaining what we mean by a miracle, we'll examine what the Bible says about Jesus's miracles. Then we'll take a closer look at exactly why most skeptics cry foul when it comes to this issue, as well as address why miracles *seem* so rare today.

What Is a Miracle?

People use the word *miracle* to describe a lot of things these days. The term gets thrown around when someone narrowly avoids a horrendous car accident or experiences a crazy coincidence that feels too good or impossible to be true. Fans say it's a miracle when their favorite sport team, against all odds, pulls off a last-second play to win the championship. Perhaps you've even used it to describe when your son or daughter uncharacteristically cleans up their room of their own free will.

While those moments may often feel "miraculous" due to their low statistical probability or unexpectedness, none of them are miracles, strictly speaking. A miracle is an event that can't be explained by our scientific knowledge. It defies our expectations and the way we typically experience the world. Although philosophers and theologians still debate this definition, a miracle is a moment when the supernatural intervenes, when natural causes alone can't offer a sufficient explanation of what occurred.

One of the ways I (Cliffe) often explain how this works on campus visits or in interviews is by the falling of an apple. If a person is sitting under an apple tree and one of its ripe apples disengages from its branch, a hundred times out of a hundred it's going to fall and hit the ground. That's how the physical force of gravity works. But if I reach my hand out and catch the apple out of the air, I've stopped gravity from pulling it down to the ground. The introduction of my hand changes the expected trajectory of the apple. I haven't contradicted the way physics works across our universe. I haven't "broken" gravity or done something illogical; I simply intervened and prevented the effect of gravity on that apple in that moment. In a similar way, a miracle is the introduction of the supernatural hand of God to change the outcome of what would naturally happen in a certain event.

The main difference between this analogy and the way God

performs miracles is that God is not a mere human being catching an apple in midair. Unlike us, God is not restrained by the limits of our material world. That's because God, who exists outside of space and time and matter, created this cosmos and established the orderly laws and scientific processes governing our universe. As a result, God can intercede momentarily in our world in ways we, as finite human beings, cannot. His divine intervention is not limited by the physical and temporal restrictions that structure our mortal lives. In that sense, miracles push back against the idea that our world is a closed system that remains untouched by some detached, impersonal deity. A miracle is a statement that a supernatural hand has been added to the equation.

What Does the Bible Say About Jesus's Miracles?

As we saw in the previous chapter, the New Testament makes it crystal clear that Jesus Christ not only served as an amazing ethical teacher but also lived out his high moral principles to perfection. Besides Jesus's ethical teachings and parables, much of the focus of the New Testament Gospels centers on his miraculous deeds. In Matthew, Mark, Luke, and John, we find more than three dozen distinct episodes where Jesus performs different types of miracles.

A large portion of these miracles fall into the category of healings. In these gospel episodes, Jesus encounters a person who is suffering some sort of physical disorder or illness and, out of compassion, he alleviates their ailment. Jesus gives blind people sight (Mark 8:22–26; Luke 18:35–43; John 9:1–12) and cures those with skin diseases (Matthew 8:1–4; Luke 17:11–19). He heals paralytics who cannot walk (Matthew 8:5–13; Mark 2:1–12; John 5:1–18) and those who have other physical ailments (Mark 3:1–6; Luke 14:1–6). Jesus restores those who suffer from serious fevers and other sicknesses (Matthew 14:34–36; Mark 1:29–31) and causes the deaf to hear and the mute to speak (Matthew 9:32–34; Mark 7:31–37).

In most of these episodes, Jesus simply speaks, touches the person, or prays to God to bring about their healing. In a couple of the gospel accounts, Jesus even cures someone from far away, simply telling the person who requests the healing to return home because their loved one has already been healed (Luke 7:1–10; John 4:46–54).

These healing accounts told by the gospel eyewitnesses certainly resonate with those of us who have experienced a serious sickness ourselves or who have watched loved ones suffer bouts with disease, injury, or chronic health issues. But for the earliest Christians, these narratives would have been especially powerful. The gift of good health was a rare commodity in the ancient Roman world. During the first century, the average life expectancy hovered around thirty-five to forty years of age. Historians estimate that roughly 20 to 30 percent of all children did not live past the first year and nearly half of them did not make it to adulthood. Malnutrition and unsafe drinking water led to birth defects or long-term health issues. Poor sanitation and hygiene practices allowed diseases to spread with relative ease, especially in the close living conditions of urban areas. And while medical treatment, herbal medicines, and surgery were potential options for those who suffered from disease and disorder, they were not always widely available and were often limited in their effectiveness. Sickness, suffering, and death were exceptionally common and disturbing realities in Jesus's day.

The inescapable presence of disease and the incredible hope that Jesus brought the sick can be vividly felt in the account of the bleeding woman (Matthew 9:18–26; Mark 5:25–34; Luke 8:40–56). According to the gospel writers, this woman had been suffering from this ailment for twelve straight years. She had spent every penny she owned seeking out the help of physicians. But no medicine or treatment had worked—they only made everything worse. Believing that Jesus might be able to heal her, she approached him in a bustling crowd and managed to touch his cloak. Instantly, she felt the bleeding stop; she had been healed. Kneeling before Jesus, she confessed to touching his cloak and told him everything. In response, he replied, "Daughter, your faith has healed you. Go in peace and be freed from your suffering" (Mark 5:34). What an extraordinary moment and powerful testimony to faith in Jesus Christ!

Elsewhere in the Gospels, we find Jesus performing exorcisms and curing people of demonic possession (Matthew 15:21–28; Mark 1:21–27; Luke 8:26–39). Occasionally, we are asked what we believe about evil and whether demons actually exist. Evil is unfortunately a tangible thing in the world, regardless of how much we hate that fact. The Bible is clear that demons and Satan are real beings. That being said, we need to admit that human beings have proven more than capable of causing copious amounts of evil on our own, no demonic help required. Much of the bloodshed, hatred, inequality, and injustice in our world can be traced back to our own selfishness, rebellion, and sin. So we're leery of any approach to evil where the Devil suddenly gives everyone an easy out for the horrible ways we treat one another.

At the end of the day, however, neither of us can claim to be experts in this area. We just don't have all the details; the Bible only tells us so much on the subject. On this point, we find wisdom in the words of C. S. Lewis from his book *The Screwtape Letters*:

> There are two equal and opposite errors into which our race can fall about the devils. One is to disbelieve in their existence. The other is to believe, and to feel an excessive and unhealthy interest in them. They themselves are equally pleased by both errors and hail a materialist or a magician with the same delight.

Several other narratives in the Gospels recount miracles in which Jesus demonstrates his control over nature. In John 2:1–11, Jesus turns water into wine at a wedding in the village of Cana. Three of the four gospels tell of Jesus calming a terrifying storm on the Sea of Galilee while traveling across the lake in a ship with his disciples (Matthew 8:23–27; Mark 4:35–41; Luke 8:22–25). In another incident on the Sea of Galilee, Jesus walks across the water to the disciples' boat floating on the lake in the middle of the night (Matthew 14:22–33; Mark 6:45–52; John 6:16–21). All of the four gospels also contain at least one report of Jesus multiplying a meager amount of food to feed thousands of people (Matthew 15:32–39; Mark 8:1–13; Luke 9:10–17; John 6:1–15).

Finally, as a sort of prelude to his own resurrection (see the next chapter), all of the four New Testament gospels recall Jesus raising people from the dead. Three tell of a man named Jairus, who came to Jesus and asked him to heal his sick daughter only to discover that, prior to arriving at his home with Jesus, she had already died. Much to the derision of the mourning crowd, Jesus consoled Jairus, telling him his daughter was merely sleeping. Upon entering the house, Jesus commanded the girl to get up, bringing her back to life (Matthew 9:18–26; Mark 5:21–43; Luke 8:40–56). In Luke 7:11–17, we find a similar episode where Jesus raised the young son of a widow from the dead by commanding him to get up. Without question, the most famous of these accounts is that of the raising of Lazarus in John 11. Jesus was informed that his friend Lazarus was deathly ill and was asked to come and heal him. Unfortunately, by the time Jesus arrived, Lazarus had been deceased for four days and had already been placed in a tomb. He had been dead long enough that Lazarus's sister told Jesus not to open the tomb because of the stench of his decaying body. However, Jesus proceeded to order the stone to be removed. After speaking a prayer, Jesus commanded Lazarus to come out, and Lazarus appeared, still wrapped in his graveclothes.

It cannot be denied that the New Testament presents Jesus Christ as a prolific healer, exorcist, and wonder-worker. Even the most naturalistic of historians, such as University of North Carolina religious studies professor Bart Ehrman, will admit as much, despite denying the reality of miracles. However, if we accept the evidence that all of the New Testament Gospels were ancient biographies that preserved historically reliable eyewitness testimony regarding the life of Jesus (as we demonstrated in chapter 5), we must also then accept that these accounts of the miraculous deeds of Jesus shouldn't be diminished as mythical interludes or legends. Just like the wise ethical teachings and parables of Jesus, these miracle accounts were recorded by the gospel writers as *credible historical testimony* to the incredible life of Jesus. He actually *did* such miraculous things.

Interestingly, the earliest nonbiblical source that mentions Jesus—the Jewish historian Josephus's book 18 of his late first-century *Antiquities*—confirms that Jesus had a reputation for performing miracles, stating that Jesus was "a doer of wonderful works." The gospel writers weren't just making these stories up out of thin air; other people had heard about Jesus's miracles too.

Why Did Jesus Perform Miracles?

Was Jesus just some sort of ancient magician?

It's a question we encounter every once in a while when we talk about Jesus's miracles. To some degree, we get why people ask it. While most folks know that Jesus healed people and performed other miraculous deeds, far fewer can identify exactly why he did such wondrous things. Was he just looking to show off or make money? Were Jesus's miracles simply purposeless acts of power? Could it be that Jesus was trying to go viral and become famous?

When we look at the New Testament, we can identify two specific reasons Jesus did miracles. First, he did so because *he felt compassion for human suffering.* When we read the four gospels, we notice that

Jesus never performed wonders as a means of self-promotion. We see no indication that he had grand political ambitions. He wasn't trying to become a celebrity or the ancient version of a social media star. We know this because in several places, the Gospels record Jesus instructing the people he healed to tell *no one* that he had healed them (Luke 5:12–16), or him healing people anonymously (John 5:13). Jesus wasn't a seeker of fame.

What motivated Jesus to perform a miracle—be it healing the sick, multiplying loaves and fish to feed the hungry, or raising someone from the dead—is that he *had compassion* on them (Matthew 9:36; 20:34; Mark 1:41; 8:2; Luke 7:13). The New Testament verb translated as "to have compassion" comes from the Greek word for one's innards or intestines (*splanchnizomai*). It can be translated more literally as "to be gut-wrenched." Jesus *ached* in his heart for the suffering of the people he encountered. In a world full of illness and infirmity, hunger and hurt, death and despair, Jesus brought to all people—young and old, rich and poor, powerful and lowly, Jews and Gentiles—healing and hope.

Second, the Gospels reveal that Jesus's miracles were *signs pointing to his identity as the Son of God*. Our natural world is constantly spiraling toward death and decay, disorder and decomposition. Because of sin, things aren't the way they were created to be. And no human solution—be it political, economic, social, or cultural—has proven even remotely capable of reversing this vicious cycle. It's a colossal mess only God could fix, and that's exactly what God did by sending Jesus Christ.

The miracles performed by Jesus point to his identity as the sinless Son of God. The supernatural creator who brought the oceans into being now shows mastery over creation by walking on the water and calming the storm. The divinity who crafted our human bodies that became marred by sin now restores them from their brokenness. The one who rained bread from heaven now multiplies bread for our stomachs and wine for our joy. The all-powerful deity who created this world and declared, "It is good," now shows command over the spiritual forces of evil. The God of life now brings the dead back to life.

No mere human could bring about such miracles; only a supernatural hand could enact such authoritative, world-restoring power. *Only God incarnate could.* As the gospel of John puts it, "Jesus performed many other signs in the presence of his disciples, which are not recorded in this book. But these are written that you may believe that Jesus is the Messiah, the Son of God, and that by believing you may have life in his name" (John 20:30–31).

Did Those Miracles Really Happen?

"But you don't *really* believe Jesus turned water into wine, healed the blind, or raised the dead, *do you*?"

"Sure, those might be great stories, but there's *no way* that stuff like that actually happened."

"How could you even rationally begin to prove something like that? Seems silly to me."

Stuart and I hear this kind of disbelief expressed at nearly every place we speak. It's not all that surprising, to be honest. We live in a culture that leaves as much room for miracles as it does for the Loch Ness Monster or Santa Claus. And it's not very quiet about it either. I don't know about you, but some days I feel like I'm being bombarded with the message that believing in God and trusting in Jesus Christ are simply naive superstitions or a retreat from reality. In those moments, doubt can creep in faster than we can expel it. It can be hard to avoid becoming consumed with the thought that maybe Jesus didn't do any of the fantastic things the New Testament authors attribute to him. Maybe those miracles are nothing but literary exaggerations. Maybe he was just a regular guy from Nazareth.

Admittedly, this kind of skepticism can be tough to wrestle with, but only if we let it intimidate us first. The truth is that many of the criticisms of the reality of Jesus's miracles aren't very imposing once we become familiar with them and understand what skeptics are actually arguing here.

Take, for example, one of the more heated conversations I (Cliffe) have had on the subject. As I stood in the shade of one of the classroom buildings at Texas State University, a male student wearing a light blue hooded sweatshirt stepped forward from the group. Without hesitation, he dramatically began to spout question after question about the historicity of the Bible and its "superstitious" miracles. Over time, the discussion became increasingly more one-sided in tone as the young man's frustration grew and his gestures became more animated. Before long, his ranting began to drown out all of the responses I was offering to his questions. It didn't matter what I was saying—if I was lucky enough to speak before being interrupted. (Frankly, I'm not sure he heard most of what I said.) His insistent and incensed chorus remained the same: "Miracles are pure nonsense."

Finally, after enduring several more fruitless minutes, I had to acknowledge the elephant in the room. It seemed clear, I told him, that nothing I said could ever change his mind—regardless of how convincing or reasonable what I had to say might be. The real issue wasn't my historical interpretation of the Bible and of Jesus's miracles; *the real issue was his philosophical presupposition of naturalism.* Yes, miracles are absolutely ridiculous *if* someone comes into the discussion with the blanket assumption that nothing supernatural exists and everything is merely material. In that case, miracles will always be impossible and "pure nonsense," since miracles, by definition, presuppose the existence of the supernatural.

Naturalism is a nonstarter when it comes to discussing miracles. By showing his ideological cards, the young man revealed he wasn't interested in having an honest or authentic dialogue. He wasn't there to grapple with his doubts or seek understanding. He wanted his gotcha moment. Needless to say, once I called him out, I didn't get the chance to talk with him about the shortcomings and self-refuting nature of naturalism as a philosophical worldview. With an exaggerated flip of his arm, the fellow in the blue sweatshirt turned around and bitterly paced away before I had the chance. I truly hope our conversation ended up changing him in some positive way. I hope he has found peace.

Another criticism Stuart and I often hear about the reality of miracles is that no one has scientifically proven them. One of the more memorable examples of this perspective was a female student who, nearly thirty years ago, said she couldn't believe in miracles like the resurrection because she'd have to observe them for herself. At the end of the day, the only convincing evidence was scientific proof. "Show me the medical charts," she yelled, "and I'll become a Christian *today*!" Over the past several decades, plenty of other conversation partners have followed suit in demanding 100 percent empirical proof of miracles. "Hand over the photographic and video evidence! Give me the lab results! Show me the science, and then I'll believe!"

Don't get me wrong, science is a wonderful tool. Our lives are far better because of it. But like any type of knowledge, science has limits to what it can and cannot do. Many forms of science can study observable physical processes, test their repeatability, investigate potential theories, and make sense of the way certain aspects of our physical world work. But science can't explain so much of what constitutes reality—including love, beauty, relationships, history, morals, and even human logic—which is why scientism (the philosophical worldview that we can only believe what we know scientifically) is so problematic. When we restrict knowledge purely to what we can determine through scientific observation, our world gets pretty small—much smaller than most of us would be comfortable with.

The main issue with demanding scientific proof for miracles is that miracles, by definition, aren't replicable or predictable events. They're unique historical events caused by the supernatural—extraordinary, once-in-a-lifetime moments that are impossible to repeat without divine intervention. Scientific knowledge often (but not always) relies on empirical repeatability and the observation of natural processes. But we can't test a miracle in a lab the same way we'd test a chemical reaction. Now, that doesn't mean there's absolutely no observable evidence for the reality of miracles. There are plenty of documented cases, for example, of medical miracles, where doctors have seen patients whose cancer or chronic ailment was suddenly cured. Something happened where the natural causes at work were contravened. An event occurred that cannot be explained without pointing to a supernatural cause.

Arguably, there is some (though limited) empirical evidence in these cases, yet such events cannot be replicated a second time by using any of the natural means at our disposal. Without supernatural intervention, a miracle can't occur—for example, an apple falling from a tree will hit the ground without a divine hand there to catch it. This means the only way we can approach many miracles is through historical inquiry. Who witnessed the miracle? What did they say happened? Is their testimony historically reliable and credible? Those are the types of questions we're able to answer and the type of evidence we need to rely on when it comes to determining whether a certain miraculous event in the past plausibly occurred.

One last point we often bring up when it comes to the existence of miracles is that Christians aren't the only ones who believe in them. Even *atheists* unknowingly accept things we call miraculous, despite their contention that there is no supernatural being. When people first hear this, they often chuckle among themselves. What a preposterous statement, Cliffe! But think about it. Take a look at these six "miraculous" things that nearly all of my atheist friends believe:

1. *Existence comes from nonexistence:* What was there before the Big Bang? There was nothing. But how can you accidentally get *something* from *nothing*?
2. *Order comes from chaos:* How is it possible for chaos to order itself, especially in a universe that physically tends toward *entropy* and *disorder* rather than *life* and *order*?
3. *Life comes from nonlife:* When was the last time any of us saw a nonliving, inanimate substance suddenly turn into a living thing out of thin air on its own?
4. *The personal comes from the nonpersonal:* How can consciousness, reason, love, and other aspects of personhood randomly appear from inanimate, raw matter?
5. *Reason comes from nonreason:* How can a rational, immaterial mind emerge from nonrational matter that lacks the ability to think logically?
6. *Morality comes from matter:* What would prompt physical matter and energy to randomly produce objective moral beliefs and human conscience?

And you say that atheists refuse to believe in miracles? Baloney! Their problem isn't the existence of miracles—none of these six statements possess natural explanations. Their real problem lies in the *existence of a miracle worker*. That's what they're really contending. But as we demonstrated earlier in this chapter, miracles by definition presuppose a supernatural miracle worker. "So," I ask my atheist friends, "which is it then? Do miracles (and a supernatural miracle worker) exist, or are they simply nonsense fantasies? You can't have it both ways."

This debate about whether miracles exist isn't a new, tectonic development. Since the beginning of the Enlightenment nearly four hundred years ago, skeptic after skeptic has expressed the same sorts of disbelief we just described about whether Jesus performed miracles. In the eighteenth century, the Scottish philosopher David Hume made the still often cited naturalist argument that it is far more likely for eyewitness testimony regarding a miracle to be defective due to faulty perception or deception than for an actual miracle to occur. Needless to say, both Hume's definition of a miracle as a violation of the laws of nature and his broader argument have been extensively critiqued by modern thinkers. Thomas Jefferson famously created his own version of the four New Testament gospels by compiling all of Jesus's ethical teachings and leaving behind all of his miracles, an eccentric approach that modern historians of every stripe find laughable today. The early twentieth-century theologian Rudolf Bultmann similarly promoted the demythologization of the supernatural and miraculous elements of the Gospels. His views have also been largely abandoned.

More recently, atheist author Richard Dawkins proclaimed, "The nineteenth century is the last time when it was possible for an educated person to admit to believing in miracles like the virgin birth without embarrassment." We beg to differ. There's no shortage of renowned philosophers, physicists, mathematicians, and scientists today who affirm belief in miracles. In fact, if you look at the data from the last four General Social Survey questionnaires regarding whether American respondents believe in miracles, you may be surprised to see that more people with undergraduate and advanced degrees believe in miracles today than they did in the 1990s.

Yes, the echo chamber of doubt and cultural cynicism may feel overpowering at times. But it's important to remember that the bark of such arguments against miracles is often far worse than their bite. It is not unreasonable or illogical to believe in miracles and trust what the Gospels say about Jesus Christ—people of faith have been doing this for centuries! I believe it's much stranger to adopt a worldview that reduces human knowledge to an absurd sliver just to avoid any acknowledgment of a supernatural miracle worker. Now *that* I'd call nonsense.

Why Don't We Experience More Miracles Today?

In November 2024, we were invited to appear on Brandon McGuire's *Daily Dose of Wisdom* podcast, a show dedicated to something both Cliffe and I feel passionate about—having honest conversations about our skepticism from a faith perspective. During the interview, Cliffe walked through the four tests of historical reliability that support the credibility of the biographical account of Jesus's life found in the Gospels (see chapter 5).

"So I'm sure you've gotten this question before," Brandon commented once Cliffe finished speaking, "but how would you respond to the person who hears this and admits, yeah, there was a real guy from Nazareth named Jesus, and there may have been a cross involved, but the miracles . . . ? C'mon! That's not real, right?"

After briefly mentioning a couple of the points we've brought up in this chapter, I (Stuart) told Brandon about my recent encounter with a student at Yale who was hyperskeptical about the reality of Jesus's miracles. During our conversation, she pressed me on how I could believe something so fanciful in our scientific age. After all, if miracles like the ones found in the Bible are real, why don't we see them happening today?

My answer to her was this: Get out of your bubble and explore this world. Why? Because the vast majority of our world's population doesn't see reality through the kind of disenchanted lenses she looks through.

We Westerners are the minority in this department. We've slowly purged the supernatural and the spiritual from our daily lives and replaced them with science, materialism, consumerism, and technology. But the rest of the world hasn't followed suit. People around the world still believe in miracles and experience them. In his massive two-volume book *Miracles,* Craig Keener examines the evidence for miracles in the Gospels, as well as contemporary examples of supernatural experiences such as faith healings. According to Keener, surveys show that more than *three hundred million* people in East Asia and India alone have reported experiencing a miracle. And that number gets even larger when we include Christians from China, South America, Latin America, and Africa. For people from these settings, to even question the reality of the miraculous would be viewed as pretty outlandish.

What's more, just because Western culture has developed a reckless cynicism regarding the reality of miracles doesn't mean no North Americans experience miracles. Cliffe and I have talked to many people who have experienced medical miracles where terminal illnesses and cancerous tumors suddenly disappeared. Can we really discount their testimony so flippantly? The same can be said about the work of the Duke University Rhine Research Center, which has published dozens of peer-reviewed studies on near-death experiences of people who, having been brought back to life, later recall floating around the hospital room and observing uncanny details concerning the room or the doctors. These cases have flabbergasted doctors. So why should we be so quick to say, "Nah, that didn't happen. *They're wrong.*"

As I told the Yale student, perhaps the problem isn't that miracles don't exist, but more so that our culture has conditioned us to ignore them or explain them away. We've spent so much intellectual time and energy telling ourselves that miracles can't be real that we simply began to presume that this is just the way things are. It's a reverberation cycle of cynicism we haven't been able to shake as a culture. We've become so closed-minded and self-assured that we won't even dignify the fact that we're the ideological minority in the world, that most people actually not only believe in miracles but also have experienced them. So I advised her that if she truly wants to know whether miracles are real, she should talk to one of the millions of people around our globe who has encountered the miraculous. Listen to their eyewitness testimony. Don't stop wrestling with your doubt.

If you visited a world-renowned bakery, would it be outside the realm of belief that they could make you a sandwich? If you met a famous artist, do you think he or she could handle filling in a coloring book? If you sat down with a brilliant Silicon Valley programmer, do you think they could install your laptop updates? I would surely hope so.

The same can be said for God and miracles. If a supernatural being outside of space and time masterfully created our universe, why is it inconceivable that he could extend his hand into our world? When we put God inside a box, when we reshape Jesus Christ to fit our naturalistic presuppositions or culturally conditioned skepticism, we ignore the eyewitness testimony of the New Testament and miss out on its true, life-changing power.

The late Tim Keller in his book *The Reason for God* had this to say about our contemporary Western misunderstanding of Jesus's miracles:

> We modern people think of miracles as the suspension of the natural order, but Jesus meant them to be the restoration of the natural order. The Bible tells us that God did not originally make the world to have disease, hunger, and death in it. Jesus has come to redeem where it is wrong and heal the world where it is broken. His miracles are not just proofs that he has power but also wonderful foretastes of what he is going to do with that power. Jesus's miracles are not just a challenge to our minds, but a promise to our hearts, that the world we all want is coming.

Amazing! And perhaps that's part of the root of our doubts when it comes to miracles. It all sounds too wonderful to be real. We've grown so accustomed to a world gone wrong that it's hard to believe such a beautiful promise. I know I (Cliffe) have pushed up against this doubt before. In those moments, I need to step back and remember that if I am convinced there is an all-powerful and eternal creator who set this well-ordered world into motion out of nothing, then surely this God will have no problem healing our ills.

There is still, however, one miracle we haven't fully explored, and it is certainly the greatest of all. That miracle is Jesus Christ, the Son of God, who was crucified to give us forgiveness for our sins, only to be raised back to life. For details about that miracle, you'll have to keep on reading.

CHAPTER 9

WAS JESUS GOD AND DID HE REALLY RISE FROM THE DEAD?

"So my theory is Jesus probably lied, but he did it in good faith." It's hard to ignore an opening statement like that. It took me (Stuart) a few seconds to pinpoint where the voice had originated. By now, the waves of UC Davis students had grown several rows deep, with dozens resorting to sitting on the pavement near our feet.

"I mean, I think it was one of the greatest lies ever told, but he did it *for* God, and I think he's probably in heaven now because of that." The guy in the black Carhartt beanie finally inched his way into view, his arms gesturing enthusiastically as he spoke. "Like, I don't think he was *physically*, in a sense, the divine Son of God. I think he was a really talented magician."

"A talented magician?" I replied. My curiosity was definitely piqued at this point.

"Yeah, I think the resurrection—I think he probably had a twin." His voice started to trail off, but his suggestion that Jesus had a doppelgänger who died in his place, thereby allowing Jesus to fake his death, was clear enough.

"I mean, that's a fascinating idea," I countered. "But if you're going to say he's just a good moral teacher or a magician, how do you deal with all the people who worshiped him as God? How do you explain the fact that so many people bought into an *actual* resurrection?"

As I went on to tell him, if we accept that the four New Testament gospels represent biographies of the life of Jesus Christ based on historical, eyewitness evidence, then Jesus can be only one of three things: a *liar*, a *lunatic*, or our *Lord* and Savior. If Jesus flat-out lied about his divinity and somehow faked his resurrection with a body double, it'd be difficult to call him an outstanding moral teacher. (Last time I checked, habitual liars don't make great ethicists.) And if Jesus genuinely *did* believe he was the Son of God but got it totally wrong, then he was completely delusional, and I think most of us can agree that no one should commit their lives to someone who lacks a firm grip on reality.

Ultimately, we can't escape the issue, no matter how hard we try. The moment we acknowledge that Jesus was a historical person, we encounter the unavoidable crux of the matter: Is Jesus truly God? Did he rise from dead, just as the Gospels claim? Or is it all just a hoax—the greatest conspiracy theory that ever existed? Chances are, if you're reading this book, you've thought about these issues. Maybe you're still lost in the weeds of your disbelief and have all but given up hope. After all, how is all this even possible? *How do you even begin to demolish doubt about something so miraculous as Jesus's divinity and resurrection?*

Don't give up yet. Miracles *are* possible. And believe us, this is the greatest miracle humankind has ever seen. It's a doubt worth wrestling with.

How Can Jesus Be God?

In the first century AD, followers of Jesus Christ were worshiping him as God. This was not a later development that occurred centuries after Jesus walked this earth. The very first believers proclaimed that Jesus Christ was God in human form.

One of our oldest nonbiblical sources that describe the early Christians confirms as much. In a letter to the Roman emperor Trajan written around AD 110, a regional governor named Pliny requests advice on how to deal with this growing new movement of Christians who, he says, "meet on a fixed day before dawn and sing responsively a hymn to Christ as to a god" (*Letters* 10.96). This likely concerned Pliny. In the ancient world, refusal to worship the Roman gods was viewed as a rejection of the authority of Roman rule. While traditional ethnic groups such as the Jews, who worshiped deities that predated the Romans, were given a pass here, movements such as Christianity, that appeared to worship new gods, weren't extended that privilege. For Pliny, the exclusive worship of Christ as God was problematic because it represented sedition against Rome.

The exaltation of Jesus as God is even more clearly emphasized in the New Testament. Across the New Testament, we read of people worshiping Jesus (Matthew 14:33; 28:9; Luke 24:52; John 9:38). In all these instances, Jesus always accepted this worship; he never corrected anyone when this happened. In contrast, when Jesus's followers performed miracles in Jesus's name and became objects of worship, they always emphatically declared that they *should not* be worshiped because *they are not God* (Acts 10:25; 14:8–18). They rejected that worship because only God is worthy of that type of praise. Jesus is the one who should be praised. So the fact that Jesus openly *accepted* worship that is meant only for God assumes his self-identification as God.

The eyewitness accounts in each of the four gospels also state that Jesus himself taught that he was God. On one of our appearances on *The George Janko Show*, George and his then-fiancée Shawna (whose wedding we officiated—congrats again, George and Shawna!) asked us about this: "Is Jesus God? And if he is God, where in the Bible does he state that he is God?"

"Good question," I (Cliffe) responded. "John chapter 8, verse 58."

"Whoa, you shot from the hip!" George slapped his thigh as his face broke into a wide grin, causing all of us to break out in laughter at his animated reply. "I am *so* jealous you can just go and do that!"

"In John 8:58," I continued after composing myself, "Jesus, speaking about himself, says, 'Before Abraham was born, I am.' Now, the Jews did not call God *G-o-d* like we do. Their main name for God was Yahweh, which comes from the Hebrew verb 'to be' (*hayah*). In the Old Testament, Yahweh is referred to as I AM WHO I AM (Exodus 3:14). So there was no misunderstanding here. By calling himself 'I am,' Jesus was identifying himself as God. That's why the Jewish opponents of Jesus picked up rocks to stone him after he said this.

"Another passage to think about here is Mark 2. Jesus is preaching to a packed house when all of a sudden the roof is ripped open and a paralyzed man lying on a mat is lowered onto the floor right before Jesus's feet. Jesus looks into the face of the paralyzed man and, seeing his faith, says, 'Your sins are—'"

"Forgiven." George beat me to the punch before I could finish quoting Mark 2:5.

"Bingo, you got it."

"And then the people there got mad and were confused," George added, alluding to the rest of the story. Once Jesus completes the healing of the paralyzed man, the teachers of the law discuss among themselves whether Jesus is blaspheming, since no one can forgive sin but God (Mark 2:6–7). Knowing what they were thinking, Jesus responds, "Which is easier: to say to this paralyzed man, 'Your sins are forgiven,' or to say, 'Get up, take your mat and walk'? But I want you to know that the Son of Man has authority on earth to forgive sins" (2:8–10).

"I've always found that so beautiful," George continued, "because there Jesus is showing that forgiving sins is way more powerful than raising a man who was crippled."

"You got it, George. By claiming to forgive the sins of that man, Jesus is claiming to be God. Only God can ultimately forgive my sins." I paused for a second, gesturing toward George. "If I treat you rotten, George, yes, I have to ask you for forgiveness, but ultimately I have to ask *God* for forgiveness, because when I trample all over you, I'm basically saying, 'Hey, God, when you created George, you did a lousy job.' Baloney! God did a wonderful job making you. So when I do wrong to you, I certainly have to ask for your mercy, but ultimately I had better ask the God who created you for forgiveness."

"We need to bring it to God first," George thoughtfully replied.

We completely agree.

We'll get into the full significance of Jesus and the forgiveness of sins later in this chapter. For now, it's important to stress that the paralyzed man didn't "do" anything directly to Jesus that required forgiveness—he had probably never seen Jesus before. So Jesus wasn't forgiving a wrong directly done to him. *He was forgiving all of the man's sins.* Jesus wasn't offering situational forgiveness for a particular misdeed. He was offering a *full cosmic pardon*, the type of grace and mercy that only the God who created this world could offer. In the words of the apostle Paul, "Through Jesus the forgiveness of sins is proclaimed to you. Through him everyone who believes is set free from every sin" (Acts 13:38–39).

Forgiving sins isn't the only action of Jesus that points to his identity as God incarnate. As we observed earlier, Jesus's performance of miracles signified his divine identity. Miracles can only occur if a supernatural hand has unexpectedly intervened, if natural causes alone cannot explain what transpired. A mere human cannot suddenly reverse blindness through a simple touch or silence a fierce storm. Even the most outstanding moral sage cannot cause a paralyzed man to walk or bring the dead back to life. No natural explanation can make sense of those events. Those miracles signaled that there is more to Jesus than his humanity. Jesus is the supernatural hand that can cause miracles. He is God.

So, too, as we discussed earlier, the fact that Jesus lived a perfect life also indicates his divinity. As the apostle Paul says in Romans 3:23–24, "*All* have sinned and fall short of the glory of God, and all are justified freely by his grace through the redemption that came by Christ Jesus" (emphasis added). No human being has ever lived (or will ever live) a perfect life, no matter how diligently they try. The reason Jesus could overcome temptation every single time is that he is more than a mere human—he is God incarnate.

The New Testament evidence indicates that Jesus was not only identified and worshiped by his followers as God but also teaches that he is God incarnate, who demonstrated his divinity through his performance of miracles and his sinless life. Jesus is unquestionably unique, the eternal presence of God living among us in human flesh (see John 1:14). He is fully God and fully human. But admittedly, knowing this doesn't make this extraordinary message any easier to swallow. The mystery of the incarnation, of God taking on human flesh, defies human comprehension. The mere thought still leaves me bewildered when I consider it, even after all these decades. God is so, so immense. How could the all-glorious, all-powerful, and all-wise God who created this world be squeezed into a human body prone to atrophy and subject to pain?

Over the years, many students have told me that such a mystery seems nonsensical, to put it lightly. Why would God ever do such a thing? How is that even *possible*? As I tell them, just because the incarnation is a great mystery doesn't mean it's impossible. Presuming as much overlooks the ability of the all-powerful God to choose to limit himself by becoming a human being. If the omnipotent and eternal God who brought this universe into existence wants to limit his power by becoming a human being, doing so is fully within his ability. God becoming a human being is *exceptional*, not impossible or irrational. It's this that makes Christianity profoundly unique—God comes near to us in the most extraordinary of ways.

In one of the most poetic portions of the New Testament, Paul says this very thing about Jesus:

> Who, being in very nature God,
> did not consider equality with God something to be
> used to his own advantage;
> rather, he made himself nothing
> by taking the very nature of a servant,
> being made in human likeness.
> And being found in appearance as a man,
> he humbled himself
> by becoming obedient to death—
> even death on a cross! (Philippians 2:6–8)

No other philosophy or religion proclaims that God loves his creation so much that he humbled himself, submitted himself to a mortal human body, and joined them in community—eating and drinking, laughing and crying, healing and suffering, alongside them. For many, this would be considered ridiculous at best and pure blasphemy at worst. For me, it encapsulates perfectly why I follow Jesus Christ.

What Happened on the Cross?

Could Jesus's death have been just one big hoax?

It's a question that comes up once in a while when we speak

about the crucifixion of Jesus. Over the past couple of centuries, there have been a number of attempts to try to explain away Jesus's death at the hands of the Romans. Perhaps Jesus simply passed out from exhaustion, and after being revived in the tomb, he walked out alive. Maybe the cross story was just made up. Or perhaps Jesus had a twin brother or look-alike follower who died in his place, allowing Jesus to escape.

Curious and entertaining as such suggestions may be (some of them sound like they could be out of *The Da Vinci Code*), none of them are based on any evidence. For starters, if there's one thing the Romans were good at, it was executing people. The crucifixion process was both incredibly grueling and impressively effective. There are no known cases of anyone surviving the ordeal. That all four gospels not only explicitly state that Jesus gave up his life on the cross but also claim that he was pierced by a Roman soldier with a spear to confirm his death discounts this imaginative theory (see John 19:34). A person doesn't walk away from that.

Additionally, both the late first-century Jewish historian Josephus (*Antiquities* 18.3.3) and the early second-century Roman author Tacitus (*Annals* 15.44) explicitly state that Jesus was executed by the Romans. Neither one mentions any rumors of his survival. When we combine this with the fact that crucifixion was a death reserved for criminals or traitors and was considered a highly embarrassing and shameful way to die, it doesn't make any sense why ancient Christians would have made up that detail about Jesus's death. (Would you have dedicated your life to an alleged criminal who would be executed in the electric chair?) Finally, there is no ancient tradition claiming that Jesus had a twin brother, much less that this twin brother may have been crucified in his place. This is a modern conspiracy theory that lacks any basis in reality.

Not surprisingly, outside of a couple fringe individuals, historians have completely discounted the notion that Jesus was not crucified to the point of death. Jesus died, pure and simple. This is a historical truth.

But why did Jesus die on the cross? What was the point?

A Cosmic Rescue Mission

What a lot of people don't realize is how interconnected these two questions are. Jesus died on the cross *because* he and he alone is fully God and fully human. The significance of Jesus's death can only be understood hand in hand with this reality.

The cross is the most unique rescue expedition in human history, a mission to save us from the weight of our sins that hold us back from the God who created us. A mere human could not accomplish that, because all humans are predisposed to dirty, rotten sin. We're trapped in it like a prison, no matter how hard we try to escape. If we wanted to free everyone in a high-security penitentiary, we would never trust one of the prisoners to get everybody out. They'd have no way to break down all the doors from the inside. We would need someone from outside the prison to do that, someone who hasn't been condemned to be locked up behind those bars. A fellow prisoner to sin would not be able to do that; they're in the same boat as everyone else. Only a person already free from the clutches of sin could open the doors and redeem everyone on the inside.

Redemption always comes at a cost. The New Testament teaching of redemption derives from the language of ancient business transactions. To redeem something means to buy it back, to pay the required ransom. Our sin comes with a tremendous debt: "The wages of sin is death" (Romans 6:23). And no one can be freed unless those wages are paid. The problem is that no human being could ever cover the cost for themselves, much less on behalf of the whole world. The cost of sin simply cannot be ignored. The God who created the universe is a just God who abhors evil. Human sin and God cannot coexist. Evil must be punished.

At times, students will express discomfort with this idea of a sin-hating, punishing God. How can a good and loving God be so vengeful and angry? What is this obsession with judgment? What about forgiveness? What often gets missed is the fact that God's justice and love go hand in hand. They are two sides of the same coin.

If God's response to the countless horrors human beings have caused—mass genocides, slavery, murder, greed, abuse, and other unfathomable acts of violence—was simply to look away and let the perpetrators of such heinous wrongdoing walk away scot-free, how can we say that God truly loves the oppressed and the marginalized? What kind of messed-up world would that be? And if God only punished some types of injustice and not others, what would that say about God's love? It'd be hard to claim that God's love is perfect and impartial if it is inconsistently doled out to a select few.

A God without perfect justice is a God without perfect love. God's wrath toward sin is not a divine temper tantrum. He is not a cosmic nitpicker or killjoy. God loves all of humanity, each and every one of us, and this perfect and universal love cannot stand the reprehensible injustice and harm we inflict on one another. A just world is a good world, one in which *all* human beings, people created in God's image, flourish in harmony. There is no room for sin in that world. True love requires true justice.

But it is here that God does something truly remarkable. As Paul puts it so beautifully, the clearest expression of God's love and justice coming together is this: "While we were still sinners, Christ died for us" (Romans 5:8). We all deserve judgment because of our slavery to sin, and there is nothing we could ever do that would change that. Our debt is far too high. But knowing that, God did not stand by idly. Instead, God humbled himself by taking on human flesh, living the sinless life that none of us could live, so that he could satisfy the debt we all bear. The author of the book of Hebrews wrote these words:

> Since the children have flesh and blood, [Jesus] too shared in their humanity so that by his death he might break the power of him who holds the power of death—that is, the devil—and free those who all their lives were held in slavery by their fear of death. . . . For this reason he had to be made like them, fully human in every way, in order that he might become a merciful and faithful high priest in service to God, and that he might make atonement for the sins of the people. Because he himself suffered when he was tempted, he is able to help those who are being tempted. (Hebrews 2:14–15, 17–18)

Jesus himself states, "For even the Son of Man did not come to be served, but to serve, and to give his life as a ransom for many" (Mark 10:45). Jesus Christ took the hit for our sin and rebellion. He served the sentence to fulfill the just punishment we deserved. As God on the cross, Christ offered the only sacrifice extravagant enough to pay the deadly wages of injustice. Only someone truly innocent of sin could offer that (Luke 23:13–16, 41).

What Jesus's Death Did for Us

By dying on the cross, Jesus achieved three things we cannot do for ourselves. First, Jesus's death brought divine forgiveness to all humanity. Forgiveness isn't free. It always costs something. To forgive requires the cancellation of a debt on the part of the person harmed. It means giving up the right to seek revenge, even when payback may seem totally justified, and it means releasing the other person from the burden of that guilt.

We have the capability to forgive those particular individuals who have hurt us and cancel their debts. But who could possibly forgive all of humanity for our collective injustice? Only God can forgive the sins of the world. Only God can offer all of us the opportunity to repent and turn away from sin because only God has the right to seek punishment for humanity's injustice. So when Jesus, God incarnate, died on the cross, he absolved the guilt for our sins—past, present, and future. Jesus made us right before the God of righteousness; he justified us before the God of justice. In the face of the curse of sin, Jesus became a curse for us (Galatians 3:13). So when Jesus pronounced from the cross, "Father, forgive them, for they do not know what they are doing" (Luke 23:34), his powerful forgiveness wasn't restricted to the Roman soldiers who nailed him up there; it is meant for us too.

Second, by dying on the cross, Jesus restored our ruptured relationship with God. As you've likely experienced at least once in your life, sin is a relationship wrecker. Marriages are torn apart by lies and infidelity. Friendships are broken by jealousy, selfish behaviors, or hateful words. Parents and children become estranged due to abuse, rebellion, and betrayal. In much the same way, sin is the great schism that has separated us from our heavenly Father since it first entered this world. When any relationship is broken, forgiveness is an important step, but mending the relationship doesn't just end here. Reconciliation is needed for true repair to occur. Forgiveness comes as one admits that a wound was received but then refuses to strike back and thus opens up the relationship to what is needed to heal the wound and draw both people together again.

When Jesus died on the cross, he didn't just absorb the punishment of our sin; he also paved the way for us to return to a right relationship with God. In the words of Paul, "God was reconciling the world to himself in Christ, not counting people's sins against them. And he has committed to us the message of reconciliation. . . . God made him who had no sin to be sin for us, so that in him we might become the righteousness of God" (2 Corinthians 5:19, 21). Paul writes elsewhere, "At one time you were separated from God. You were enemies in your minds because of your evil ways. But because Christ died, God has brought you back to himself. Christ's death has made you holy in God's sight. So now you don't have any flaw. You are free from blame" (Colossians 1:21–22 NIrV).

Jesus spanned the relational distance between us and God by taking upon himself the brokenness and loneliness that once filled that chasm. The crucifixion was not a pretty sight to behold. To watch a bleeding Jesus pull up his tattered and raw back against the splinter-covered wood of his cross, using his nail-impaled feet and hands as leverage, just to alleviate the weight of his hanging body and take a labored breath of air had to have been a traumatic sight. He died one of the most excruciating deaths possible. But perhaps most devastating of all is that in his moment of terrible suffering, Jesus also endured the colossal cosmic rejection that once divided us from our creator. When Jesus cried out, "My God, my God, why have you forsaken me?" (Matthew 27:46), we hear the words of someone who is experiencing the full weight of absolute divine abandonment. In that moment, Jesus brought us back together with our creator, such that we could once again call ourselves the children of God (John 1:12). He "suffered once for sins, the righteous for the unrighteous, that he might bring us to God" (1 Peter 3:18 ESV).

Third and finally, Jesus died on the cross to bring us eternal life. When a group of people become caught in a riptide and are dragged mercilessly out to sea, a lifeguard will brave the dangerous current to rescue them. But saving them can sometimes come at a great cost. We've all read a number of tragic stories where lifeguards succeed in pulling victims to safety only to lack the strength to overcome the unrelenting waves themselves. In those instances, the lifeguard freely gives their life as the ultimate sacrifice. Their perishing brings others life.

The sacrifice of Jesus Christ, in much the same way, saves us from drowning in the waves of death. Through his sacrificial death on the cross, Jesus overpowered the forces of sin and death for us. No amount of good behavior could have ever kept our metaphorical heads above the waves. Heaven isn't something we can obtain through good deeds, any more than we can become a gold-medal swimmer simply by putting on a pair of goggles. None of us can possibly tread water well enough to reach the safety and security of eternal life. But by using the cross as a life preserver, Jesus has thrown humanity a rope of salvation, one that cost him his life. In the lavish words of what is arguably the most famous Bible verse in history, "For God so loved the world that he gave his one and only Son, that whoever believes in him shall not perish but have eternal life" (John 3:16). Jesus gave himself over to the waves of death so that we might be set free from its control.

It was necessary for Jesus to die because there had to be a substitute that could withstand the punishment we deserved, some kind of ultimate antidote to the issue of sin, some kind of gracious and glorious payment to cover the ransom that our empty wallets couldn't afford. No ordinary mortal being could ever do this. Only Jesus Christ, fully divine and fully human, can bridge the harrowing divide between a just God and a sin-infested humanity and bring forgiveness, reconciliation, and eternal life.

What Evidence Do We Have for the Resurrection?

"Do you believe that historical methods can prove the resurrection of Jesus?"

By now, the inquisitive University of Massachusetts student in the matching gray sweatshirt and ball cap had been patiently waiting for quite some time for his turn to speak. We've been having these campus discussions long enough that it's gotten pretty easy to tell the difference between the students who have really thought long and hard about their questions versus those who just rattle off the first thing that comes to their mind. Both of us could tell by the look in his eyes that this guy was the former type.

"Well, I can't prove *anything* to you," I (Cliffe) responded, getting a good-natured chuckle from my conversation partner. "I can't *prove* that I'm not just some bad dream you're having. But there's overwhelming evidence that your eyes and mine are perceiving reality right now. I don't base my life on proof; I base it on evidence."

"Well I have a lot more faith that this is real than I do in the resurrection," he admitted with an inviting smile. "So how would you best present why you believe that Jesus rose from the dead?"

Like the many other times I've answered this question—easily hundreds of instances over the past four and a half decades—I admitted off the bat that for a person who doesn't believe in the existence of the supernatural, believing in the resurrection is impossible. As Stuart and I mentioned in the previous chapter, the presupposition that there is no God automatically nullifies the possibility of a miracle, since miracles by definition require a supernatural hand that intervenes in a way that cannot be explained by natural causes. No God means no resurrection. But if our amazing universe was created by a supernatural being, an eternal creator who brought time and energy and matter into a well-organized existence, then there's nothing that prevents that creator from acting in our world in ways that may contravene the expected natural processes. If God exists, the resurrection is surely possible.

This then brings us to the big question: *What evidence do we have for the resurrection?*

Over the past few decades, we've seen an explosion of scholarship centered on the historicity of the resurrection. Well-known academics like William Lane Craig, Michael Licona, and N. T. Wright have all written one (or more) books on the subject. Every year it seems like some new and exciting piece of evidence emerges, be it archaeological, historical, or philosophical. Increasingly, we're seeing the claims of Jesus's real, historical resurrection are being taken seriously by scholars, including by those who do not profess to believe in God.

Perhaps none of these figures have been more influential than Gary Habermas, whose four-volume research project on the resurrection is arguably the most comprehensive work ever written on the subject. Habermas is perhaps most famous for his "minimal facts," a collection of strongly attested evidence drawn from the four gospels. The vast majority of critical scholars, regardless of religious affiliation, accept these as being probable historical facts. While we don't have nearly enough time to run through all of Habermas's "minimal facts," we want to focus on three points we've found especially convincing and helpful in our ministry.

The Empty Tomb

First, all four gospels mention that Jesus was buried in the tomb of a man named Joseph of Arimathea, but when a group of women came to the tomb on the third day after his death, his body was no longer there. *The tomb was empty.*

There are several reasons why the evidence suggests that the claim of the empty tomb should be taken as a historical fact. For one thing, the shared mention of Joseph of Arimathea is far too specific a detail to be made up, especially considering that Joseph is known to be a member of the Jewish Sanhedrin that had worked to get Jesus killed. This would be an odd detail to add if it weren't true.

Moreover, it would also be odd if all four gospels fabricated the detail that several women were the first ones to see the empty tomb. Women in that day were typically not considered to be dependable witnesses. Later rabbis prohibited women from testifying in court in certain cases (Mishnah Shevuot 4.1; see also Josephus, *Antiquities*, 4.8.15). If the gospel authors were just concocting an empty tomb, it would have been far more credible to depict a couple of *male* disciples discovering the empty tomb, not a group of grief-torn women.

Finally, the idea some have proposed that someone stole Jesus's body from the tomb seems extremely unlikely when we consider that the only ancient source to actually mention this theory is the gospel of Matthew, which describes how the Jewish chief priests bribed the soldiers who were guarding Jesus's tomb to tell people they fell asleep and the disciples stole the body (Matthew 28:11–15). If Jesus's followers really did take his body, only to create a conspiracy theory that he had been raised from the dead, it seems extremely unlikely that they'd say as much in any capacity.

All of Our Earliest Sources Profess a Bodily Resurrection

Second, it is crucial to note that the belief in the resurrection of Jesus wasn't something that developed a few decades after the Christian movement began. All of our earliest Christian sources unanimously emphasize that *Jesus experienced a bodily resurrection.* These include the New Testament Gospels, all of which were written within thirty to sixty years after Jesus's death.

Between the four of them, the Gospels record six separate incidents (seven if you include Acts 1:3–9) where Jesus physically appeared to his disciples. The gospel eyewitnesses report that the disciples not only saw Jesus but also touched him, feeling his nail wounds and even eating with him. The disciples were not experiencing a grief-driven group hallucination. A hallucination can't be grabbed (Matthew 28:9–10). A hallucination doesn't have a full-on conversation with you and your friend during a long walk (Luke 24:13–35). A hallucination doesn't make breakfast either (John 21:7–13). But the resurrected Jesus did just that.

Even earlier than the four gospels is the testimony found in 1 Corinthians 15, a text we discussed earlier in chapter 4. Written by Paul around AD 53–55, 1 Corinthians contains a section that many scholars have suggested may represent part of an early Christian creed written *within a few years of Jesus's death*:

> For what I received I passed on to you as of first importance: that Christ died for our sins according to the Scriptures, that he was buried, that he was raised on the third day according to the Scriptures, and that he appeared to Cephas, and then to the Twelve. After that, he appeared to more than five hundred of the brothers and sisters at the same time, most of whom are still living, though some have fallen asleep. Then he appeared to James, then to all the apostles. (1 Corinthians 15:3–7)

This message "passed on" by Paul to his Corinthian readers not only asserts that Jesus died, was buried, and rose again, but also lists a bevy of eyewitnesses who professed to have seen him: Cephas (the Hebrew name for the disciple Peter), the Twelve (shorthand for the twelve disciples), five hundred other individuals (including some who were still alive when Paul was writing), James (the brother of Jesus), then all the apostles, and finally himself (see Acts 9). That's a *massive* list of eyewitnesses!

Now, if Jesus's earliest followers did just fabricate the accounts of his resurrection out of thin air, why would they list *so many independent witnesses* who could potentially tell someone, "Yeah, I didn't see him. Those guys made that whole resurrection thing up." If you don't want to get caught lying, you don't tell folks the names of the people who can prove you wrong. Big mistake. What seems far more likely is that the New Testament authors are telling the truth.

Jesus's Followers Suffered and Died Defending the Resurrected Jesus

Third and finally, the last time we checked, no one in their right mind will risk their well-being for something they don't authentically believe is true. Why would someone ruin their life for something they know to be false? So the fact that nearly *all* of Jesus's earliest followers preached his resurrection, some to the point of suffering and even death, suggest that the resurrection wasn't just some feeble cover-up narrative. Jesus's followers were *entirely convinced that he rose from the dead.*

During my (Stuart's) discussion with the UC Davis student mentioned at the beginning of this chapter, he brought up the point that it's entirely possible that the disciples all got together following Jesus's death and agreed to pass along the same story about the resurrected Jesus. "You know, they still could have done this in good faith, for a good reason," he reasoned (seemingly on the fly), "but I think it wouldn't have to be true for them to believe it."

As I told him, that would have been an extremely costly lie. Early followers of Jesus experienced an array of hardships because of their belief. They lost property, experienced social scorn and mockery, underwent familial upheaval, experienced periodic persecution, and sometimes paid the ultimate cost—their lives. Ancient church traditions say as much with regard to Jesus's closest disciples. Acts 12 states that James the son of Zebedee was beheaded due to his faith. Ignatius of Antioch, writing at the beginning of the second century, states that Paul was martyred, perhaps in Rome (*Letter to the Ephesians* 12.2). Regarding James the brother of Jesus, the Jewish historian Josephus records that he and several other apparent followers of Jesus were stoned (*Antiquities* 20.9.1). A letter written by Clement of Rome at the end of the first century recounts that Peter was martyred for his faith (1 Clement 5.4), with later traditions claiming he was crucified upside down. Thomas is said by early Christian tradition to have been torn into two while spreading the gospel in India.

These don't sound like the actions of people covering up a blatant lie. They were, without question, absolutely convinced that Jesus, the Son of God, truly did rise from the dead.

It's too good to be true. So often in life we face disappointment when the promise of something good goes sour. No wonder hyperskepticism and disbelief are so pervasive! Truly good news seems so rare these days. Hatred and hurt can drown out hope so quickly in this broken world. We've all been burned more times than we can count. So both of us get why something so mysterious, miraculous, and momentous as Jesus's divinity, salvific death, and resurrection is the source of so much doubt. *How can I possibly trust something so extraordinary?* Some days, we struggle with that question too.

But when we look at the evidence with open minds and hearts, it becomes clear that Jesus's death and resurrection aren't just well-advertised hoaxes. It is far more reasonable to have faith in the eyewitness testimony of the New Testament message than it is to speculate that a ragtag group of uneducated fisherman duped the entire world with the greatest fib ever told. It is far more reasonable to believe that Jesus Christ, fully God and fully human, died on the cross for our sins and then rose from the dead than it is to speculate that he was nothing more than an accomplished liar or a convincing lunatic. This isn't to say that the disbelief you bear isn't heavy. It isn't to say that faith should be easy and painless. But the most powerful and transformative hope in human history is here in front of you, great good news that outshines the darkness of even the most substantial doubts.

We've all seen this darkness in our lives. During one campus visit, we were introduced to a mother whose eighteen-year-old son was a devoted follower of our *Give Me an Answer* YouTube channel. Standing beside her son's girlfriend, she smiled as they both recounted how excited he was at the prospect of meeting us here. But as she spoke, their eyes started filling with tears. Her voice quivered as she recounted how, two weeks earlier, her son was tragically killed by a man who, in an act of malicious road rage, followed her son home and shot him right in front of her eyes. By this point in the telling of her story, her deceased son's girlfriend was openly weeping. On full display was the sorrow of human sinfulness, the wretchedness of an unjust world. We embraced them tightly in prayer.

How do we even respond to such a raw moment of loss?

I'm not even remotely sure what my atheist or agnostic friends would say to that mother. Would they simply express their sympathies? Would they angrily wave their fist at the idea of God? What kind of hope could they offer, if any? If there is no God, there is no hope. But for the four of us, in that painful moment of profound grief, there was also profound comfort. For we shared faith in the resurrected Jesus Christ. Each of us trusted that the death of Jesus has paid the cost of our sins and brought us eternal life, one where God "will wipe away every tear from [our] eyes, and death shall be no more" (Revelation 21:4 ESV). Together through the tears, we could look at one another with a gentle smile of understanding, because we knew that death is not the end.

This mother will see her son again. We will see her again. And in that joyful moment, those doubts that once shook us so fiercely will seem so small and trivial compared to the greatness of Jesus's gracious gift to us.

Jesus is risen. He is risen indeed. There is hope, even in the darkness.

How Social Media Has Changed Our Ministry

If you would have told me (Cliffe) a decade ago that reels of Stuart and me would be viewed and shared by millions of people across the internet, I would have responded, "You've got to be kidding me. I think you've lost a few marbles there, friend."

When we first started exploring the potential of using social media as a ministry tool, I wasn't too sure about the whole thing. I didn't know how to use Instagram or Facebook (much less my smartphone), and I didn't really have an interest in learning how either. I'm a pretty old-fashioned guy when it comes to that stuff. Not to mention, I couldn't picture what sort of young people would actually want to watch some gray-haired geezer in a sweater and khakis debating college students about the existence of God. It didn't exactly sound like riveting material to me.

I'm glad to say I was wrong. The last few years have been quite a ride. I'll admit I'm still not any more skilled at using Twitter (which I guess is called "X" now) or YouTube than I was ten years ago. And my feelings haven't really changed about social media. If every platform out there shut down tomorrow, I wouldn't lose a wink of sleep. I'm far from what you'd call an "influencer." That being said, I'm truly thankful that, despite my personal feelings about social media, God has used it (and is using it) as an instrument for evangelism.

Social media attention is a strange thing. It's hard to believe we have thousands of "internet fans" and "subscribers" out there. It's even harder to believe people repost clips of Stuart and me that end up getting a million views. It's still new territory for me. On the whole, though, it's been a great experience. To arrive at a university to find a pack of students waiting for us is a big departure from the years of speaking to audiences that numbered in single digits. Having random celebrities—politicians and professional athletes, actors and models—contact us to ask questions and want to talk about Jesus Christ has also been a fascinating experience. (It's still shocking that people we see on the daily news or the movie theater screen know who we are.) We've loved the opportunities we've had to appear on podcasts with a wide array of people from all sorts of religious backgrounds and speak to them about Jesus Christ. It has also been wonderful to develop friendships with other religious content creators. To be able to gather together, pray for one another, and share this passion for bringing the gospel to the world has been a truly worthwhile experience.

We've been delighted to see a number of young people come to visit us at Grace Community Church. To hear their stories and see the powerful ways God is working in their lives is a huge blessing. It surprises me sometimes just how far people will come just to attend our Sunday morning service and talk with us after worship. One twentysomething man rode an overnight bus from Canada to New York City, took the train to Connecticut, and then walked six *miles* in a snowstorm to get to our 9:30 a.m. service. Another fellow drove through the night from Kentucky (eleven hours!) just for a handshake and a hug. Recently, two young women from Australia took five different planes to attend one of our services. As we talked with them, their kindness, energy, and ability to memorize some of our theological arguments blew us away (they had the "Knechtle Stance" down pat too). Even more awesome is the fact that they documented their whole trip on TikTok, demonstrating to millions of viewers their love for Christ. I've heard some folks my age complain about the up-and-coming generation. Not me. I deeply admire the radical faith and excitement displayed in so many of these young people. God is doing something amazing among them.

Of course, everything isn't a bed of roses. Not every moment of public recognition or interview experience has been positive. To know that millions of people are constantly watching every single thing we say is a pretty odd feeling too. Most of all, however, I wonder at times if all the attention may be preventing us from reaching those students who really need to be challenged in their skepticism and disbelief. More and more these days, the crowds we attract are made up of believers who've seen our videos and follow us on social media rather than agnostics, atheists, or people from other religious backgrounds. Don't get me wrong; I love meeting with and encouraging fellow Christians. At the same time, though, I can't help but think of Luke 5:30–31 and Jesus's response to the Pharisees after they accused him of fraternizing only with tax collectors and sinners: "It is not the healthy who need a doctor, but the sick." When I began this ministry four and a half decades ago, I always tried to keep those folks front and center. Nowadays, it feels like a greater challenge. Even the most outspoken atheist or materialist might think twice about debating someone about the resurrection when they're surrounded by two hundred Christians. A part of me definitely misses those early days. So when I get to have a deep and challenging conversation with a student, I always embrace the opportunity.

In this season of ministry, we've been busier than ever. When God puts an opportunity in our lap, we need to have faith and run with it. We definitely have. But if there's one thing social media hasn't changed about our ministry, it's the placement of Christ at the very center of all we say and do. That's the reason we do any of this. Not entertainment. Not financial gain. Not the fame that comes from clicks and subscribers. All that matters is Jesus Christ.

PART 4

WHAT SHOULD I DO NEXT?

Sometimes the final leg of the journey is the longest.

We began this book by addressing the question of whether God exists. After exploring several arguments for God's existence and reflecting on God's status as creator, we asked where we can learn more about this creator God. From there, we examined the Bible as the Word of God to humanity and addressed its historical reliability, along with covering several other social and cultural issues. We also made the case for why one should follow Jesus Christ over other religious truth claims. The third part of this book addressed what the Bible says about Jesus, including his ethical genius and sinlessness, his miracles and divinity, and finally his death to defeat sin and his resurrection promise of eternal life.

But the quest to demolish unhealthy doubt doesn't stop here. If anything, it's only just begun. It's only when we dare to live out this knowledge and conform our hearts and desires to God's will that the adventure truly begins. In the final chapter and conclusion, we'll describe in fuller detail what it means to accept Jesus Christ as your Savior and commit your life to him, as well as explore what you can do to grow spiritually in your relationship with God.

It's here that God goes from something real to a real relationship.

CHAPTER 10

HOW DO I COMMIT MY LIFE TO JESUS CHRIST?

But why is it so *hard* to trust in Jesus?" asked a female student dressed in a dark gray T-shirt and ripped black jeans. A few people in the crowd nodded and murmured in agreement with her sincere question. "We discuss all these topics and have all these debates, but why is it *still* so hard to have faith? Is it just pride? Is it, like, the things of this world? What do you think is the problem?"

Why is it so hard to commit to Christ?

That's a question that I (Cliffe) can wholeheartedly relate to. As I admitted to that honest young woman, it's hard for *me* to commit *myself* to Jesus Christ because, deep down, *I want to be God*. It doesn't matter how extensively I *know* about the evidence for God's existence and for the reliability of Jesus Christ. None of that changes the fact that I don't like God making my choices for me. I want to make *my own choices*. But if I've committed my life to Christ, I can't do that. These two things can't coexist. So when I've got God telling me what to do, well, it can feel pretty off-putting.

And I'm not alone in that feeling either. A lot of folks who reject Christ don't do so solely because of intellectual objections or theological disagreement. The barrier that often holds them back from Christ is that they don't want to submit to God. *They want to submit to themselves.* They want, just like me, to live by the mantra, "I'm gonna do my life my own way." It's a problem that extends beyond the mind. It's an issue of the will. It's a dilemma of the heart.

Demolishing doubt isn't just about overcoming the intellectual arguments that hinder your faith. You need *commitment* to empower such knowledge to change your behavior and truly allow Jesus to transform your life. Otherwise, you are still dwelling in your doubts.

For the rest of this chapter, we're going to examine what it means to commit ourselves to Jesus Christ. We'll explore what this response looks like, what steps a person has to take to begin that relationship, and what sorts of hardships we might face in the process. We'll also briefly explore some things we can do right here and now to grow stronger in our spiritual relationship with God. For some of you reading this, you may see this as a big leap of faith that you're not sure you're ready to take. Others of you may already be years down the road toward putting Christ in the center of your life, but perhaps you're at a point in your life where you need some insight and clarity. Regardless of where you find yourself at this moment, we want to walk alongside you on that journey, no matter what obstacles you may be encountering along the way.

What Do You Mean by "Commitment to Christ"?

Commitment to Christ involves more than just thinking about your faith. Intellectual discussions, like the ones Stuart and I have with university students, are delightful opportunities to help people navigate their doubts or rethink their hyperskeptical approach to God. But such talks only scratch the surface when it comes to committing one's life to Christ. Like any other healthy relationship, true commitment to Christ requires an intentional and personal response. *It requires actively putting Christ in the center of our lives.*

Faith without a personal commitment is a contradiction. You can't claim to believe something but then act like you don't believe it. When our belief in Christ does not come with a commitment, our lives call into question our beliefs. Either we're not totally convinced or we're just too complacent and cavalier to care. Both of these attitudes are tragedies. It's not the way anyone should live their life. This should be no one's approach to something as important as what they believe.

Now, you may be thinking, *Hey, Cliffe, does putting Jesus Christ in the center of your life mean you're supposed to be nearly perfect?* No, definitely not. If it did, I would have totally missed the mark, and I'm not being harsh on myself either. Like all of you reading this, I have plenty of my own struggles. I can be selfish and stubborn. At times I lose my temper. I struggle to love people consistently and well. And don't even get me started on the warped motives and ambitions that are underneath the surface (see Mark 7:20–23). As I've told countless students, if I were to put up a projector screen and broadcast all the thoughts I had during the day, well, I'd be way too embarrassed to show my face. I'm a dirty, rotten sinner. *We all are.* Sin is a universal human problem that we can't escape on our own (see Romans 3:23), which is exactly why every one of us needs Jesus Christ. We need to commit our lives to him because we are so imperfect.

Commitment to Christ doesn't have perfection as a prerequisite. It requires dedication to change, not unblemished excellence. It requires persistence, not flawless execution. Putting Christ at the very center of your life will not magically make sin and selfishness cease to exist. Nor will it cause doubt to vanish into thin air. But it will change the way you try to live your life. It will make you rethink the priorities and allegiances you once thought were so important. It will cause you to question your behaviors, as well as the way you treat others. It will compel you to seek out new habits that fuel spiritual growth.

Don't let an unrealistic notion of perfection keep you from committing yourself to Christ.

What Do I Need to Do to Commit My Life to Christ?

One morning after I preached at Grace Community Church, one of the most physically intimidating gentlemen I've ever seen approached me. I mean, this guy was absolutely *huge*. His hand engulfed mine as he gave me a firm and friendly shake.

After warmly introducing himself, his voice became more heartfelt and reflective. "When I went to fight for the United States in Afghanistan, I was an atheist. For much of my adult life, I had been skeptical about everything to do with God. But during my tour of duty, I began to watch *Give Me an Answer*. I really appreciated how clearly you presented the evidence for the credibility of the New Testament writings and the reliability of Christ. And when you spoke about your own struggles with doubt, I felt like you got where I was coming from. After hearing you challenge students to read and test all of the gospels for themselves, I finally decided to do that for myself. And after I did, I decided to commit my life to Christ."

He paused for a second as he reached to pull something out of his pocket, handing me a faded metal object. "I wanted to come and personally thank you. And I wanted to give you the dog tags I wore in Afghanistan. You'll notice they say atheist on them. I went to Afghanistan to fight as an atheist in the service of my country. I returned a follower of Christ." What a privilege it was to hear about that soldier's commitment to Christ and be on the receiving end of that joyous bear hug.

Putting Christ at the center of your life is a radical, life-changing move, as my veteran friend so clearly illustrated. It's not something to take lightly. But what does this commitment look like? What steps must someone take to commit their life to Christ?

Respond to Christ's Commitment to You

The first step has already been taken.

People I talk to often assume that a commitment to Christ is all about what *they* need to achieve. What often gets neglected is the fact that much of the work has already been done. *Christ has already committed himself to you.*

As I said earlier in this book, one of the four aspects of following Jesus Christ that I've found so convincing is that it's not about achievement or earning salvation. Working overtime to become more pious or enlightened than anyone one else won't do it either. What makes the message of the gospel so powerful is that it's all about *grace*. On the cross, Jesus did for us what we, as sinful and selfish human beings, could never have done for ourselves. He paid the price for our wickedness. He made right our broken relationship with God. He extended to us the promise of eternal life.

God's grace isn't cheap. This love came with a heavy price. Jesus was beaten to a pulp, forced to haul a splinter-covered, eighty-pound crossbeam up a hill, and then nailed to that beam, all while bearing the sin of all humanity on his shoulders. He did it all for you and me. Talk about true commitment!

We do not need to climb up on that cross and save ourselves. Jesus already did that for us. But when we choose to ignore that reality, discount the significance of that sacrifice, and disregard Christ's commitment to us, we've effectively looked that gift of grace in the face and said, "No thanks." Just because Jesus dragged his cross for us doesn't mean he can drag us out of hell kicking and screaming. That's not how it works. We must *respond* to Christ's commitment.

Paul writes in Galatians 3:22, "We are all prisoners of sin, so we receive God's promise of freedom only by believing in Jesus Christ" (NLT). Christ has set us free from bondage; he ransomed us from our imprisonment. But if we keep sitting in an open jail cell and don't actually walk out the door to freedom, we have no one to blame but ourselves. If we refuse to own our beliefs, to choose to accept Christ's generous love, then nothing has changed.

Repent and Accept Forgiveness

The word *repentance* gets a bad rap. A lot of students have admitted that just the sound of the word brings to mind uncomfortable church pews, stodgy evangelists, and a fire-and-brimstone judgment trip. In a contemporary world that sees things in relativistic, "my way or the highway" terms, repentance feels like a dinosaur, an uncomfortable shame-filled relic we've outgrown. Who wants that kind of buzzkill negativity in their lives? Who needs repentance anymore?

When we reduce repentance to a dry religious word, we miss out on something profoundly important. As I (Stuart) told a group of students at the University of North Carolina recently, repentance isn't really about shame, self-pity, or beating yourself up. Repentance is about *change*. The Greek New Testament word for repentance is *metanoia*, which means to turn around or change one's mind (*nous*). Repentance, biblically speaking, is the process of heading in one direction and then turning around and going in a different one, much like what you do when you accidentally take the wrong route on a road trip. In that sense, repentance is a really good thing. It's a conscious decision to correct course and get back on track.

It's here that guilt comes into play. We cannot change our course unless we first acknowledge that we took the wrong turn. Much like the GPS in our cars that tells us we've strayed from the intended route, guilt is how the conscience that God created within us lets us know we've lost the way and need to make a change. The uneasy emotional feeling that we've missed the mark motivates us to repent. Like repentance, guilt isn't inherently bad but rather can be the internal nudge we need in order to make a positive change in our lives—to decide to be a better friend, coworker, sibling, spouse, child, or parent.

That's why it's so painful to watch students (and people in general) feel a need to sidestep guilt by buying into the idea of being their "authentic self." *It's* my *life. It's just how* I *do things. I'm living out* my *truth. Nothing's going to get in* my *way.* Okay, but what kind of life is that? It's one where meaningful change and growth become increasingly rare. When we ignore the warning signs that we've strayed off course, we'll just get more and more lost. And convincing ourselves that we're just following our own way and we'll eventually get back on track isn't a promising strategy. We need to change course. We need to turn around.

Turning around isn't easy. It doesn't always feel great to admit, "Hey, I messed up." When I think about repentance, one biblical text that often comes to mind is Luke 7:36–50, which tells the story of a sinful woman who tearfully approached Jesus during a dinner, washed his feet with her tears, and doused them with expensive perfume. The religious leader whom Jesus was eating with disdained the woman, thinking to himself, *How could such a sinful person dare to bother such outstanding moral teachers like Jesus and me?* But Jesus didn't see it that way. After correcting the religious leader, Jesus embraced the woman's sincere and heartfelt act of repentance, forgiving her of her sins. Jesus didn't despise her; he openly *praised* her for her faith.

It undoubtedly wasn't easy for the woman to approach Jesus. She could have easily ignored the guilt sitting heavy in her stomach, justified her way of life, and avoided the uncomfortable moment altogether. But that approach would not have resulted in change. The story wouldn't have ended in forgiveness and the joy and relief that accompany it.

Commitment to Christ requires a response, and a huge part of this response is repentance. When we make Jesus the center of our lives, it will dramatically alter how we understand everything else that revolves around this center. Suddenly, the destination we were heading toward will change. Those things in life that seemed so important will lose some of their shine. The ways we've acted in the past will begin to feel radically inappropriate.

Commitment to Christ means embracing a new way of doing things. When we approach Jesus in our guilt and admit we've been going the wrong way, we're not only guided back on the right path but are also given forgiveness that washes away that guilt. Repentance isn't a dirty and dour word. There is *extravagant joy* in repentance, because in that moment, all the guilt we've spent so much effort trying to hide, explain away, or shake off is erased by Jesus's grace and love. We're set free. His work on the cross cleanses us from the wrongs of our past. We're given a new, clean slate and put back on course.

In his famous spiritual work *The Ladder of Divine Ascent*, the sixth-century monk John Climacus writes, "Repentance is a contract with God for a second life." Through Jesus Christ, forgiveness and a new life has already been purchased for us. We just need to sign the contract.

Take Up Your Cross

Genuine commitments aren't solely intellectual affairs. Anyone can conclude that they have reasons to make a commitment. But it's an entirely different thing to live out that decision. Ask anyone who has been married for a while, and they'll back us up on this one.

In this book, we've worked through loads of evidence supporting the existence of God, his creation of the universe, the credibility of the four New Testament gospels, the historicity of Jesus Christ, and the reality of his death and resurrection. That's all deeply important stuff, especially when it comes to demolishing unhealthy doubt. But possessing this knowledge only takes us so far. What matters just as much is *living out this knowledge*.

When thinking about what it means to live out my commitment to Christ, I (Cliffe) continually come back to Mark 8:34–35, one of my favorite pieces of Scripture: "Then [Jesus] called the crowd to him along with his disciples and said: 'Whoever wants to be my disciple must deny themselves and take up their cross and follow me. For whoever wants to save their life will lose it, but whoever loses their life for me and for the gospel will save it.'"

Putting God at the center of our lives is a choice to accept the call to follow Jesus. And when Jesus says, "I am the way and the truth and the life" (John 14:6), the way is the way of the cross. When we repent to God for our sins, accept his forgiveness, and change the direction of our lives, the way of the cross is where God directs us to go.

But what does it actually mean to take up our cross? It means a radical change of identity. It means acknowledging we have been freed by God's sacrificial grace from the chains of sin, walked out of that prison never to return, and entered a new life with Christ as our center. The old self has been put to death. As Paul so powerfully declares, "I have been crucified with Christ and I no longer live, but Christ lives in me" (Galatians 2:20). Commitment to Christ is an act of self-crucifixion. It is, in the words of Mark 8:34, a denial of self, a deference to God's will over our selfish wants. No longer do we inhabit the center of our own little universes, for together we revolve around Christ.

Sometimes the students we meet express confusion over this notion of denying oneself. Does denial of the self mean we're supposed to let folks walk all over us like a doormat? Is Jesus instructing us to adopt some sort of ascetic or monastic lifestyle? Not at all (at least not for most of us). Denial of self doesn't mean we can't stand up for ourselves. It's not that we need to deprive ourselves of all the good things life has to offer or engage in self-deprecation. What it does mean, however, is that neither ourselves nor the earthly things we love can take the ultimate spot of priority. *Self-denial means complete loyalty to Christ.* Self-denial means that nothing else in our lives—be it our political ideology, philosophical beliefs, cultural clout, social status, economic achievements, university degrees, or ethnic background—can serve as our primary identifier. Who we are is defined by Jesus Christ.

Commitment to Christ isn't a part-time job or side hustle that takes a back seat to your job, romantic partner, hobbies, financial goals, or even your family. That's not to say those things don't matter. They're all incredibly important. But when those things displace Christ as your central commitment, well, then, you've got a problem. *You're worshiping an idol.*

Contrary to what some people think, idolatry isn't something that was found only in the ancient world. Our contemporary culture is full of idols, and it's only getting worse. Think about how many things you've placed on an altar other than Christ this week. I know my list is way longer than I want to admit. It's far too easy in this world that is consumed with instant gratification, consumption, and selfish pride to find glossy things to pursue instead of God's will. So we try to juggle our self-absorbed desires with our commitment to Christ, thinking maybe we can be devoted to Jesus *and* some of these other nice things. But we're only fooling ourselves. In the words of James 1:8, "A double minded man is unstable in all his ways" (KJV).

No one can carry more than one cross. Nobody can serve two masters (Matthew 6:24). Our allegiance to God cannot play second fiddle to anything else in our lives, even the relationships you hold most sacred (see Luke 14:26–27). The paradoxical truth is this: It is only when we put Christ first and embrace wholeheartedly his commitment to us that we can fully commit our lives to others. It is only when our love is rooted in the firm foundation of Jesus Christ that we can freely offer healthy, genuine, and sacrificial love to other people, from our closest family members and deepest friends to our most distant neighbors and remote strangers.

Obey Christ

Obedience is an essential aspect of any commitment. It's where the rubber hits the road. No true commitment can lack obedience. Without it, the commitment falls apart. If we commit to doing our job but don't show up and do the work, we've broken our commitment. In the same vein, if we do our job but our employer neglects to pay us, then they haven't fulfilled their end of the relationship.

Obedience goes beyond simply professional commitments. Every loving relationship we have requires some degree of obedience. Disobedience is a relationship breaker because it suggests that we don't value or respect that relationship. It tells the other person that we're not all in, that we've got something better to do, that their desires and needs automatically come second to ours. It's a sign we're not truly committed.

Obedience to Christ goes hand in hand with the self-denial we undertake when we carry our cross. If we've truly placed Christ in the center, then our lives will reflect it. This is the message of the epistle of James, which emphasizes over and over that one's commitment to Christ lacks authenticity if it is not consistent with one's actions:

> What good is it, my brothers and sisters, if someone claims to have faith but has no deeds? Can such faith save them? Suppose a brother or a sister is without clothes and daily food. If one of you says to them, "Go in peace; keep warm and well fed," but does nothing about their physical needs, what good is it? In the same way, faith by itself, if it is not accompanied by action, is dead. (James 2:14–17)

According to James, faith that lacks action isn't the life-giving commitment that God wants from us. If Christ has ransomed us from the prison of our sin, we shouldn't be living out our freedom as if we're still incarcerated. At that point, we're squandering God's grace.

If we've truly repented of our sins, accepted God's forgiveness, and placed Christ at the center, then our actions should reflect that, pure and simple.

But does this mean James is advocating that we have to *earn our salvation*? A while back, we talked with evangelist and content creator Bryce Crawford, who came to Connecticut for a couple of days to share some fellowship and interview us for his podcast. Bryce is an outstanding young man whose articulate passion for God conveys wisdom far beyond his years. Even without his patented "I ♥ Jesus" T-shirt, everyone can see that Bryce is a guy committed to bringing others to Christ.

During our chat about the teachings of James and Paul, Bryce remarked, "So, Cliffe, I understand that it's by faith in Jesus Christ that we're saved, but Jesus also says that if we love him, we'll obey his commands. So does that mean our faith is proved genuine because of our actions, not that our actions get us there?"

I responded with deep appreciation for his thoughtful and practical question:

> You know, Bryce, the apostle Paul taught that we're saved by grace through faith, but that this grace is shown in the fruit of the spirit—love, joy, peace, and the like (Galatians 5:22–23). Paul never preaches a cheap grace. He preaches that our experience of God's love changes our hearts so that this fruit grows within us.
>
> I don't think the epistle of James disagrees with this. James is not addressing whether we can get to heaven by our deeds. That's not his point. James clearly assumes that faith is essential. James 2 says that *sincere* faith will be reflected in our lifestyle. So we had better question where our faith is if we're insincerely living in habitual sin. Faith is not just intellectual gymnastics. Real faith involves our mind, emotions, will, and heart—every bit of us actively obeying Christ.

Being determined that our actions accurately reflect our sincere commitment to Christ should certainly not be confused with *earning our salvation*. The point here is not that we have a certain bar we must reach to achieve "gold-level salvation status." God has no expectation that we'll be even remotely perfect. Obedience is a lifelong process for the Christ follower. It's a marathon, not a sprint. It's a race that will have bumps and bruises along the way. But if we truly dedicate ourselves to loving God and carrying our cross, we will see changes in how we love and respect others, from our closest family members to our worst enemies.

How Can I Keep Growing Spiritually?

Commitment means change. And change means growth. Every new commitment we'll ever make—be it a high school sports team or club, job, marriage, child, or social responsibility—will transform who we are. To fulfill our commitments, we will find ourselves learning new skills, adopting new habits, and building new relationships with those we entered into that commitment with. In that sense, commitments aren't simply something we take on; *they're something we grow into.*

That's why spiritual growth is so important. Spiritual growth is the next big step once we've decided to commit our lives our Christ, take up our cross, and live in obedience to his will. Spiritual growth isn't so much about *achievement* as it is about *relationship*. It is ultimately a relationship-building exercise, one that brings us closer to God.

Growing closer to God is like almost anything else we want to experience growth in: It takes *practice*. One might make a rough comparison with learning how to play a new instrument or studying a new language. But neither of those is a truly relational pursuit. We don't ever develop a deep, personal relationship with our guitar, regardless of how much we might like playing it. Spiritual growth is all about connection. It's about desiring God's will and having our habits authentically echo this desire.

But what does this look like in the living out of our lives? In the pages we have left, we'll focus on three particular practices that can serve as an excellent starting point for experiencing growth in your relationship with God.

Studying Your Bible

Reading and studying God's Word is one important way of getting to know God on a more personal level. As we stated earlier, the Bible is God's voice speaking to us, a special revelation beyond what we can learn about God through his creation. Through the Bible, we can learn who God is, what God has done in history, and the depth of God's love for us through the sacrifice of Jesus Christ. In some ways, we can even say that the Bible is God's love letter to us.

It's important to remember that the Bible isn't a horoscope where we can just flip to some random page, put our finger down on a paragraph, and receive a secret message from God about how we should live our lives. As I (Cliffe) told a Harvard student who said as much, if that were the case, then you'd be seeing me doing so whenever I had any sort of tough decision to make (like whether I should buy a Kenmore or a Whirlpool dishwasher). But that's not how the Bible works. God doesn't speak to us through a magic biblical code. Healthy relationships don't rely on secret codes as their primary means of communication.

The first key thing we need to do when reading the Bible is to come to it with listening ears and an open heart. The Bible is full of deep comfort for and insight into our lives. However, God's Word also calls us to reassess how we construct our identities and challenges how we live our lives. As some have put it, the Bible has the power to comfort the afflicted and afflict the comfortable. We may not always like the message we read. Believe me, I know what that's like. When I read the Sermon on the Mount, I am struck by its beauty and wisdom—it truly is the work of an ethical genius. But when I think about what it means to live out those teachings, suddenly those words take on a lot heavier weight. Why would I desire to be someone who is poor in spirit, who mourns, or who is meek? That's not what I want. I'm not interested in being persecuted. Just give me the cushy life for now, God, and I'll get to the other stuff later.

Yet that's not how it works.

God's Word calls us to rethink where our desires are leaning. It will challenge our previous conceptions of the world, sometimes even radically so. It will compel us to go beyond the intellectual and to change how we treat others. But only if we let its words sink in. Only if we're open to God pushing us a bit further than we're comfortable going.

Second, as we mentioned earlier, like any book, the Bible must be interpreted. Biblical interpretation is remarkably difficult. Scholars have spent their entire career learning ancient languages, studying history and archaeology, and writing lengthy commentaries and books in their quest to better understand how to interpret the Old and New Testaments. And most of them admit they *still* have plenty of questions they haven't had answered yet, even after decades of work.

Of course, this doesn't mean that if you're not a historian or biblical scholar, you're not qualified to read the Bible. If that were the case, Stuart and I would be in the same boat. My point is that part of reading the Bible is learning how to do it well, and a huge component is knowing the right people and resources to help guide us in that process. Talking to a pastor or an experienced spiritual mentor is a good place to start. Another helpful source of information is BibleProject (https://bibleproject.com/), an online resource set up by Tim Mackie and Jon Collins that provides helpful articles, videos, Bible study guides, and even classes (many of which are free) to give insight into the Bible and its interpretation. Finally, be sure to check out the For Further Reading and the Notes sections in the back of this book, where we've listed several resources that can provide a great starting point for learning how to read the Bible.

Third and finally, encountering God through reading the Bible isn't just a private discipline; it's a communal practice as well. From the very beginning of the Christian movement, people gathered to read Scripture with one another. It brought people together from different places, ethnicities, genders, economic and educational levels, and social tiers. God's Word was never meant to be read in total isolation. It was meant to be tackled as a team of believers, to draw people together in unity. Naturally, this doesn't mean reading Scripture together won't on occasion result in disagreement. Again, interpreting the Bible isn't easy. We need to extend grace and love to those we disagree with and seek to understand their perspectives rather than simply cut them off. But in a way similar to doubt, those disagreements can be a fruitful place where we can learn about who God is if we let them.

Studying the Bible encompasses far more than just reading another old book. There is life to be found there, a relationship to be built. Meditating on the Bible, memorizing its words, and studying it, both alone and in community, can build a deep connection with the God who speaks in its pages. In the words of Hebrews 4:12, "For the word of God is alive and active. Sharper than any double-edged sword, it penetrates even to dividing soul and spirit, joints and marrow; it judges the thoughts and attitudes of the heart." From Genesis to Revelation, the Bible points out that our only hope is found in God's grace and forgiveness. It is in Scripture that we get to know God personally.

Engaging in Prayer

"Why does prayer matter if God is all-knowing? It doesn't make sense."

"Doesn't prayer just turn God into a genie in a magic lamp?"

"What's the point of asking God to heal my mom if he hasn't done so already? Shouldn't God have done something by now?"

We've gotten a lot of questions about prayer over the years. Many of them have been incredibly tough and very personal in nature. In these moments when the suffering and brokenness of our world hits home hard, sometimes it feels like all we can do is ask God to do something, *anything*, to fix the mess. And when God doesn't respond in the way we were hoping he would, well, then what?

Prayer is a mysterious spiritual practice. When we truly think about it, the idea that we can communicate freely with the eternal God who created the universe is overwhelming. So it's no wonder that many people tend to approach prayer with a less than full picture of how it works. And one of the major misconceptions people have when it comes to prayer is that it's just some sort of cosmic wish list of goodies. The truth is, prayer isn't an experiment in getting; it's *an exercise in intimacy*. The point of prayer isn't to twist God's arm to get the slick BMW I want, the promotion I've been working toward, or even the healing I long for on behalf of a loved one. *The purpose of prayer, first and foremost, is to draw us closer to God.*

Of course, it's not easy to think of prayer this way when so much can and does go wrong in our lives. If anything, prayer in those dire moments can feel like a *struggle*. Yes, you heard me right. In prayer, we sometimes wrestle with God's will for us and express our disappointment, anger, and confusion about the way things are.

Perhaps no one has experienced this reality more deeply than Jesus Christ the evening before his death. Matthew 26 describes how Jesus, in his darkest hour, knowing an excruciating death awaited him, fell on his face in prayer to God the Father, asking if there could be another way. There wasn't, and Jesus knew it. But in his great sorrow (the Greek word *perilypos* means "encircled by grief"), Jesus did not tell the Father to get lost; he didn't bail out. In the face of a struggle that none of us could even imagine undergoing, Jesus aligned himself with the will of the Father. He drew closer to him.

Prayer is most powerful when we look beyond the transactional stereotype, when our approach shifts from "God, I need this; please give me what I want" to "God, I need you; please work in me so that my hopes align with your will." Prayer truly enters into the realm of spiritual practice when its focus shifts from our desire for *our world to change* to our desire for *God to change us*. To paraphrase the famous Danish philosopher Søren Kierkegaard, "The function of prayer is not to influence God, but rather to change the nature of the one who prays."

Remembering the four basic answers that God gives our prayers of supplication (a prayer in which we ask for fulfillment of a specific need) helps me (Cliffe) keep this focus. Meditating on the meaning of these answers can make a huge difference in how we respond to them.

First, God may say, *No*. I can't say I like hearing this answer, especially when things seem really dark. And I've heard it a lot in my life. No one prays in the hope that they'll get a negative response. But like Jesus did on the night before his crucifixion, we must accept God's will. In that moment, we can ask God for strength, insight, and comfort as we learn to align with God's plan, incomprehensible or unthinkable as it might feel to us. We can also share our hurt and frustration with God in prayer. We often forget that sadness and anger are not forbidden when it comes to prayer. Read Psalms if you don't believe me. Almost 40 percent of the prayers in the book are straight-up psalms of lament—hymns written to God expressing profound grief, confusion, and indignation (see, for example, Psalms 6; 13; 22; 42; 44; 60; 88; 130; 142). If King David could declare, "My soul is in deep anguish. How long, LORD, how long?" (Psalm 6:3), then we can too. Don't forget that the God you pray to is the same God who hung on the cross for your sins. That's not a God who is unfamiliar with suffering.

Second, God may say, *Slow. Now is not the time.* This isn't an easy answer either. It's hard to align God's will to your desires when you're an impatient rascal like me. It's hard not to let exasperation get the better of you when God tells you, "Yes, but on my time, Cliffe, not yours."

In many ways, moments like these are opportunities for healthy trust to grow. God has a plan. It's all in his hands—*everything*. Now he just needs *you* to get with the program too. Here I think of the words of Isaiah 55:8–9:

> "For my thoughts are not your thoughts,
> neither are your ways my ways,"
> declares the LORD.
> "As the heavens are higher than the earth,
> so are my ways higher than your ways
> and my thoughts than your thoughts."

Life is filled with so much mystery, so many things we don't understand. God is so far above us. In those moments when God says, *Slow down*, we need to take a deep breath and reaffirm our trust in him. We need to thank God for tending to our needs and ask for patience and understanding as we wait for his good work to come to fruition. We need to trust God's flawless timing.

Third, God may say, *Grow*. He may tell us that the trial we're going through has a purpose, that he has put us exactly where we're supposed to be. I've often come to God in bewilderment at what has taken place in my life or in the lives of those around me. I've prayed for many escapes from difficult situations that never came. But the suffering was not meaningless. By means of those trials, God shaped me as a person. Through my pain and confusion, God taught me how to rely on him and other people he put in my life. Through my brokenness, God gave me the opportunity to grow spiritually and to enter into a much deeper relationship with him, one characterized by trust and love. In those moments, we may not see the purpose in the suffering. We may not know why life feels so unfair. But we must remember that we worship a fair and just God who, in the words of Paul, "works for the good of those who love him, who have been called according to his purpose" (Romans 8:28). We must pray that God will do that hard work within us and provide us the wisdom we need to grow through our suffering.

Fourth and finally, sometimes God may say, *Go*. God may give us the answer we've been hoping for. But that doesn't mean we stop praying once we've gotten what we want. When God's will aligns with our hopes and desires, we must remember to thank God for his loving-kindness and ask for continued guidance as we embrace the opportunity he has given us. What's more, we cannot let a single divine yes derail our practice of daily prayer. Far too often, when the problem disappears, we suddenly forget that we desperately need God. We allow ourselves to become so distracted by the *gift* that we lose sight of the *divine giver*. That's the challenge we face when God says, *Go*. Even in the wonderful moments of relief, we must not stop asking God to conform us to his will.

So what does true prayer look like as an exercise of intimacy with God? How do we begin doing this? As Stuart and I explained to Graham Stephan and Jack Selby on *The Iced Coffee Hour* podcast, authentic prayer is simply the *real you* talking to the *real God*, just as if God is sitting right next to you. It's no easy task. You have to get in touch with the real you. No faking it. No trying to skirt around the reality of things, no matter how dark, dirty, or desperate it might feel. Authentic and intimate prayer does not mince words.

At the same time, you must also know who the real God you're praying to actually is. This is another reason why reading the Bible is so important. Without a regular practice of Bible reading, we tend to envision God in our image. We want to pray to a God who looks like us and talks like us, a God who holds the same political, social, and cultural views we do. But prayer isn't about constructing the type of God we wish existed—a God who will just let us do "business as usual." That's not a recipe for spiritual growth. That's a fake relationship. True prayer is about reaching out to the creator God of the Bible, the God who died on the cross for our sins. God exists beyond our imaginations. Make sure you're praying to the real God, the God who reveals himself in Scripture, and not to an empty chair.

Finally, authentic prayer consists of four main things: adoration, confession, thanksgiving, and supplication (ACTS). First, we offer *adoration* to God. We praise God for his attributes—his unconditional love, his power, his providential care, and his mercy. We express our awe of who God is and admit that he is God and we are not.

Second, we offer *confession* of our sins to God. A number of people have said that confession sounds prudish or old-fashioned. But confession is vitally important. It's an acknowledgment that we are not sinless, that we have caused harm, and that we need God's help in every minute of every day. We gossip and lie. We lust after power, sex, and money. We act out of selfishness, pride, and rage. It's only when we are honest about our sins that we can accept God's forgiveness and find repentance (see the previous chapter). As we take responsibility for our wrongdoing, God reaches out to set us right.

Third, we offer *thanksgiving* to God. We must take every opportunity to show gratitude to God for all of his good gifts to us, beginning with his gracious promise of eternal life. It is all too easy to become calloused to the simple goods of life, to become distracted by the many things we don't have. Taking a moment to reflect on the small and large goods God has given us is a transformative act of gratitude. Opportunities to express gratitude should never be overlooked in our times of prayer.

Finally, we offer *supplication* to God. We ask God for strength, mercy, and forgiveness, alongside all the other needs we've encountered throughout the day. If we let supplication become the center of our prayers, however, we will reduce it to shooting up spiritual flares calling for help. Only when we have an authentic relationship with God—when we come to know and worship his awesome attributes, share our inner heart with God, and truly appreciate all that God has done for us—can our supplication become meaningful and lead us to genuinely understand the answer (be it *no*, *slow*, *grow*, or *go*) that God sends our way.

Prayer is not a mindless, memorized formula; it is a sacred relational practice. It pulls us out of our desire to exalt ourselves and instead places our attention and love on the one true God. It is where our hunger and thirst for God find fulfillment. In the words of Psalm 42:1, "As the deer pants for streams of water, so my soul pants for you, my God."

Finding Community

Occasionally, students will declare that while they're deeply convinced that Jesus Christ is the Son of God who died for their sins, they're hesitant to go to church. Some say it's because they feel uncomfortable with the stuffiness of "institutional religion." Others confide that they've had a traumatic experience in the past with a certain church and haven't gone back since. Still others admit they've never been to church and don't understand why it matters in the first place. We certainly empathize with each of them. It's hard to build community, especially when it feels foreign or carries with it deep wounds. But community is an essential part of what it means to grow as a follower of Jesus Christ. Spiritual growth isn't simply an individual activity; it's a communal one.

Since the very beginning of his earthly ministry, Jesus Christ promoted a life of community. It's the reason he traveled to Judea with a group of disciples. It's why he shared meals with people from all walks of life, even those judged to be sinners by society at large. It's why he talked with outcasts and healed with his touch those who were considered untouchable. Even while on the cross and suffering horrific pain, Jesus didn't stop building community. In his last moments, when one of the thieves crucified on a cross next to him asked Jesus to remember him in his kingdom, Jesus responded, "Truly I tell you, today you will be with me in paradise" (Luke 23:43). And when the resurrected Jesus ascended into heaven, he didn't instruct his disciples to go out and seek personal enlightenment and wisdom. No, he commissioned them to "go and make disciples of all nations, baptizing them in the name of the Father and of the Son and of the Holy Spirit, and teaching them to obey everything I have commanded you. And surely I am with you always, to the very end of the age" (Matthew 28:19–20). Jesus commanded his disciples to build communities that are committed to God.

Finding a Christian community is an important step in spiritual growth for many reasons. To begin with, it's a place where God can work through other believers to help us move forward in our faith. As human beings, we all have struggles and shortcomings that we're incapable of seeing or unable to overcome. We all have temptations and flawed inclinations that frustrate our attempts to build Christlike behaviors and habits. Going through life solo doesn't make our efforts any easier. And so God established the church, giving us the gift of other believers to help guide us on our journey. Believers who have experienced what we're struggling with and can offer practical support and gracious encouragement. Believers who keep us accountable in our moments of weakness without judgment. Believers who challenge us when it comes to how we live our lives. In a world full of distractions, God provided a community to keep us focused on the road ahead, to teach us the lessons we can't teach ourselves, and to provide us more ears to discern where God is calling us to go.

Second, Christian community is where we can become fully integrated into the body of Christ. As the apostle Paul puts it in several places, the church is the body of Christ, the hands and feet of our risen Savior:

> For just as each of us has one body with many members, and these members do not all have the same function, so in Christ we, though many, form one body, and each member belongs to all the others. We have different gifts, according to the grace given to each of us. If your gift is prophesying, then prophesy in accordance with your faith; if it is serving, then serve; if it is teaching, then teach; if it is to encourage, then give encouragement; if it is giving, then give generously; if it is to lead, do it diligently; if it is to show mercy, do it cheerfully. (Romans 12:4–8)

This image of a body with many members is what makes the community of Christ such a powerful space for believers. Together, the church in its diversity can encourage each member to use their God-given gifts and talents to contribute to the whole. Individually, we find fulfillment and growth through our participation in the body of Christ. But this personal fulfillment and growth only exists because it is part of the larger whole. Without being part of Christ's body, an eye cannot see, an ear cannot hear, and a hand cannot touch. And it's only when they work together that God's love can be most effectively extended to the world. That's why I tell people who declare, "Well, I believe in Jesus, but I don't want to belong to a church," to rethink what they're saying. Authentically living out our belief in Christ only reaches its full, intended potential when we do it in community.

Third, it is in community that we can best experience the growth that comes from Christian service. It is how we as the body of Christ can visibly embody God's love to others by combating the unfairness and injustice of life. Service is love wearing work boots. It is spiritual growth through action. Biblical spirituality was never meant to be a retreat from the world around us. We've always been called to extend God's love to all people, whether they are family, friends, fellow believers, strangers, and even enemies. And although Christian service is something we can carry out individually, such work is most meaningfully done in community. Communal Christian service is what prevents spirituality from being an opiate of the masses, an excuse for laziness, or a trip into irrelevance.

Service is an act of worship, a hymn of praise to God. It is how we can bring his coming kingdom a little bit closer to earth. But our voices are loudest and our impact is strongest when we work together. It is serving in community that we as Christ's body can most fully experience the spiritual growth that comes from being his hands and feet.

We could say so much more about commitment and spiritual growth. We cannot say enough how deeply we encourage you to make this commitment and keep growing in your spiritual life with God. Read your Bible. Research the deep questions that won't go away. Pray intentionally and continually. Find a Christian community where you can experience understanding, encouragement, and growth. Serve God and others through acts of restorative love. Investing in your commitment to Christ is one of the most important steps you can take as a believer. Just as eating healthily, working out, and staying current on doctor visits can help prevent various health problems from occurring, so, too, engaging in practices of spiritual growth can help stave off the affliction of unhealthy doubt.

But again, all of these steps of commitment are a matter of the will and the heart, not merely the intellect. The famous church father Augustine once wrote, "You [O Lord] have made us for yourself, and our heart is restless until it rests in you" (*Confessions* 1.1.5). Defeating our doubts doesn't end with our minds. It's not until our hearts conform to God's will that we can truly experience freedom from our disbelief. It's not until our loves and desires come into alignment with God's plan that our faith can begin to grow deeper and richer.

And that's not something knowledge can achieve on its own. We can memorize as many philosophical and theological arguments as we want, but it won't make a lick of difference if our hearts refuse to live out the depths of that knowledge.

CONCLUSION

One of my (Cliffe's) favorite biblical characters is Thomas. I can empathize with the guy. As one of the twelve disciples, Thomas knew Jesus just about as well as anyone else on earth. He shared meals with Jesus, walked across Judea and Samaria with him, and listened to him preach and saw him perform miracles. Thomas was committed to Jesus, so much so that he expressed willingness to follow Jesus *to his death* (John 11:16). Talk about being a dedicated and faithful follower.

Three days after Jesus was crucified, he appeared to the women at the tomb and eventually to all of his disciples (John 20:19–22)—*all of them except Thomas*. You see, according to the gospel of John, Thomas was not with the disciples when the resurrected Jesus appeared to them. And when the rest of the gang excitedly told him, "We have seen the Lord!" Thomas didn't buy it one bit. He hadn't been there to see it for himself, so how could he believe something so miraculous and extraordinary as this? "Unless I see the nail marks in his hands," Thomas told them, "and put my finger where the nails were, and put my hand into his side, *I will not believe*" (John 20:25, emphasis added).

Thomas, the disciple who had been willing to die for Jesus, hit the wall of doubt.

But the story doesn't end there. A week later, all of the disciples, Thomas included, were gathered together when suddenly Jesus appeared to them again. Looking at Thomas, Jesus said, "Put your finger here; see my hands. Reach out your hand and put it into my side. *Stop doubting and believe*" (John 20:27, emphasis added). John's gospel never states whether Thomas actually touched Jesus's scars. It is entirely possible he was too awestruck to move (I know I would have been). All we have is Thomas's verbal reaction: "My Lord and my God" (20:28). Thomas saw and believed.

Over the centuries, Thomas has gotten a bad rap. I mean, he's the namesake behind the epithet "Doubting Thomas," a phrase used to label cynics who refuse to believe anything without personal experience. Personally, though, I think it's about time we stop ragging on Thomas. In fact, as I hope we've made clear in this book, I think it's about time we stop ragging on doubt in general.

Thomas wasn't an unfaithful fool or a hardened skeptic who fought tooth and nail to disagree on principle. *Thomas was just like all of us.* Unsure. Confused. Searching for answers. Hurt by disappointment. Looking for glimmers of light in the darkness. Yearning for proof. Fearing the pain and embarrassment that come with being mistaken. There was nothing sinful or strange about Thomas's doubt. If there was, then I'm in deep trouble too, because I'm there with him. I've got my doubts. I've got my reasons not to believe. And like Thomas, I want physical proof too. There are plenty of days when I wonder why Jesus doesn't simply appear in person, show me his nail wounds, and prove once and for all that he's not just some character in a fairy tale.

Doubt isn't a shortcoming experienced only by the weak. It's not a type of spiritual apathy. It's not a sign that one's faith is too fickle, infirm, or stagnant to function in daily life. On the contrary, doubt only arises when one has engaged their beliefs beyond the surface level. It's a necessary stop on a long and difficult journey to truth.

Thomas never abandoned this journey. He didn't outright deny the possibility of the resurrection. He never told the disciples they were hallucinating idiots and just walk away. Thomas still joined them a week later. He had his doubts, to be sure, but he also desired to uncover the truth. Thomas's doubts did not sound the death knell to his belief. If anything, they were what propelled him to encounter Jesus Christ for himself. Doubt gave his faith the opportunity to grow in abundance.

All this to say, we need to destigmatize doubt.

I've always struggled with doubt. It has come at different times and in different ways over my lifetime, but it's almost always been there. At times, I've risen to the occasion and embraced my doubt as an opportunity for growth. I've allowed God to fill the space of my skepticism, expand my understanding, and refine my attitude and actions. I've searched my Bible and theological books for answers, reflected long and hard, prayed for guidance, and sought wisdom from others. In other moments, however, I've stuck my head in the sand like an ostrich, ignoring the nagging questions in front of me. In the face of doubt, I've refused to approach the issues with an open mind and instead indulged in intellectual and spiritual laziness.

To some extent, the problem with doubt isn't merely the doubt itself, but rather our reaction to it. When we neglect to address our doubts and allow them to run rampant, they can turn into monsters pretty quickly. Healthy skepticism becomes hyperskepticism. Critical questioning morphs into ideological cynicism. A deep desire for scientific proof warps into materialist naturalism. Polite relativism becomes meaningless nihilism. When we don't take the initiative to confront and demolish our uncertainties, they're bound to become unhealthy. When we're too afraid to struggle with skepticism, we become consumed by it. When we lose sight of the truth through the fog of doubt, we begin to sink into disbelief.

But it doesn't have to be that way. Doubt doesn't have to be an untamable beast. One of the chief reasons we wrote this book is to encourage people to embrace doubt as an opportunity to spark intellectual growth and spiritual transformation. The deep questions that hinder belief have answers. Yes, we may not have absolute proof for the existence of God, but we do have several strong arguments that support the idea that our universe has been crafted in immaculate detail by an intelligent and eternal creator. Yes, we don't have photographs of Jesus Christ, but we do have a boatload of trustworthy signs and the reliable eyewitness testimonies in the Bible about his life. Of course, none of us were there to see Jesus appear to the disciples after his death, but the historical details we possess largely defy any other explanation besides the physical resurrection of Jesus from the dead.

Do we have *all* the answers? Not a chance. Are all the answers easy to grasp? No, they are not. But should we then throw in the towel and surrender to disbelief? Never. It's in those moments when despair sets in, when like Thomas we yearn to see the nail marks, that we need to rely on God for strength, seek the wisdom of others for guidance, and remember that we're not alone in this fight.

Sometimes when I'm wrestling with doubts, I find that it helps to stop for a minute, move my questions to the side, and look at the bigger picture. Doubt can seem far more intimidating when we're in the thick of the fight. Stepping back to put everything in perspective can help ease our anxiety and frustration by setting our doubt into context.

For example, think about this: Jesus Christ walked this earth nearly two thousand years ago. Two millennia is a long time. Lots of brilliant people, folks far smarter than any of us, have lived and died during that span of time. Yet none of those people have ever ultimately knocked the underpinnings out from under belief in Christ. No detractor has ever delivered a fatal blow that has definitively proven the central tenets of faith to be false. So why should we be so worried that *our* questions and doubts, big as they may feel, could demolish what generations of people have tried and failed to destroy?

Something else I try to keep in mind when doubt feels heavy is that if we authentically search for the truth, we can't go wrong. Truth should not be a reason for us to give way to fear. Jesus himself said, "The truth will set you free" (John 8:32). I've heard quite a few people over the years admit that they've avoided dealing with their doubts because they're scared that what they discover might threaten their current beliefs. I get that. It's not fun to be confronted with an inconvenient truth. But facing doubts head-on is a necessary part of the journey of belief. Sometimes the trail we're on may feel unsafe or scary, but that doesn't mean we turn around. In those moments, we need to keep the summit in view. In those moments when confronting the truth is difficult, we have to remind ourselves that if God is truth, we have nothing to fear.

One other encouragement for me when doubt feels challenging is to reflect on the spiritual revival we're seeing arise among the youth in our country. Several surveys taken the past few years have revealed that Christianity is not only growing like wildfire across the world, especially in Africa and East Asia, but also among young people in America.

Until recently, we've been told that Christianity is on the decline, that fewer and fewer people believe that God exists, and that churches are becoming empty graveyards. I didn't anticipate I'd see this trend change direction in my lifetime. My hope was always to plant seeds for the future without any expectation that I would live to see any of the fruit of such labor. But today, I see a new spiritual passion brewing among young people, a growing desire to learn more about Jesus Christ and make the commitment of faith. There is a revival of faith moving in this world, despite the weight of immense suffering, political conflict, social injustice, familial breakdown, moral relativism, personal tragedies, and issues of identity. In the midst of this turmoil, more and more students are finding stability and security in Jesus Christ. To see God at work in this current generation gives me tremendous hope when the darkness of doubt feels gloomy.

Finally, when doubt feels dire, I remember that the God who created this world, died on the cross for my sins, and is now bringing spiritual renewal to people around the globe is the same God who is working within the dirty, rotten sinner I am. This God faithfully committed himself to me first, long before I committed myself to him. This God brings a stability and security I could never conjure on my own. This God is faithful and gracious, offering the gift of eternal life, even when I'm distrustful and uncharitable. This God loves unconditionally and calls me his child, even when I'm selfish and prideful. This God gives me wisdom to admit what I don't know and strength to seek out the truth. There's nothing more powerful than this.

We're so grateful that you've taken this step with us in the journey to belief. It's a lifelong quest, one with many obstacles along the way. But we can tell you from experience that it's a truly good journey, one that will change your life forever. We'd love to get the chance to meet all of you on one of our university campus visits—you can follow us on Instagram (@Stuart_Knechtle) to know what college campus we will be at next—or at our Sunday morning service at Grace Community Church.

We thank our God every time we remember you. In all our prayers for all of you, we always pray with joy because of your partnership in the gospel from the first day until now, being confident of this, that he who began a good work in you will carry it on to completion until the day of Christ Jesus. (Philippians 1:3–6, paraphrased)

FOR FURTHER READING

In addition to many of the sources mentioned in the Notes section of this book (which we highly recommend you also check out), the following resources provide additional insight into the topics dealt with in this book, as well as engage issues and questions not treated in this volume. Unlike some of the works cited in the Notes, a majority of the more than two dozen resources listed below are also fairly accessible to the general reader, including teens and college students. We hope these suggestions strengthen you and give you guidance as you continue your faith journey. We'll be praying for you!

Bishop, Robert C., Larry L. Funck, Raymond J. Lewis, Stephen O. Moshier, and John H. Walton. *Understanding Scientific Theories of Origins: Cosmology, Geology, and Biology in Christian Perspective*. InterVarsity, 2018.

Chatraw, Joshua D., and Mark D. Allen. *Apologetics at the Cross: An Introduction for Christian Witness*. Zondervan Academic, 2018.

Collins, Francis S. *Belief: Readings on the Reason for Faith*. HarperCollins, 2010.

Copan, Paul. *How Do You Know You're Not Wrong?: Responding to Objections That Leave Christians Speechless*. Baker, 2005.

Craig, William Lane. *God, Are You There?: Five Reasons God Exists and Three Reasons It Makes a Difference*. Wipf & Stock, 2023.

Geisler, Norman L., and Frank Turek. *I Don't Have Enough Faith to Be an Atheist*. Crossway, 2004.

Green, Michael. *Running from Reality*. InterVarsity, 1983.

Groothuis, Douglas. *Christian Apologetics: A Comprehensive Case for Biblical Faith*. InterVarsity, 2022.

Keller, Timothy. *The Reason for God: Belief in an Age of Skepticism*. Penguin, 2008.

Knechtle, Cliffe. *Give Me an Answer That Satisfies My Heart and My Mind*. InterVarsity, 1986.

Knechtle, Cliffe. *Help Me Believe: Direct Answers to Real Questions*. InterVarsity, 2000.

Lennox, John. *Can Science Explain Everything?* Good Book Company, 2009.

Lewis, C. S. *Mere Christianity*. Macmillan, 1951.

McDowell, Josh, and Sean McDowell. *Evidence for Jesus: Timeless Answers for Tough Questions About Christ*. Thomas Nelson, 2023.

McDowell, Josh, and Sean McDowell. *Evidence That Demands a Verdict: Life-Changing Truth for a Skeptical World*. Thomas Nelson, 2017.

McDowell, Sean, ed. *Apologetics for an Ever-Changing Culture: A Biblical and Culturally Relevant Approach to Talking About God*. Harvest House, 2025.

McLaughlin, Rebecca. *Confronting Christianity: 12 Hard Questions for the World's Largest Religion*. Crossway, 2019.

McLaughlin, Rebecca. *10 Questions Every Teen Should Ask (and Answer) About Christianity*. Crossway, 2021.

Moreland, J. P. *Scientism and Secularism: Learning to Respond to a Dangerous Ideology*. Crossway, 2018.

Neill, Stephen. *Christian Faith and Other Faiths*. InterVarsity, 1984.

Orr-Ewing, Amy. *Is the Bible Intolerant?* InterVarsity, 2006.

Orr-Ewing, Amy. *Why Trust the Bible? Answers to Ten Tough Questions*. Rev. ed. InterVarsity, 2020.

Sire, James W. *Habits of the Mind: Intellectual Life as a Christian Calling*. InterVarsity, 2000.

Stott, John. *Being a Christian*. InterVarsity, 2016.

Wallace, J. Warner. *Cold-Case Christianity: A Homicide Detective Investigates the Claims of the Gospels*. Expanded Edition. David C. Cook, 2023.

Wright, Christopher J. H. *The God I Don't Understand: Reflections on Tough Questions of Faith*. Zondervan, 2009.

ACKNOWLEDGMENTS

We have come to learn that writing a book is at once a lonely and collaborative endeavor. There were times when it involved a blinking cursor and the transfer of thoughts to a page that comes only with determined thought and a not insignificant amount of prayer. There were just as many times that this book came into existence only because of the determined efforts of a few people who kept the project on track and on deadline. We are deeply grateful for the many individuals who encouraged and helped us on this journey.

First and foremost, our hearts overflow with gratitude to God, whose truths and Holy Spirit, we pray, have sustained this work and whose mercies encourage us to spread the gospel.

Our families were extraordinarily patient with us as we worked on the manuscript. Sharon, you are the matriarch of our family and the one without whom nothing would be possible.

Though we had been approached to write a book several times over the years, Keith Urbahn of Javelin approached us with the plan and enthusiasm to make it a reality. Our mutual connection to New Canaan brought this dedicated advocate to our corner, and we are grateful for his counsel throughout the process.

Zondervan and the team at HarperCollins Christian Publishing saw the potential in this project from the start. We are indebted to Webster Younce, who acquired the project, and Andrea Palpant, who expertly edited it and saw it to its completion.

Blake Jurgens was an extraordinary collaborator without whom our book would almost certainly have remained a collection of notes in the form of dozens of draft emails. Blake worked to make this book a better, more coherent version of itself and to combine our voices and experiences into a singular narrative.

Last but not least, there is no way we can adequately express our gratefulness for the people of Grace Community Church in New Canaan, Connecticut. They are real partners in the ministry. Their prayers and support mean so much.

NOTES

Introduction

page 9: *In the pages to follow*: Regarding the relationship between faith and doubt, see Anthony C. Thiselton, *Doubt, Faith, and Certainty* (Eerdmans, 2017); Sean McDowell and John Marriott, *Set Adrift: Deconstructing What You Believe Without Sinking Your Faith* (Zondervan, 2023).

Chapter 1: Is God Real?

page 17: *Nearly every significant thinker*: The quotes in the introduction come from René Descartes, *Meditations on First Philosophy*, ed. and trans. John Cottingham (Cambridge University Press, 2013); Friedrich Nietzsche, *Twilight of the Idols and The Anti-Christ*, trans. R. J. Hollingdale (Penguin, 1990); G. K. Chesterton, "Where All Roads Lead," in *G. K. Chesterton: Collected Works*, vol. 3 (Ignatius, 1990); Francis S. Collins, *The Language of God: A Scientist Presents Evidence for Belief* (Free Press, 2006); Sam Harris, *Letter to a Christian Nation* (Knopf, 2006). The George Bernard Shaw quotation was commonly recited by him in lectures and conversations.

page 20: *Albert Einstein is reported to have said*: While widely attributed to Einstein, this quote cannot be found in any of his verified writings or speeches.

page 20: *As any biologist or physicist will tell you*: On the role of probability in scientific research, see Antony Eagle, "Probability," in *The Oxford Handbook of Philosophy of Science*, ed. Paul Humphreys (Oxford University Press, 2014).

page 21: *Faith is belief rooted in trust*: For thinking about the relationship between faith, trust, and knowledge, see Carolyn McLeod, "Trust," *Stanford Encyclopedia of Philosophy*, last revised August 10, 2020, https://plato.stanford.edu/entries/trust/.

page 23: *The first key piece of evidence*: For sources used regarding the design of the universe as evidence for God, see the notes for chapter 2.

page 24: *often attributed to Albert Einstein*: While widely attributed to Einstein, this quote cannot be found in any of his verified writings or speeches.

page 24: *One textbook on molecular biology*: Bruce Alberts et al., "Chromosomal DNA and Its Packaging in the Chromatin Fiber," in *Molecular Biology of the Cell*, 4th ed. (Garland Science, 2002), www.ncbi.nlm.nih.gov/books/NBK26834/.

page 24: *our miniscule cells each contain*: For the remarkable properties and structure of DNA as evidence for God, see the chapter "Deciphering God's Instruction Book: The Lessons of the Human Genome," in Collins, *Language of God*.

page 25: *British philosopher Bertrand Russell*: The quote from Russell comes from the chapter "Science and Values" in *The Impact of Science on Society* (Routledge, 2016), 83, 86.

page 27: *there are moral absolutes*: For some wonderful insights about the moral argument for God, see David Baggett, "Moral Arguments: An Abductive Moral Argument for God," in *Two Dozen (or so) Arguments for God: The Plantinga Project*, ed. Jerry Walls and Trent Dougherty (Oxford University Press, 2018); Sean McDowell and

Jonathan Morrow, "Can People Be Good Without God?" in *Is God Just a Human Invention? And Seventeen Other Questions Raised by the New Atheists* (Kregel, 2011).

page 27: *Christian philosopher Alvin Plantinga*: Concerning Alvin Plantinga's argument against naturalism, see his *Where the Conflict Really Lies: Science, Religion, and Naturalism* (Oxford University Press, 2011). Offering a great summary of his ideas is William Lane Craig, "Plantinga's Evolutionary Argument Against Naturalism," Reasonable Faith, November 8, 2020, www.reasonablefaith.org/question-answer/p10/plantingas-evolutionary-argument-against-naturalism-707.

Chapter 2: Did God Create the Universe?

page 31: *Several ancient Hindu texts*: Detailing these and many other creation myths, see David Adams Leeming, *Creation Myths of the World*, 2 vols. (Bloomsbury, 2008).

page 32: *As we'll explore in this chapter*: Engaging and helpful summary treatments of the topics engaged throughout this chapter can be found in William Lane Craig and James P. Moreland, eds., *The Blackwell Companion to Natural Theology* (Blackwell, 2009).

page 34: *God is the first principle*: On historical arguments for God's existence as first or uncaused cause, see William Lane Craig, *The Kalam Cosmological Argument* (Barnes & Noble, 1979); Sean McDowell and Jonathan Morrow, "How Did the Universe Begin?," in *Is God Just a Human Invention?*

page 36: *The naturalist can't allow free will*: Concerning immaterial realities, such as consciousness and beauty, as evidence for God, see chapter 9 of Richard Swinburne, *The Existence of God* (Clarendon, 1979); J. P. Moreland, *Consciousness and the Existence of God: A Theistic Argument* (Routledge, 2010).

page 36: *The only real option for the naturalist*: Richard Dawkins in several places argues that free will is an illusion. See especially his

The Selfish Gene (Oxford University Press, 1979). Making similar points is the more recent work by Sam Harris, *Free Will* (Free Press, 2012).

page 37: *analogy most famously used by . . . Michael Behe*: The notion of irreducible complexity is developed by Michael Behe in *Darwin's Black Box: The Biochemical Challenge to Evolution*, 2nd ed. (Free Press, 2006).

page 39: *existence of life in our solar system*: Concerning the specific scientific details regarding our universe's meticulously balanced and unique life-producing qualities, see Paul Davies, *Cosmic Jackpot: Why Our Universe Is Just Right for Life* (Harcourt, 2007).

page 41: *God created this fine-tuned universe*: Some of the recent approaches to fine-tuning that have influenced our understanding include Robin Collins, "A Scientific Argument for the Existence of God: The Fine-Tuning Design Argument," in *Reason for the Hope Within*, ed. Michael J. Murray (Eerdmans, 1999); Alister McGrath, *A Fine-Tuned Universe: The Quest for God in Science and Theology* (Westminster John Knox, 2009).

Chapter 3: What Is the Bible and Why Does It Matter?

page 47: *2024 study by the American Bible Society*: "State of the Bible: USA 2024," American Bible Society, September 2024, https://1s712.americanbible.org/state-of-the-bible/stateofthebible/State_of_the_bible-2024.pdf. Interestingly, there has been a massive growth in Bible sales over the last couple years in the United States. See Christopher Kuo, "In a Bible Publishing Boom, All Scripture Is Profitable," *Christianity Today*, January 30, 2025, www.christianitytoday.com/2025/01/bible-sales-boom-christian-publishers/.

page 47: *We're still a biblical illiterate society*: For a recent treatment of the idea of biblical illiteracy, see Joe Holland, "Are We More Biblically Illiterate Than Ever?," *Ligonier Ministries*, March 28,

2025, https://learn.ligonier.org/articles/are-we-more-biblically-illiterate-than-ever.

page 50: *second-century Christian writers like Papias*: Papias of Hierapolis's naming of the gospel writers was preserved in Eusebius, *Church History* 3.39. For an accessible treatment of all four of the New Testament gospels, including authorship, see Patrick Schreiner, *The Four Gospels: Jesus, the Hope of the World* (B&H, 2024).

page 52: *most translated book in the entire world*: Regarding the history of the transmission of the Bible among Christians, see Neil R. Lightfoot, *How We Got the Bible*, 3rd ed. (Baker, 2003).

page 55: *Bible speaks to God's historical relationship*: For more on the amazing amount of historical information we find in the Bible that has been confirmed by other nonbiblical sources and archaeology, see J. Daniel Hays, *A Christian's Guide to Evidence for the Bible* (Baker, 2020); David A. deSilva, *Archaeology and the World of Jesus: A Visual Guide* (Baker, 2025).

page 60: *dozens of massive commentaries*: There are many helpful introductions to the Bible of varying degrees of complexity and historical detail. Some solid ones discussing the details mentioned here include D. A. Carson and Douglas J. Moo, *An Introduction to the New Testament* (Zondervan, 2005); Bill T. Arnold, *Introduction to the Old Testament* (Cambridge University Press, 2014).

page 61: *interpret the Bible fluently*: For a helpful approach to biblical interpretation, see W. Randolph Tate, *Biblical Interpretation: An Integrated Approach*, 3rd ed. (Baker, 2008).

Chapter 4: Can We Trust What the New Testament Says?

page 67: *They are first-century biographies*: Regarding the historical language and the literary genre of the Gospels as *bioi* (Greco-Roman biographies), see Craig Keener, *Christobiography: Memory, History, and the Reliability of the Gospels* (Eerdmans, 2019).

page 68: *sign that Luke wants his readers*: Looking at Luke as a historian, including the language of Luke 1, is I. Howard Marshall, *Luke: Historian and Theologian*, 3rd ed. (InterVarsity, 1998).

page 68: *discuss this passage in more detail*: For more information on 1 Corinthians 15, see the notes for chapter 9.

page 69: *Lewis writes regarding the Gospels*: Lewis's quote is from his essay, "Modern Theology and Biblical Criticism" in *Christian Reflections*, ed. Walter Hooper (Eerdmans, 1967), 155.

page 70: *corroborate some of their specific details*: Concerning the general historicity of the New Testament, see Benjamin Shaw, *Trustworthy: Thirteen Arguments for the Reliability of the New Testament* (InterVarsity, 2024). Discussing the historicity of the Gospels, see Craig L. Blomberg, *The Historical Reliability of the Gospels*, 2nd ed. (InterVarsity, 2014).

page 70: *Archaeologists have even discovered*: For an essay on the historical and archaeology data surrounding the Capernaum synagogue and other synagogues mentioned in the four gospels, see Eric Meyers, "The Synagogue in the Time of Jesus and the New Testament," in *Behind the Scenes of the New Testament: Cultural, Social, and Historical Contexts*, ed. Bruce W. Longenecker et al. (Baker, 2024).

page 71: *Luke 3:1–2*: Offering a detailed assessment of Luke 3:1–2 is James Edwards, *The Gospel According to Luke* (Eerdmans, 2015).

page 72: *a group of excavators*: For a good summary of the archaeological data we have for the pools of Bethesda and Siloam, see James H. Charlesworth, "The Tale of Two Pools: Archaeology and the Book of John," *Near East Archaeological Society Bulletin* 56 (2011): 1–14.

page 73: *possible mention of Christ*: For an essay summarizing the extrabiblical accounts mentioned in this chapter regarding Jesus, see Casey D. Elledge, "Josephus, Tacitus, and Suetonius: Seeing Jesus Through the Eyes of Classical Historians," in *Jesus Research:*

New Methodologies and Perceptions, ed. James H. Charlesworth et al. (Eerdmans, 2014).

page 73: *inform our archaeological knowledge*: Regarding the relationship of the New Testament to archaeology, see Jonathan L. Reed, *The HarperCollins Visual Guide to the New Testament: What Archaeology Reveals About the First Christians* (Zondervan, 2007).

page 75: *Gospels are accurate historical accounts*: Concerning the different details found in the four gospels, see Michael R. Licona, *Why Are There Differences in the Gospels? What We Can Learn from Ancient Biography* (Oxford University Press, 2016).

page 79: *manuscripts we possess accurately transmit*: Regarding the reliability of the New Testament manuscripts, see F. F. Bruce, *The New Testament Documents: Are They Reliable?*, 6th ed. (InterVarsity, 1981).

page 80: *infinitesimal level of overlap*: A wonderful digital resource for those interested in the study of New Testament manuscripts is *The Center for the Study of New Testament Manuscripts* website (www.csntm.org/). This project is run by Daniel Wallace of Dallas Theological Seminary, one of the preeminent scholars on New Testament manuscripts in the country.

Chapter 5: Isn't the Bible Problematic?

page 84: *questions are important to address*: For a general resource addressing many of the questions encountered here, see Dan Kimball, *How (Not) to Read the Bible: Making Sense of the Anti-Women, Anti-Science, Pro-Violence, Pro-Slavery and Other Crazy-Sounding Parts of Scripture* (Zondervan, 2020), as well as several of the sources listed in the For Further Reading section in the back of this book.

page 84: *We hear this counterpoint*: Regarding the question of whether the New Testament authors could have made stuff up, see Norman Geisler and Frank Turek, "10 Things You Should Know About the

Reliability of the New Testament Writers," *Crossway*, February 1, 2022, www.crossway.org/articles/10-things-you-should-know-about-the-reliability-of-the-new-testament-writers/.

page 87: *New Testament Apocrypha*: Regarding the New Testament Apocrypha in general, see J. Christopher Edwards, *Early New Testament Apocrypha: Ancient Literature for New Testament Studies* (Zondervan Academic, 2022).

page 88: *Gnosticism*: Among other works, a broad historical analysis of Gnosticism and early Christianity can be found in Pheme Perkins, *Gnosticism and the New Testament* (Fortress, 1993).

page 89: *distinct from the other texts*: For a detailed treatment of why the four New Testament gospels are distinct from other noncanonical works such as the Gospel of Peter, see Simon J. Gathercole, *The Gospel and the Gospels: Christian Proclamation and Early Jesus Books* (Eerdmans, 2022).

page 89: *most reliable witnesses to Jesus*: For an overview of how the Old and New Testament canons were formed and the criteria behind their formation, see Michael J. Kruger, *Canon Revisited: Establishing the Origins and Authority of the New Testament Books* (Crossway, 2013).

page 90: *relationship between the Bible and slavery*: On the topic of the Bible and slavery, see James M. Hamilton, "Does the Bible Condone Slavery and Sexism?," in *In Defense of the Bible: A Comprehensive Apologetic for the Authority of Scripture*, ed. Steven B. Cowan and Terry L. Wilder (B&H, 2018); see also several chapters in Paul Copan, *Is God a Moral Monster? Making Sense of the Old Testament God* (Baker, 2011).

page 93: *treatment of women in the Bible*: Concerning sexism and the Bible, see the Hamilton essay noted in the previous note, as well as Donald G. Bloesch, *Is the Bible Sexist?* (Wipf & Stock, 2001).

page 93: *leadership roles in worship*: Regarding the active role of women in the early church, see Ben Witherington III, *Women in the Earliest Churches* (Cambridge University Press, 1991).

page 94: *disorganized worship practices*: Dealing with 1 Corinthians 14 and the reason for Paul's instruction is Kenneth E. Bailey, *Paul Through Mediterranean Eyes: Cultural Studies in 1 Corinthians* (IVP Academic, 2011), 409–18.

page 95: *proper integration of these women*: For an informative and thoughtful approach to 1 Timothy 2 and Paul's discussion of women, including the worship of Diana of Ephesus in the ancient world, see John Stott, *The Message of 1 Timothy and Titus* (IVP Academic, 1996).

page 96: *Isn't that genocide?* Looking critically at accusations of genocide in the Bible are Paul Copan and Matt Flannagan, *Did God Really Command Genocide? Coming to Terms with the Justice of God* (Baker, 2014).

Chapter 6: But What About Other Religions?

page 102: *diverse array of religious traditions*: The statistics regarding the number of world religions comes from Pam Wasserman, "World Population by Religion: A Global Tapestry of Faith," *Population Education*, January 12, 2024, https://populationeducation.org/world-population-by-religion-a-global-tapestry-of-faith/.

page 104: *religious pluralism as a worldview*: For a summary of religious pluralism as a social and political aim (that is, the peaceful coexistence of different religions and religious communities), see the essays in Charles L. Cohen and Ronald L. Numbers, eds., *Gods in America: Religious Pluralism in the United States* (Oxford University Press, 2013). An excellent overall summary of religious pluralism both as a social virtue and a worldview (that is, the belief that all religions point to the same deity) is Michael Barnes Norton, "Religious Pluralism," *Internet Encyclopedia of Philosophy*, accessed November 4, 2025, https://iep.utm.edu/rel-plur/#SH3c.

page 104: *Golden Rule*: Luke 6:31 in the New Testament. Comparing variations of the Golden Rule in other religious traditions, see

Jacob Neusner and Bruce Chilton, eds., *The Golden Rule: The Ethics of Reciprocity in World Religions* (Bloomsbury, 2008).

page 108: *Why should I trust Jesus?* An interesting discussion of the uniqueness of Jesus Christ versus other religions can be found in Gavin D'Costa, Paul Knitter, and Daniel Strange, *Only One Way? Three Christian Responses on the Uniqueness of Christ in a Religiously Plural World* (SCM, 2013).

page 109: *Gandhi*: The quote is found in Mohandas Gandhi, *The Wit and Wisdom of Gandhi* (Dover, 1951), 187.

page 109: *C. S. Lewis*: For the story of C. S. Lewis's identification of grace as the unique aspect of Christianity, see Scott Hoezee, *The Riddle of Grace* (Eerdmans, 1996), 42, italics added. Hoezee says Peter Kreeft shared this anecdote in a speech at Calvin College.

page 113: *G. K. Chesterton*: While widely attributed to Chesterton, this quote cannot be found in any of his verified writings or speeches.

page 117: *God calls us to be tolerant*: Offering a basic summary of the idea of religious tolerance is Josh Moody, "Does the Bible Promote Tolerance or Intolerance?," *The Gospel Coalition*, August 24, 2018, www.thegospelcoalition.org/article/bible-tolerance-intolerance/.

page 117: *Dorothy Sayers*: The quote from Dorothy Sayers comes from her book *Letters to a Diminished Church: Passionate Arguments for the Relevance of Christian Doctrine* (W Publishing, 2004), 98.

page 118: *sloppy tolerance*: Noting some of the dangers of a "sloppy" type of tolerance, see D. A. Carson, *The Intolerance of Tolerance* (Eerdmans, 2012).

Chapter 7: Was Jesus an Ethical Genius?

page 128: *Jesus's ethical teachings*: For an in-depth overview of various ethical aspects of Jesus's ethical teachings and the ethical teachings of the New Testament writers in general, see Greg Goswell and Andreas J. Köstenberger, "The Ethics of Jesus: What Do the Four

Gospels Reveal?," *Crossway*, August 11, 2024, www.crossway.org/articles/the-ethics-of-jesus-what-do-the-four-gospels-reveal/.

page 128: *unprecedented ethical teacher*: A treatment of Jesus as an ethical and wise teacher can be found in Pheme Perkins, *Jesus as Teacher* (Cambridge University Press, 1990).

page 132: *could have sinned at any time*: Looking at Jesus's sinless life in relationship to his divinity and its full significance in Christian thought is Jeffrey S. Siker, *Jesus, Sin, and Perfection in Early Christianity* (Cambridge University Press, 2015).

page 134: *Robert Coles*: See Philip Yancey's chapter on Coles in *Soul Survivor: How Thirteen Unlikely Mentors Helped My Faith Survive the Church* (WaterBrook, 2003), 111. Some sources reference a similar statement about the Sermon on the Mount that is attributed to Robert Coles: "All ethical teachings over the past two thousand years are simply footnotes to the Sermon on the Mount" (see Raymond B. Kats, "Why Jesus Was an Ethical Genius," Medium, June 21, 2025, https://medium.com/@rkataz/why-jesus-was-an-ethical-genius-b2a1648092f3).

page 134: *Franklin Roosevelt*: The Franklin Roosevelt quote comes from his October 1, 1938, speech "Greeting to the National Eucharistic Conference," *The American Presidency Project*, www.presidency.ucsb.edu/documents/greeting-the-national-eucharistic-congress.

page 134: *Sermon on the Mount*: Among many other interpretations of the Sermon on the Mount, see Jonathan T. Pennington, *The Sermon on the Mount and Human Flourishing: A Theological Commentary* (Baker Academic, 2017).

page 137: *"Blessed are the meek"*: For an accessible treatment of meekness in the Roman world and in the Beatitudes, see Derek Rishmawy, "Meekness Is Not Weakness," *Christianity Today*, June 2019, www.christianitytoday.com/2019/05/meekness-is-not-weakness/.

page 139: *Abraham Lincoln*: Lincoln made this remark to Joseph Gillespie, found in a letter from Gillespie to William H. Herndon,

January 31, 1866 (see Douglas L. Wilson and Rodney O. Davis, eds., *Herndon's Informants: Letters, Interviews and Statements About Abraham Lincoln*, www.abrahamlincolnsclassroom.org/abraham-lincoln-in-depth/abraham-lincolns-values-and-philosophy/index.html).

page 141: *what makes someone pure*: For an in-depth, technical treatment of Jesus's understanding of purity, see Craig Blomberg, *Jesus the Purifier: John's Gospel and the Fourth Quest for the Historical Jesus* (Baker, 2023).

page 144: *viewed many of their emperors as gods*: Regarding the cult of the Roman emperor and their deification, see Ittai Gradel, *Emperor Worship and Roman Religion* (Clarendon, 2002).

page 144: *died globally for their faith*: For more on the high level of persecution for Christians globally, see the 2025 Open Doors World Watch List, accessed November 11, 2025, www.opendoorsus.org/en-US/persecution/countries/.

page 145: *Gandhi*: Gandhi's remark is found in Mahadev Desai, *With Gandhiji in Ceylon* (Gansesan, 1928), 143–44.

Chapter 8: Did Jesus Really Perform Miracles?

page 149: *event that can't be explained by our scientific knowledge*: A much-beloved overview of the reality of miracles is C. S. Lewis, *Miracles: A Preliminary Study* (Macmillan, 1947).

page 149: *moment when the supernatural intervenes*: Offering a detailed but accessible summary of philosophical discussion about miracles is William Lane Craig, "The Problem of Miracles: A Historical and Philosophical Perspective," *Reasonable Faith*, accessed November 11, 2025, www.reasonablefaith.org/writings/scholarly-writings/historical-jesus/the-problem-of-miracles-a-historical-and-philosophical-perspective.

page 150: *centers on his miraculous deeds*: Regarding miracles in the

New Testament and their reality, see Craig S. Keener, *Miracles: The Credibility of the New Testament Accounts* (Baker Academic, 2011) and his *Miracles Today: The Supernatural Work of God in the Modern World* (Baker, 2021).

page 150: *In Matthew, Mark, Luke, and John*: For an accessible approach to Jesus's miracles and their purpose, see Sean McDowell, "Why the Miracles of Jesus Are Unique," *Sean McDowell.org*, February 23, 2021, https://seanmcdowell.org/blog/how-the-miracles-of-jesus-are-unique. See also Amy-Jill Levine, *Signs and Wonders: A Beginner's Guide to the Miracles of Jesus* (Abingdon, 2022).

page 150: *category of healings*: Concerning healing and health care in the ancient world, including statistics surrounding ancient mortality, see Helen Rhee, *Illness, Pain, and Health Care in Early Christianity* (Eerdmans, 2022).

page 151: *did not live past the first year*: For information about life expectancy and the mortality rates of children in the first-century world, see the Wikipedia article, "Life Expectancy," accessed November 11, 2025, https://en.wikipedia.org/wiki/Life_expectancy.

page 152: *C. S. Lewis*: The quote from C. S. Lewis is found in *The Screwtape Letters* (HarperSanFrancisco, 2001), ix.

page 154: *Bart Ehrman*: Regarding Bart Ehrman's point, see his *How Jesus Became God: The Exaltation of a Jewish Preacher from Galilee* (HarperOne, 2014).

page 154: *He actually did such miraculous things*: For an overview of Jesus as a miracle worker in his historical environment, see Graham Twelftree, *Jesus the Miracle Worker: A Historical and Theological Study* (InterVarsity, 1999).

page 154: *Josephus*: Josephus's quote from book 18, chapter 3, of *Antiquities of the Jews* can be viewed at the University of Chicago's website, accessed November 11, 2025, https://penelope.uchicago.edu/josephus/ant-18.html.

page 157: *criticisms of the reality of Jesus's miracles*: A much-beloved overview of the reality of miracles is C. S. Lewis, *Miracles: A Preliminary Study* (Macmillan, 1947).

page 159: *evidence for the reality of miracles*: Among those defending the real possibility of miracles today are J. P. Moreland, *A Simple Guide to Experience Miracles: Instruction and Inspiration for Living Supernaturally in Christ* (Zondervan, 2021); R. Douglas Geivett and Gary Habermas, eds., *In Defense of Miracles: A Comprehensive Case for God's Action in History* (InterVarsity, 1997).

page 161: *Hume . . . Jefferson . . . Bultmann*: Hume's views on miracles are summarized in a study guide written by the Fiveable content team, "Hume's Critique of Miracles," *Fiveable.me*, accessed November 11, 2025, https://fiveable.me/science-sacred/unit-6/humes-critique-miracles/study-guide/E9NjN4RXXYexJro5. Information on Jefferson's Bible can be found in the Wikipedia article, "Jefferson Bible," accessed November 11, 2025, https://en.wikipedia.org/wiki/Jefferson_Bible. For a summary of Bultmann and his demythologization approach, see the study guide written by the Fiveable content team, "Rudolf Bultmann," *Fiveable.me*, accessed November 11, 2025, https://fiveable.me/key-terms/introduction-christianity/rudolf-bultmann.

page 161: *Richard Dawkins*: The quote from Richard Dawkins derives from his book *The God Delusion* (Bantam, 2006), 187.

page 161: *General Social Survey*: The General Social Survey data is engaged by Ryan Burge, "Do You Believe in Miracles?," *Graphs About Religion*, September 19, 2024, www.graphsaboutreligion.com/p/do-you-believe-in-miracles.

page 163: *reported experiencing a miracle*: The global data listed about people reporting miracles comes from Keener, *Miracles*.

page 163: *Duke University Rhine Research Center*: For more on the Duke University Rhine Research Center and various accounts of near-death experiences, see the essays in Bruce Greyson et al., eds., *The*

Handbook of Near-Death Experiences: Thirty Years of Investigation (Bloomsbury, 2009).

page 164: *Tim Keller*: The quote from Tim Keller comes from chapter 6 of his *The Reason for God: Belief in an Age of Skepticism* (Dutton, 2008), 95–96.

Chapter 9: Was Jesus God and Did He Really Rise from the Dead?

page 168: *a liar, a lunatic, or our Lord and Savior*: The "Liar, Lunatic, or Lord" trilemma is posed by C. S. Lewis in book 2, chapter 3, of *Mere Christianity* (Macmillan, 1951), 56.

page 169: *worshiping him as God*: A number of excellent studies have been published on the worship of Jesus Christ by the first Christians. See especially James F. McGrath, *The Only True God: Early Christian Monotheism in Its Jewish Context* (University of Illinois Press, 2009).

page 169: *Pliny*: On Pliny the Younger's *Letters to Trajan* and their discussion of Christianity, see chapter 1 of Robert Louis Wilken, *Christians as the Romans Saw Them*, 2nd ed. (Yale University Press, 2003), 1–30.

page 170: *Jesus himself taught that he was God*: For general assessments of Jesus's claims to divinity and their significance, see Greg Lanier, *Is Jesus Truly God? How the Bible Teaches the Divinity of Christ* (Crossway, 2020).

page 170: *Is Jesus God?* Looking at different aspects of the discussion of Jesus's divinity in the gospel of John, including John 8:58 and 10:30, are the essays in Christopher M. Blumhofer et al., *Early High Christology: John Among the New Testament Writers* (Fortress, 2024).

page 171: *a full cosmic pardon*: Offering a technical assessment of both Jesus's act of forgiveness and its ties to his divinity, as well as other aspects of forgiveness in biblical literature, is Tim Carter, *The Forgiveness of Sins* (Clarke, 2016).

page 172: *The mystery of the incarnation*: For a popular-level approach to the incarnation of Jesus Christ, see Melvin Tinker, *Veiled in Flesh: The Incarnation—What It Means and Why It Matters* (InterVarsity, 2019).

page 174: *discounted the notion that Jesus was not crucified*: Concerning the historicity of Jesus's crucifixion and its ancient context, see John Granger Cook, *Crucifixion in the Mediterranean World*, 2nd ed. (Mohr Siebeck, 2018). Offering a detailed assessment of the crucifixion narratives in the Gospels is Raymond Brown, *The Death of the Messiah: From Gethsemane to the Grave*, 2 vols. (Yale University Press, 1998).

page 175: *But why did Jesus die on the cross?* Regarding Jesus's crucifixion and its salvific significance, see Simon Gathercole et al., *What Did the Cross Accomplish? A Conversation About the Atonement* (Westminster John Knox, 2019).

page 180: *historical methods can prove the resurrection*: Major research works on the historicity of the resurrection include William Lane Craig, *Assessing the New Testament Evidence for the Historicity of the Resurrection of Jesus* (Wipf & Stock, 2024); Michael R. Licona, *The Resurrection of Jesus: A New Historiographical Approach* (IVP Academic, 2010); N. T. Wright, *The Resurrection of the Son of God*, vol. 3 of *Christian Origins and the Question of God* (Fortress, 2003).

page 182: *Gary Habermas*: For Gary Habermas's "minimal facts," see volume 1 of his *On the Resurrection: Evidences* (B&H Academic, 2024–2026), 89–152, 283–748.

page 182: *Mishnah Shevuot*: The quote from Mishnah Shevuot 4 can be viewed at the Sefaria website, accessed November 11, 2025, www.sefaria.org/Mishnah_Shevuot.4; the quote from Josephus, *Antiquities of the Jews*, book 4, can be viewed at the University of Chicago's website, accessed November 11, 2025, https://penelope.uchicago.edu/josephus/ant-4.html.

page 183: *early Christian creed*: Regarding the creedal material of

1 Corinthians 15:3–8, see James Ware, "The Resurrection of Jesus in the Pre-Pauline Formula of 1 Cor 15.3–5," *New Testament Studies* 60 (2014): 475–98; and chapter 10 of volume 1 of Habermas, *On the Resurrection: Evidences*, 367–436.

page 185: *martyred for his faith*: For a close look at the martyrdom of Jesus's disciples, see Sean McDowell, *The Fate of the Apostles: Examining the Martyrdom Accounts of the Closest Followers of Jesus*, 2nd ed. (Routledge, 2025).

Chapter 10: How Do I Commit My Life to Jesus Christ?

page 200: *turn around or change one's mind*: A helpful resource on the practical and theological aspects of repentance is Mark J. Boda, *"Return to Me": A Biblical Theology of Repentance* (InterVarsity, 2015). Regarding repentance (*metanoia*) in the New Testament, see ChoongJae Lee, *Metánoia (Repentance): A Major Theme of the Gospel of Matthew* (Wipf & Stock, 2020).

page 202: *Climacus*: The quote from John Climacus is from step 5 of his *The Ladder of Divine Ascent*, trans. Archimandrite Lazarus Moore (Harper & Brothers, 1959), 47.

page 204: *culture is full of idols*: For a helpful summary of idolatry in modern life, see the interview with John Piper, "What Is an Idol?," *Desiring God*, January 3, 2022, www.desiringgod.org/interviews/what-is-an-idol.

page 206: *chat about the teachings of James and Paul*: Among others who read James and Paul and hold a shared theological view with differing (but complementary) points of emphasis, see Donna Hughey, *James Through the Eyes of Paul* (Wipf & Stock, 2014).

page 207: *spiritual growth is so important*: General guides for spiritual formation and growth include Alex Sosler, *A Short Guide to Spiritual Formation: Finding Life in Truth, Goodness, Beauty, and Community* (Baker, 2024); Henri J. M. Nouwen, *Spiritual*

Formation: Following the Movements of the Spirit (HarperOne, 2015); Dallas Willard, *The Spirit of the Disciplines: Understanding How God Changes Lives* (HarperSanFrancisco, 1988).

page 208: *listening ears and an open heart*: For helpful recent resources that approach the spiritual discipline of Scripture reading from different angles, see David Platt, *How to Read the Bible: A Simple Guide to Deeper Intimacy with God* (Nelson, 2025); Dave Ripper, *Experiencing Scripture as a Disciple of Jesus: Reading the Bible like Dallas Willard* (InterVarsity, 2025). See also the Old and New Testament introductions listed in the notes for chapter 3.

page 210: *it's a communal practice*: Looking at communal Scripture reading and study in the early church, even as early as the first century, is Brian J. Wright, *Communal Reading in the Time of Jesus: A Window into Early Christian Reading Practices* (Fortress, 2017).

page 211: *draw us closer to God*: For an accessible book on the discipline of prayer, see Pete Greig, *How to Pray: A Simple Guide for Normal People* (NavPress, 2019); see also Henri J. M. Nouwen, *The Only Necessary Thing: Living a Prayerful Life* (Crossroad, 2008).

page 212: *Søren Kierkegaard*: Most paraphrases of Kierkegaard's statement on prayer derived from "On the Occasion of a Confession," as found in Kierkegaard, *Three Discourses on Imagined Occasions*, ed. and trans. Howard V. Hong and Edna Hong (Princeton University Press, 1993), 23.

page 212: *psalms of lament*: Looking at the psalms of lament with practical application in mind, see Glenn Pemberton, *Hurting with God: Learning to Lament with the Psalms* (Abilene Christian University Press, 2012).

page 216: *community is an essential part*: For two must-read works on Christian community, see Dietrich Bonhoeffer, *Life Together*, trans. John W. Doberstein (HarperOne, 2009); Henri Nouwen, *Community*, ed. Stephen Lazarus (Orbis, 2021).

page 217*: Finding a Christian community*: Regarding the importance of church and Christian community, see Jonathan R. Wilson, *Why Church Matters: Worship, Ministry, and Mission in Practice* (Brazos, 2006).

page 217: *In a world full of distractions*: Looking at different aspects of Christ-centered communities, see Mark Dever and Jamie Dunlop, *The Compelling Community: Where God's Power Makes a Church Attractive* (Crossway, 2015); Jim Wilder and Michel Hendricks, *The Other Half of Church: Christian Community, Brain Science, and Overcoming Spiritual Stagnation* (Moody, 2020).

page 218: *a body with many members*: Thinking through the biblical concept of the church as the body, especially in a post-COVID-19 context, see Collin Hansen and Jonathan Leeman, *Rediscover Church: Why the Body of Christ Is Essential* (Crossway, 2021).

Conclusion

page 225: *growing . . . among young people in America*: For a recent study on this topic, see the Barna Group research summary, "New Barna Data: Young Adults Lead a Resurgence in Church Attendance," Barna, September 2, 2025, www.barna.com/research/young-adults-lead-resurgence-in-church-attendance/.

From the Publisher

GREAT BOOKS

ARE EVEN BETTER WHEN THEY'RE SHARED!

Help other readers find this one

- Post a review at your favorite online bookseller
- Post a picture on a social media account and share why you enjoyed it
- Send a note to a friend who would also love it—or better yet, give them a copy

Thanks for reading!